Female Ascetics

RELIGION & SOCIETY IN SOUTH ASIA SERIES

Also in the same series:

Religious Conversion Movements in South Asia
Continuities and change, 1800–1900
Edited by Geoffrey A. Oddie

Paths of Dalit Liberation in Kerala
Interaction with Christianity and Communism, 1854–1966
George Oommen

Religious Traditions in South Asia
Interaction and Change
Edited by Geoffrey A. Oddie

Female Ascetics

Hierarchy and Purity in an Indian Religious Movement

Wendy Sinclair-Brull

CURZON

First published in 1997
by Curzon Press
St John's Studios, Church Road, Richmond
Surrey, TW9 2QA

Typeset in Baskerville by LaserScript, Mitcham, Surrey
Printed in Great Britain by
Biddles Ltd, Guildford and Kings Lynn

British Library Cataloguing in Publication Data
A catalogue record for this book is available from the British Library

Library of Congress in Publication Data
A catalogue record for this book has been requested

ISBN 0–7007–0422–1

Contents

Illustrations

Acknowledgements

The fieldwork on which this book is based was funded by an Australian Post-Graduate Award for Doctoral Research, together with a generous grant from the Carlyle Greenwell Bequest, through the Anthropology Department of the University of Sydney.

I am deeply indebted to the South Sydney Rotary Club for requesting assistance from Trichur Rotary on my behalf. Dr KPB Nair and his wife were most generous in their hospitality, and I would like to thank them most sincerely.

Pavanan of the Kerala Sahitya (Literary) Akademi, was not only an entertaining and reliable source of a Marxist-atheist perspective of local affairs, but also was able to provide me with archival historical material kept by the Akademi.

The distinguished P Chitran Nambudiripad of Trichur introduced me to Nambudiri culture, and through him I met the irrepressible A Madhavan Menon. The latter discussed former Nayar beliefs and practices in a highly frank manner, proving an excellent informant.

The late Satto Koder of Cochin and his dear wife Gladys provided me with a home away from home when I needed respite from the field. I was able to make use of the Koder's extensive and valuable library, containing many rare books and documents, unavailable elsewhere.

Many of the insights into village life could not have been provided without the confidence and trust shown to me by my Harijan and Izhava village friends, and my research assistant, PN Valsala. I cherish her friendship.

Several venerable Nayar women contributed background information whilst I was in Kerala, recalling details of the past, and reminiscing about the days of Kerala's great matrilineal families. But, none can surpass the wealth of detail supplied by S Leelamani of Sydney, a truly remarkable and perceptive lady.

My cousin Jean Soames deserves a special mention, for offering me a perfectly situated London base for my post fieldwork library research. I thoroughly enjoyed my time with her.

Before leaving for fieldwork I sought advice from world-renowned Anthropology Professor MN Srinivas, who was visiting Australia at the time. He told me to start at the centre and follow my sources outwards, in ever widening concentric circles. That is exactly what I did: collecting data became simple. He also gave me his Bangalore home address and phone number, for which I am eternally grateful.

One night his wife received a frantic long distance call from me. I had reached a low point, commonly experienced by anthropologists in the field. I found myself the next day on her doorstep, where she took me into her home, sight unseen. I remained there, together with her daughters Lakshmi and Tulasi, for a week, during which time I learned a considerable amount about College girls in Karnataka.

Professor Srinivas has scrutinised the manuscript of this book, making any helpful comments and observations, on both content and style. I feel flattered by his attention.

Professor Michael Allen, then Head of the Anthropology Department of the University of Sydney supervised the initial research on which this book is based. Without his help, I would not have received the required funding. I remain indebted to him for his support.

My thanks are also due to my husband Zoltan (for legal advice), and to our sons Jeremy (for help with the photographic work), and Michael (for assistance with the Index).

Finally, I wish to pay tribute to the late Professor Peter Lawrence, who first encouraged me to pursue a career in Social Anthropology. I remember him with affection.

Foreword

I have used a number of essential Sanskrit, Malayalam and Bengali words. Wherever possible, I have transliterated these with diacritical marks. Sanskrit words used in a Bengali or Malayalam context are spelled as written, not as pronounced. Names have been rendered in the most current local form. However, variations in spelling may occur in quotations used.

My use of the word 'community' needs some clarification. For the fourfold division of Hindu society, I use the term *caste* or *varṇa.* To denote the divisions within a *varṇa,* in the Kerala context I do not use the term *jāti.* Instead, I use the word 'community', which is both in common and official usage. 'Community' is a useful term in Kerala, where birth ascribed groups include not only Hindu *jātis* but other religions and their divisions. Thus, in the Trichur region, the population can conveniently broken down into Nambudiri, Nayar, Izhava, various artisans, Harijan and its divisions, and either Christian or Muslim *communities,* depending on the location. In this type of breakdown, the term *jāti* could not be applied. You could not, for example, speak of a clash of interests between the Nayar, Izhava and Christian *jātis.*

Although the word Harijan has fallen out of favour, I retain it, as the newer term Dalit had not been adopted at the time of my fieldwork.

Glossary

adharma	lack of dharma (righteousness)
ambalavāsi	community of temple personnel (Kerala)
amma	mother (Kerala)
ārati	form of worship in which five elements are offered symbolically to a deity
āśrama	one of the four phases of life. A hermitage
avarṇa	outcaste
avatār	incarnation of a deity
beedi	a type of Indian cigarette
bhadralok	urban gentleman (Bengal)
bhajan	devotional song
bhakti	devotion. One of the four paths of yoga
bhasmam	sacred ashes
brahmacāri	celibate student (m). The first stage of life
brahmacārini	celibate student (f)
brahmacārya	celibate studentship
Brahmin	highest of the four Vedic castes
cakra	six 'wheels' or nerve centres of body
caṇḍala	outcaste
charkha	spinning wheel
chaver	suicide squad (Kerala)
chechi	elder sister (Kerala)
chetan	elder brother (Kerala)
darśan	'have sight of', be in presence of a holy person or deity
dharma	righteousness
divya	'divine' type of spiritual aspirant
dosa	pancake, usually of rice and lentil flour (Kerala)
ekādaśi	eleventh day of lunar fortnight
gāyatrī	mantra recited by Brahmin males

gerua	ochre, used to dye robes of saṃnyāsins
ghee	clarified butter
gṛhastha	householder. The second stage of life
guru	religious teacher
Harijan	"untouchables". The lowest in the Hindu social order
himsa	violence
homa	sacrificial fire
illam	home of Brahmin (Kerala)
japa	repetition of mantra
jāti	sub caste
jnāna	wisdom or knowledge. One of the four paths of yoga
Kali Yuga	last of the four Cosmic Eras. Era of destruction
kāmini-kāncana	'women and gold'
kāraṇavan	oldest male of taravād (Kerala joint family)
kāristhan	property manager of taravād (Kerala)
karma	law of cause and effect. Duty. One of the four yogas
kasavu	gold thread used in cloth (Kerala)
kavi	ochre used to dye robes of saṃnyāsin (Kerala) Same as gerua
kṣatriya	second of the four varṇas (castes). Warrior caste
kohl	black soot, used to enhance eyes
kumkum	red powder offered to deities and often worn on forehead
kuṇḍalinī	spiritual energy, latent in all people, symbolised by a snake
kutty	child (Kerala)
leela	earthly play of a deity
lingam	symbol of the god Siva
luchi	deep fried, round, unleavened bread, like a small air-filled cushion
madamu	'European' woman
mahut	elephant's keeper
mālā	flower garland, rosary of 108 beads
mana	home of Brahmin (Kerala)
mangalāratī	type of ritual worship, especially at dawn
mantra	sacred Sanskrit formula
marumakkathāyam	matrilineal descent rules (Kerala)
Mataji	Revered Mother, as saṃnyāsinis are called in the Order

Maya	illusion
medha	special nerve in central canal developed by yogi. Intelligence
mokṣa	release from cycle of rebirth
mundu	lower wearing cloth, worn from waist to ankles (Kerala)
nakśetram	ascendant star
nalekettu	four sided house with inner courtyard (Kerala)
namaskar	a type of greeting with palms held together at chest or forehead level
nellikay	small, round acidic fruit used for pickle (Kerala)
nirvikalpa samādhi	Realisation of Formless Brahman
onera	undergarment for women (Kerala)
pāndit	a Brahmin scholar
papadum	fried lentil wafer
paraṃguru	guru's (teacher's) guru
paraṃpara	guru-disciple succession
paśu	'animal' type of spiritual aspirant
pāyasam	grain such as rice or semolina simmered in sweetened milk
pranām	prostration before a deity or revered person
prasād	food or other item that has been offered to a deity or revered person
prasādi	adjectival form of above
pūjā	ritual worship
punya	religious merit
r̄aja	'royal'. One of the four paths of yoga
sādhaka	spiritual aspirant
sādhana	religious disciplines
śakti	Female Principle. Cult of Goddess
samaram	industrial strike (Kerala)
sambandham	form of sexual relationship (Kerala)
saṃkīrtan	type of devotional singing
saṃnyāsa	vows of renunciation
saṃnyāsin	member of a Hindu Order of ascetics. The fourth stage of life
saṃnyāsini	female form of above
saṃsāra	social world
saṃskāra	tendencies inherited from past lives
Sangha	Buddhist religious Order
Satī	burning of widow on husband's funeral pyre

sattvik	pure
serpu kavu	serpent grove (Kerala)
sevika	personal attendant
shenai	instrumental music (Bengal)
sīkhā	tuft of hair at crown of head, as worn by Brahmin males
sneham	goodwill, loyalty (Kerala)
śraddha	faith. Care and attention
śrāddha	a funeral rite
sudra	the lowest Vedic caste
suṣumṇa	central spinal nerve, through which kuṇḍalinī rises
tapas	'heat'. Austerities.
taravād	matrilineal joint family (Kerala), or joint family home
tāvazhi	smaller division of taravād
thekkini	open hall in traditional taravād
tīrtham	sacred water used in worship
tithi	a day of lunar fortnight
tol	Sanskrit school (Bengal)
upanāyana	sacred thread ceremony
veedu	house of Nayar (Kerala)
vesti	upper body cloth (Kerala)
viraja	homa used during samnyasa rites
viveka	knowledge, discrimination
vairāgya	dispassion
vaṇaprastha	forest hermit. The third stage of life
varṇa	one of the four Vedic castes
Vedas	a Hindu sacred text
vesti	upper wearing cloth (Kerala)
vīra	'heroic' type of spiritual aspirant
visesam	news (Kerala)
yoga	union of Individual with universal Soul

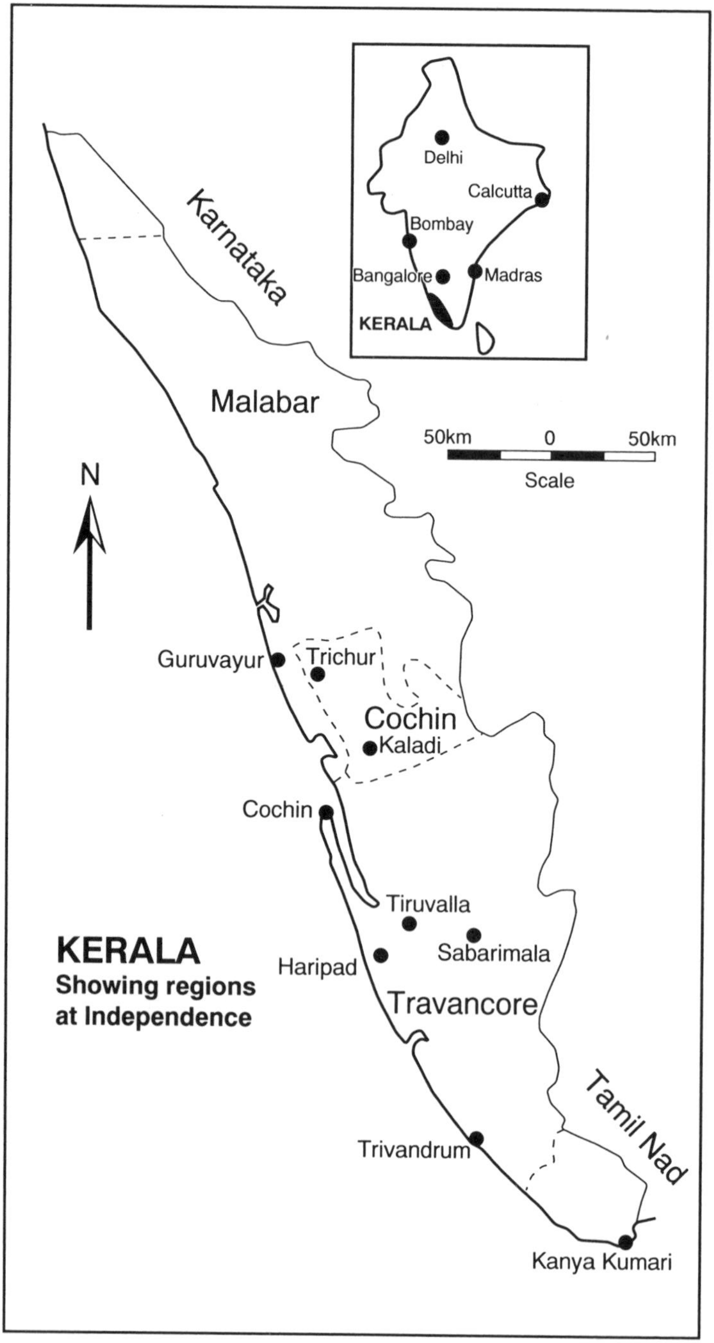

KERALA
Showing regions at Independence

Introduction

The aim of life for a Hindu is *mokṣa,* release from the cycle of birth and rebirth. Central to this notion is the development of *vairāgya,* dispassion and the eventual realization of the illusory nature of the social world of phenomena known as *saṃsāra.*

As the pursuit of *mokṣa* entails *vairāgya,* asceticism[1] in its various forms has been an integral part of Hinduism since Vedic times. A religious Order of ascetics known as *saṃnyāsins* was said to have been founded by Sankaracarya in the eighth century, and the Orders which exist today mainly trace their origins to this. An understanding of *saṃnyāsa* is crucial for an understanding of Hindu society, since it is the *saṃnyāsin* who has vowed himself to a life of *vairāgya,* and the pursuit of *mokṣa.* In forsaking the complexities of Hindu social life, within the realm of family, *varṇa* (caste), village, and occupation, the *saṃnyāsin* exists as the antithesis of the Hindu householder. However, although Hindu society has been intensively studied by sociologists/anthropologists from the perspective of the householder, the *saṃnyāsin* and in particular the *saṃnyāsin* Orders have been almost entirely ignored.

Since the time of Sankaracarya, the majority of *saṃnyāsin* Orders have been almost exclusively reserved for Brahmin males. According to orthodox Brahmin notions, *saṃnyāsa* was the fourth optional stage of life, to be undertaken after a man had discharged his family duties and satisfied his worldly desires.[2] In becoming a *saṃnyāsin,* a man should thus no longer be concerned with *saṃsāra.* Dumont (1970) has followed the 'ideal' notion of *saṃnyāsa,* and has located the *saṃnyāsin* as therefore living outside of Hindu society (1970:43). Since a *saṃnyāsin* is not bound by the constraints of society, Dumont thus concludes that he is 'an individual-outside-the-world', as opposed to the householder, the 'man-in-the-world', who is trapped by the concerns of family, caste, and the rigours of hierarchy, purity and pollution. This view of Dumont's has remained so far undisturbed, through the power of the mystique surrounding the *saṃnyāsin*, and the lack of ethnographical data of the *saṃnyāsin* within his social context.

Asceticism in India in general has received far less attention than this important topic deserves. Miller (1976) has made a comparative study of 22 monasteries of various sects and Orders in the city of Bhubaneswar, followed by Tripathi (1978), who examined 100 monasteries in the state of Uttar Pradesh. So far, no ethnography has undertaken the study of a single Order or institution, nor ventured to examine the main concerns of Hindu society as expressed within the context of *saṃnyāsa*. Thus, the questions of hierarchy, authority, purity and pollution within a monastic framework so far remain unasked and so, unanswered.

Yale (1961) has provided a valuable insight into organised Hindu monasticism in his study of the Ramakrishna Order, and although not intended as an academic work, his book is well researched and carefully undertaken, providing a wealth of detail, and thus filling a void.

Daner (1976) in her study of the Hare Krishna Movement in the USA comes closer to an anthropological work on Hindu monasticism. But, the subjects of her investigation are Western converts to Hinduism, and moreover, the Hare Krishna devotees do not constitute a monastic community, but include lay members as well as *saṃnyāsins*, married couples as well as single men and women.

This brings us to an important consideration. The prohibition on women and non-Brahmins studying the sacred Vedic texts or participating in Vedic rites has effectively barred them from embracing *saṃnyāsa*[3] except as members of unorthodox sects. Orders founded by leaders of the *bhakti* movement, which stressed devotion to a deity, rather than the non-dualist Advaita philosophy of Sankaracarya grew up between the eleventh and thirteenth centuries, and reached a peak in Bengal with the advent of Chaitanya in the sixteenth century. Chaitanya declared devotion a path open to all, and accepted non Brahmins into his fold. But, it was not until the mid-twentieth century that women were finally openly accepted into major religious Orders, although individual *saṃnyāsins* possibly accepted female monastic disciples at various times. Commonly, though, female ascetics lived away from their homes in 'holy' cities such as Varanasi either alone or in groups, but did not take monastic vows. Thus they retained lay status.

The anthropology/sociology of female Hindu ascetics is almost a total blank. Apart from scant and fleeting references to their existence, only Ohja (1981) appears to have addressed this area so far. In her study of ascetics in Varanasi, she concluded that although individual *gurus* have granted *saṃnyāsa* to women, 'no organised order of their own exists' (1981:282).[4] Nor does disciplinic succession through a female line exist, heralding the beginnings of a self-perpetuating female Order, or branch of an existing Order. She concludes thus: that female ascetics exist as 'nothing else than the total sum of women who, at a given time, belong to the different orders' (p. 282), and that in the holy city of Varanasi, she met only 45 women who could be so described (p. 267).

Though Ohja noted that female ascetics belonging to the 'Ramakrishna Mission' existed in a tiny community in Varanasi, she did not include them in her work (1981:61, note 6). Here she would have found the monastic organisation which she believed lacking among female ascetics. For, these women indeed belong to a well structured monastic Order run by and for women exclusively. The community she mentioned in passing in fact belongs to Sri Sarada Math, a completely autonomous monastic organisation, run by the Ramakrishna Order of Samnyasinis.[5] Though run on parallel lines to the Ramakrishna Order of Samnyasins, the two are legally separate entities in every way. The parallel organisation to the Ramakrishna Mission, the Ramakrishna Sarada Mission, is likewise legally separate, and undertakes charitable, medical and educational work, as does its male counterpart. During my fieldwork, which I undertook between 1980 and 1981, I examined this Female Order in some detail, and especially, a large and highly organised monastic community (known as Sri Sarada Mandiram), in the southern state of Kerala, near the rural town of Trichur.

In 1979 I had completed an honours thesis on the topic of death ritual in two Kerala communities, Nambudiri and Nayar and so was familiar with the extant literature of the region when I undertook fieldwork for a PhD.

Before undertaking fieldwork in the village in which Sarada Mandiram was situated, I stayed for three months with a high ranking Nayar family in the Trichur township. From here I conducted preliminary research, especially into recent developments in Kerala society, as I realised that once within the confines of Sarada Mandiram, my freedom of movement might be somewhat curtailed, as indeed it was.

The opportunity to live in and study a monastery of a Hindu female monastic Order I regarded as unique. Due to the conservative nature of this and other religious Orders I believe it will remain so. The book traces the foundation of the Ramakrishna Movement in the late nineteenth century in the city of Calcutta, and its spread throughout the main cities and towns in the sub continent. In particular, I focus on the growth of the Movement in the southern state of Kerala, and the establishment of an educational Institution run by the Ramakrishna Order in the rural town of Trichur.

Simultaneously, I follow the move to form a separate Order for women by the Dedicated Women Workers attached to Ramakrishna Mission centres, leading to the subsequent formation of the Ramakrishna Order of *saṃnyāsinis*. I then describe the establishment of Sri[6] Sarada Mandiram Trichur, a branch of this Order, against the background of its evolution from a Harijan Hostel under the auspices of the Ramakrishna Mission. As the book covers a period of almost a century, I constantly refer to the great social upheavals which took place in Kerala during this time, so that developments within the Ramakrishna Movement in Kerala are described against a background of the social history of the region.

I examine Sarada Mandiram in a series of chapters dealing with the recruitment, training and re-socialisation of monastic candidates, and the topics of hierarchy and ritual purity within the Institution, and then look at the members of the Institution in a broader social context, in their relationship with the local villagers. Here I found a major focus of my work. Sarada Mandiram was established when there was still a vestige of the former aristocracy in Kerala, and was modelled on the aristocratic *taravād*.[7] As the aristocracy and the old *taravāds* became abandoned, Sarada Mandiram, still operating on an outmoded social model, became a symbol of a despised past and focus for local hostility.

In the concluding section I look at the present state of Sarada Mandiram, in the light of a number of problems threatening its future viability, and offer some possible resolutions.

This book, I trust, fills a number of important gaps in the body of knowledge concerning *saṃnyāsa*, not merely as an ideology, but as a social reality in the form of the monastery. Moreover, the monastic inmates are not elderly Brahmin former-householders. They are, in fact, most unorthodox: recruited mostly as young unmarried women, and include Sudras and Harijans as well as Brahmins. The added setting of the social ferment of Kerala poses a number of interesting conundrums, which I attempt to resolve, and in the process present a new interpretation of hierarchy, purity and pollution.

From the outset at Sarada Mandiram I endeavoured to join in the

Chapter 1

The Hindu Revival

Background to Nineteenth Century Calcutta

The foundation of the Ramakrishna Movement in the late nineteenth century is closely linked with the growth of the metropolis of Calcutta, and the emergence of a number of individuals who sought to change the structure of Bengali society. It is therefore beneficial before discussing the Ramakrishna Movement itself, to first understand some of the main currents of thought working within Calcutta during the mid-nineteenth century, the time when most of Ramakrishna's disciples were in their youth.

The British gained a strong footing in India after 1765, when the East India Company took over the collection of revenue, following the defeat of Indian soldiers in the Battle of Plassey in 1757. Gradually the Company's administration grew in complexity, as it tightened its grip on the economy of Bengal. Administrators and clerks were brought in from England, young men lured by the promise of the fabulous wealth that could be made in India. An historian Nemai Sadhan Bose comments:

> The servants of the East India Company, who came to India with a small salary, succeeded in accumulating, within an amazingly short period, enormous fortunes (1969:6).

The Company had a monopoly on foreign trade, but had to operate in India through local businesses. In Calcutta certain families saw an opportunity to act as brokers and financiers, and thus a class of *banians* or merchants was born (Mukherjee 1977:12–15). At the same time the Company recruited Bengali men, largely of Hindu families, as junior clerks, so that by 1840 there were 102,055 'Natives' in its employ. The population of Calcutta swelled by almost 50,000 between the two official Surveys, carried out in 1821 and 1837 respectively (1977:5–7), as literate young men moved to the city in search of employment. Europeans and Natives (as the two categories of citizens were called) lived in separate areas of Calcutta, the former boasting a number of grand mansions set in large shady gardens, whilst the latter consisted of closely packed houses in narrow lanes, very overcrowded and with poor sanitation. Very few Bengalis lived in spacious houses, and even fewer mixed socially with Europeans.

The Missionaries

Alongside the East India Company, European influence was to make its presence felt in another sphere of Bengali society. For, with the arrival of the British merchants and administrators came Christian missionaries, not to take home the treasures of India, but to bring the Bible to a heathen land. William Carey's arrival in 1793 was a milestone not only in mission annals, but also in the history of Bengal. Despite opposition of the Company to interference in the religion of the local people, Carey and two colleagues set up the Serampore Mission in 1800, and from there published the first Bengali edition of the Bible, followed by a cascade of books, journals and tracts on a wide variety of topics. Their strategy was clearly defined. Firstly, they made an intensive study of some of the Sanskrit texts of the Hindu religion, compiling in the process a grammar of Sanskrit. Armed with a knowledge of Hinduism they hoped to challenge its conclusions, thereby making way for the acceptance of Christianity. They aimed their strategy at the educated of Bengal, the emerging urban middle class, those who had received a traditional Bengali education, and who had already come into contact with the British.

Through the printing press, missionaries launched a scathing attack on Bengali society, especially on the 'corruption' that had seeped into Hindu practices under the guise of Tantra, and various issues regarding the plight of Hindu women. At the time, girls of respectable families were married before puberty, and could not remarry on the death of their husbands, regardless of whether the marriage had been consummated. The treatment of these women, and the virtual seclusion enforced on all Hindu women of such families, were some of the topics raised in mission publications. The language used in mission journals was simple, everyday Bengali, presenting the literate public for the first time with a wide range of new knowledge and opinions.

The net result of all these missionary activities was that the

Bengalis became curious and interested in the wider world (Bose 1969:22).

Surely though, the curiosity of the citizens of Calcutta had already been aroused by the presence of the British and other Europeans, whose whole way of life was so manifestly different from that of the Bengali. Moreover, a desire to participate in this world, and in the opportunities afforded by the Company and the growing private commercial concerns, brought many young men to Calcutta to seek their fortunes, leaving the security of family behind.

Despite their efforts, the missionaries succeeded in converting very few Hindus. Instead of their literature stimulating thinking Hindus to abandon their religion as corrupt and superstitious, it caused leaders to arise from among their ranks, to rid their religion of certain undesirable practices. With this arose a movement to reform Hindu society, and at the same time to fight missionary propaganda. Foremost among Bengali leaders of the coming Bengali Renaissance (as the new era was to be known) was Raja Rammohun Roy.

Rammohun Roy and the Brahmo Samaj

Rammohun Roy (b.1772) was widely read in both Arabic and Sanskrit when he joined service in the East India Company. He soon mastered English, and became an avid reader of papers and journals, which he managed to borrow from his employer, John Digby. The more Roy read and discussed Hindu society, he compared it with what he read on other societies, and the more he was convinced that idol worship was 'the root evil of the prevailing ignorance and superstition' (Bose 1969:30). When he retired in 1815, he decided to devote his energy towards spreading this conviction, and founded an Atmiya Sabha or Friendly Society, for the discussion of religious and related issues. Rammohun's strong personality soon attracted some of the leading gentlemen of Calcutta into the circle, from the new class of *bhadralok*, the urban, educated elite. The Sabha ceased to exist after 1819, but Roy continued his work through the publication in Bengali of five of the *Upanisads*, and the *Vedanta Sutras*, Hindu texts hitherto unavailable in the vernacular. These texts were chosen by Roy as representing Hinduism in its purest form, after the era of Vedic sacrifices and before the introduction of the Bhakti or devotional sects. The latter brought to Hinduism the worship of a multitude of deities, some of whom possessed all-too-human characteristics, as missionaries often emphasised.

Access to the *Upanisads* had been restricted, at least from the time of Manu,[1] to members of the three upper *varṇas* (Brāhmin, Kṣatriya and Vaiśya) but in practice mainly Brahmin scholars studied them, as only they had a deep knowledge of Sanskrit, and the time and interest to devote to the task. The *Upanisads* advocate neither sacrifice nor worship, but the realisation of Brahman, the Supreme Self, the Supreme Being. For Roy, a return to the *Upanisads* was a return to pure Hinduism, which was more truly monotheistic than the missionaries' Christianity which (he pointed out) was largely Trinitarian (Bose 1969:34). This Roy announced in a book published in 1820, after a thorough examination of Christian doctrine, which included reading the original texts in both Greek and Hebrew.

As a result of his activities, Roy became the victim of a backlash by both orthodox Hindus and Christian missionaries, but the more they denounced him, the more he received publicity, and the further support of his admirers. His stand on the Trinity brought him close to Unitarianism, and for some time he and his followers actually attended a Unitarian church each Sunday (Bose 1969:37).

In 1828 Roy decided to establish an association for the propagation of the Hinduism of the *Upanisads*. He called it the Brahmo Samaj. The Samaj became active not only in promoting the workship of the Supreme Being, rather than the worship of the various deities of Hinduism, but also for its vigorous campaign for social reform. The missionaries had drawn attention to some of the ills of Hindu society in Bengal, and Roy was determined to prove that these were not due to the Hindu religion itself, but to a degeneration of society. He published in 1822 *Brief Remarks Regarding Modern Encroachments on the Ancient Rights of Females,* showing that in Vedic times women had high status. Child marriage, polygamy and *satī*[2] were all modern corruptions. He asserted that in Vedic times women were permitted to study the scriptures, and thus he defended the rights of women to education and to participation in the performance of religious exercises, long denied them (Bose 1969:38).

Roy was convinced that English education was necessary for the spread of modern knowledge, and he started a school for Hindu boys in 1816, in which science and Western thought were taught, at the same time encouraging missionaries to do likewise. He was received in England and later in France as a distinguished ambassador from India, and was instrumental in the abolition of *satī*, his arguments overriding those of the representatives of orthodoxy. His unexpected death in England in 1833 left a vacuum in the leadership of the Brahmo Samaj for quite some years to come.

The Bengali Renaissance

In 1826 the Portuguese-Indian by the name of Derozio was appointed as teacher to the Hindu College, an educational institution founded in 1817. It was ironical that Roy (despite his role in the College's foundation) had been excluded from the College Committee, as he was considered too radical. Derozio proved to be far more radical than Roy, for he gathered around him many of the brightest students, under the banner of the Academic Association, essentially a debating Club (Bose 1969:64). Under the inspiration of their mentor, students began to publicly denounce and even ridicule some of the most sacred institutions of Hinduism. By 1831, so alarmed were the College authorities by Derozio's influence, that his dismissal was sought. Derozio was informed, and tendered a bitter letter of resignation (1969:68). He died the same year, two years before Roy.

The influence of Derozio had spread far beyond the walls of the Hindu College, as ex-students maintained their links with each other through journals and associations, and their ideas spread through these means to other institutions also. The followers of Derozio were known as Young Bengal and they, like the followers of Roy, campaigned for the furtherance of Western education, and the need for public debate and discussion on questions of social reform. However, there was a major difference between the emerging Brahmos (members of the Brahmo Samaj) and Young Bengal.

Whilst Roy believed that Bengali Hindu religion was corrupt *as practised*, he staunchly upheld that the Hinduism of the *Upanisads* was both noble and sublime, and felt a mission to make available to a wide readership the philosophy of these texts. On the other hand, Young Bengal followed the lead of Derozio in dismissing Hinduism in its entirety, paving the way for 'scientific' atheism. Theirs was a protest movement, which became increasingly insensitive to their own Bengali tradition, whilst the Brahmos agonised as to how pride in their own traditions and heritage could be restored, in the face of missionary propaganda. By the mid-nineteenth century, the Young Bengal Movement had faded, lacking both a new leader, and a fresh supply of students, to revitalise its membership. In the meantime, the Brahmos increased in strength, under Devendranath Tagore, who was chosen by Roy as his successor (Bose 1969:122). From this time on the Samaj was persistently plagued by power struggles and personality clashes from among its own ranks, which resulted in numerous factions and splinter groups being formed, to the detriment of the movement as a whole.

Devandranath spent much of his energy in defending Hinduism against detractors, in particular the Presbyterian missionary and educator, Alexander Duff. Duff had hoped that the religious vaccum created by the rejection of Hinduism by Young Bengal could be filled by Christianity. But, the positive movement of the Brahmos towards social and religious reform within the boundaries of Hinduism, had a stronger appeal, and few converts to Christianity were made among the educated of Calcutta. Not only was the relative appeal of a return to Upanisadic Hinduism stronger than the call of the Gospels, but acceptance of Christianity would have caused the convert estrangement from both family and friends. As there was no possibility of total acceptance by European Christians either, a convert would find himself in a very alienated position indeed.

Keshab Chandra Sen

The year 1858 proved another milestone in the Bengali Renaissance, for it was in that year that Keshab Chandra Sen joined the Brahmo Samaj, embuing it with a new direction and viability. In 1861 Keshab had become a full-time worker for the Samaj and the publisher of its bi-weekly journal, the *Indian Mirror*. Keshab, like Rammohun Roy, was also enthusiastic in his support for the education and emancipation of Hindu women, and he became the minister of the women's branch of the Samaj (Bose 1969:132). Gradually, a rift began between Keshab and the more conservative Devendranath, culminating in the formation of a separation of the followers of the two leaders. The Brahmo Samaj of India under Keshab was founded as an autonomous organisation in 1866 and, unhampered by older, more conservative members of the former Samaj, went its own way.

Keshab had a different emphasis in his Samaj to Devendranath's. Instead of the scholarly study of the *Upanisads*, Keshab believed that Brahman could be known through devotion, through worship. To this end a Brahmo Mandir (temple) was opened in 1869, where regular services were held. Keshab had long been an admirer of Jesus and had made a thorough study of the Bible. From the Christian format of communal worship he devised a Brahmo order of service, which included prayer, a sermon and Brahmo hymn singing, based on the Vaisnava *saṃkīrtan* style, already familiar in Bengal. Keshab's popularity increased until the mid-1870s, when some of the younger leaders of the Samaj found Keshab himself to be too conservative and autocratic.

Ultimately, some of Keshab's own followers broke away, following the betrothal of his 14 year old daughter to a Maharajah of 15, despite the fact that both parties were below the minimum age set down for Brahmos to marry, and the groom was, moreover, from an idol-worshipping family (Bose 1969:139). Again there was bifurcation, and many of Keshab's former supporters deserted him for the rival camp, led by Sivanath Sastri. Keshab and his Brahmo Samaj had come to a crossroad, and had to determine which direction the Samaj would take, if it were to survive. The new direction the Samaj was to take was partly determined by a fortuitous meeting that took place between Keshab and a Hindu ascetic, Ramakrishna, in March 1875, just as the storm within the Samaj was at its height (*LSR*:225–32).

Ramakrishna

Unlike the leading figures of the Bengali Renaissance mentioned to date, Ramakrishna had no Western education and was barely literate in his own language, Bengali. He was born in 1836 in a remote village, and had no connections with the English administration, Calcutta reform movements or educational institutions. He wrote no articles in the many Calcutta journals, and published no books. He founded no organisation during his lifetime, and he did not believe in social reform. Yet, no discussion of the Bengali Renaissance is complete without reference to Ramakrishna, and the part which he played as a link between the Brahmo Samaj and the emergence of the Hindu Revival Movement.

An authoritative biography entitled the *Life of Sri Ramakrishna* (referred to as *LSR*) was compiled in 1924, thirty eight years after his death, by monks of the monastic Order founded in his name. It is based on two main sources, the *Gospel of Sri Ramakrishna* (referred to as *GSR*) and *Sri Ramakrishna the Great Master* (referred to as *SRGM*). The former comprises a collection of conversations between Ramakrishna and various visitors and disciples, from 1882–86, and the latter a hagiography by a monk of the Ramakrishna Order, who had been a lay disciple of Ramakrishna during his youth.

The life story of Ramakrishna is one of great complexity, open to many interpretations. Hence, although the Ramakrishna Movement is a main focus of this book, I feel that a detailed examination of Ramakrishna's life and personality are not quite appropriate or indeed necessary for an understanding of his role as catalyst in the new Revival. I have, however, examined the personality of Ramakrishna in some detail elsewhere (Sinclair 1982). For the present purpose, which is to understand his role in unwittingly changing the direction of the Brahmo Samaj, a brief sketch of his life will suffice.

Ramakrishna[3] was born in 1836 of rustic Bengali Brahmin parents of humble means. The family owned half an acre of paddy fields, which provided rice, their staple food. At the time of Ramakrishna's birth, his father was sixty-one, considered a very advanced age, and his mother forty-five. At the age of seven his father died, and the family was supported by Ramkumar, the eldest son, who was thirty-eight at the time of his father's death. He and Ramakrishna's eldest brother tried to make a living by performing religious rites, but finding the income insufficient in their village, went to Calcutta to open a *tol* or Sanskrit school there.

The family underwent a series of misfortunes, not the least of which was Ramakrishna's reluctance to study. He became very indrawn and pious, and suffered from repeated bouts of loss of consciousness. I have phrased this last statement carefully, because while biographies of Ramakrishna and numerous scholarly articles regard these forms of behaviour as signs of religious ecstasy even in childhood, a few have ventured to suggest that he suffered from *petit mal*, a form of epilepsy (see for example, Schneiderman 1969:62). At this stage it becomes almost impossible to separate fact from fiction in the life of Ramakrishna, since scholars have only the original biography and the *Gospel* (written by a fervent lay disciple) on which to base their conclusions. While the latter work has been hailed as an almost stenographic record, the former is highly interpretive and liberally sprinkled with 'signs and miracles'.

The facts of Ramakrishna's life from this point appear to be as follows: Ramakrishna went to stay with his brother in Calcutta at the age of sixteen, and three years later was appointed a priest at the new Dakshineswar Kali temple, where Ramkumar was priest to the goddess, to whom the main temple was dedicated. On the sudden death of Ramkumar the following year (1856) Ramakrishna was appointed to his place.

It is at this stage that, according to Mission Literature,[4] Ramakrishna had his first vision of the goddess Kali, after standing before her basalt image in the temple shrine day after day, pleading for her to 'reveal Herself'. Whatever his inner state, it now became impossible for Ramakrishna to carry out his duties, for he frequently lost consciousness or did not carry out the rites in the prescribed manner. He either sat inert, or laughed or sang before the goddess, for hours at a time. So increasingly bizarre was his behaviour that the temple authorities wrote to Mathur, the son-in-law of the temple founder, who generally managed the affairs of the temple. Ramakrishna stepped aside as priest, and was put under the care of a physician for his 'nervous state' (*LSR*:72).

In 1858 Ramakrishna's cousin took over as priest and Ramakrishna was sent to his village home where his mother arranged for his exorcism, believing that he was possessed by an evil spirit. After a few months at home, his condition appeared to improve, and his mother decided that it would be an opportune time to find him a wife, since he was then twenty-three years old. It was hard to find a bride though, as firstly his mother was very poor, and secondly on enquiry the parents of prospective girls could find out that Ramakrishna was not a wise choice. Eventually a girl of five from a nearby village was found, and the wedding took place soon afterwards. The girl returned to her parents a few days later, following a dispute over ornaments borrowed for the occasion, and Ramakrishna spent another one and a half years in his village, in the company of his mother and elder brother.

In 1860 Ramakrishna returned to Dakshineswar, but after a short time as priest, he once more was placed under medical treatment, as he had a relapse of his former strange condition. According to the *Gospel*, Ramakrishna is reputed to have discussed the early years of his life as the time of many and varied visions and flashes of 'realisation', the years in which he saw and talked with gods and goddesses and during which the 'Truth' of the scriptures was made known to him. According to Schneiderman, a psychologist, Ramakrishna's behaviour at this time was psychotic. He was fixated on the goddess Kali and suffered from 'ritualistic compulsions', centering on her worship (1969:69). Though from a Western psychological standpoint Ramakrishna's behaviour may appear psychotic, it should be emphasised nevertheless that to some extent his behaviour was acceptable or even sanctioned by the society in which he lived. As a devotee and priest of Kali, his belief that the goddess was his mother was entirely in line with the *bhakti* or devotional attitude chosen by countless other Hindus towards the goddess. His 'ritualistic compulsions' were born of the strict training received by Brahmin youth of priestly families. Each rite was to be performed to the most exacting specifications, by those who chose this occupation. The paradox is, that if we can rely on published accounts, Ramakrishna was relieved of his duties not for his 'ritualistic compulsions', but for *failing to perform the rituals according to rule*, and for scorning many personal observances in his everyday life. Ramakrishna abandoned the rigid format of worship because he was convinced that the goddess was real, and that he could approach her directly, as a child does his mother, without any formality. Rituals become superfluous in such a relationship.

Ramakrishna continued to stay within the temple compound, though he was no longer a priest. The temple owner had died, and her son-in-law was now wholly in charge. He was convinced that Ramakrishna was a mystic, and ordered that he be left alone by the temple staff, and be allowed to live in his own way.

The Brahmani

It was not long after this that a female ascetic arrived at the temple, and offered to become Ramakrishna's spiritual teacher. He was twenty-five at the time, and she around forty (*LSR*:96). In Bengal terms, she was old enough to be his mother. Indeed, she regarded herself as Yasoda, the mother of the god Krishna, and began to look on Ramakrishna as her divine son. Krishna is regarded as an Incarnation of God, and soon the ascetic, whom Ramakrishna called the 'Brahmani' or Brahmin woman, was proclaiming that Ramakrishna was no less than God Incarnate. A small band of scholars was called to the temple, and (if we can rely on available sources) proclaimed the Brahmani's assertion to be true (*LSR*:105,108).

Now Ramakrishna was to embark on a rather different period of his life. Until he met the Brahmani he had been a lone figure, without any guide in his spiritual quest. He had not until now followed any of the prescribed methods of spiritual disciplines, as outlined in the various religious texts. The Brahmani offered therefore to initiate him into the school of Tantra, in which she was an adept.

It is not easy or perhaps even possible to ascertain the nature of the Brahmani's relationship with Ramakrishna during his Tantrik *sādhana* (spiritual disciplines), or indeed to ascertain the precise nature of the disciplines themselves. The aim of Tantrik disciplines is to cause a current within the body, known as *kuṇḍalinī* to rise from its resting place at the base of the spine, passing through six nerve centres known as *cakras*,[5] until it reaches the brain. The god Siva is believed to reside in the highest *cakra*, in the cerebrum, and represents the Cosmic Mind, while *kuṇḍalinī* represents Cosmic Power, also known as Sakti. Thus the attainment of the highest *cakra* by *kuṇḍalinī* is also the union of Siva-Sakti. The spiritual aspirant who experiences this, 'realises' the oneness of the universe within himself, and thus attains *mokṣa,* liberation. He has, through his raising of *kuṇḍalinī,* realised his own oneness with the Cosmic Mind, Siva. He will not be reborn.

Tantra prescribes various methods of raising *kuṇḍalinī,* but one of the most prevalent at the time of Ramakrishna was the discredited Vamacara of 'Left Handed' path. *Kuṇḍalinī* resides in the lower *cakras* of the worldly person. These are situated below the navel, because that is also where his consciousness is centred: to put it bluntly, on lust and greed. *Kuṇḍalinī* can only be made to rise by a corresponding rise in consciousness, to higher, spiritual concerns. Vamacara invites the aspirant to do this by testing his control in the face of temptation. Five types of temptations are offered during the associated rites,[6] and the aspirant has to partake of each in turn without losing his equanimity. The final rites involve sexual intercourse, in which the mind must concentrate on 'the unity of Siva-Sakti' (*Abridged GSR*:587). Female partners are used in these practices, and at the time of which we are speaking, Tantra was regarded by many of the educated of Calcutta as no more than secret and perverted sexual rites practised in the name of religion.

It is stated that Ramakrishna restored purity to Vamacara, by performing the rites strictly in the spirit in which they were intended, that is without any thought of sexual gratification (*LSR*:122). But, at the same time, there is some disagreement as to how he accomplished this while still maintaining lifelong celibacy, as is also claimed.

Vamacara aspirants are divided into three categories: *paśu* or animal-like (devoid of self control), *vīra* or heroic (able to withstand temptation), and *divya* or divine (those who have transcended sense enjoyment). Only *vīra* aspirants actually partake of the fivefold rites, but the various sources disagree as to which category of aspirant Ramakrishna was. The *Gospel,* reputed to be an almost verbatim account of Ramakrishna's conversations gives few clues, but Ramakrishna's original biography (*SRGM*) has him declare that he performed rites after the *vīra* mode of worship (vol.1:227), a statement confirmed and discussed by the author (vol.1:229–30). In this work, Ramakrishna states, moreover, that an aspirant with an animal nature will conquer this by performing *paśu* mode ritual, thereby raising himself to the *vīra* level. When he has perfected the *vīra* mode, he can then, through self control progress to *divya* (vol.1:229).

The Indian-published *Life of Sri Ramakrishna* suggests that he not only practised but restored the heroic rites to their former purity. However, the biography of Ramakrishna published as an introduction to the *Abridged Gospel*, published in New York for Western Readers, denies (despite earlier evidence to the contrary), that Ramakrishna had anything to do with the heroic mode. I believe that the latter viewpoint is a concession to the Western reader, who may find it difficult to accept a deity (such as Ramakrishna is claimed to be by the Ramakrishna Movement) who indulged in rituals of a sexual nature, however refined their technique. The *Abridged Gospel* furthermore, does not only modify earlier statements on Ramakrishna's practice of Tantra, but also omits a number of 'earthy' stories and frank references to sexuality which appear in the larger English edition published in India. The Bengali *Gospel* is even more explicit.

Sādhana

Ramakrishna now embarked in earnest on unremitting *sādhana*, the practice of spiritual disciplines. It was three years after he became a disciple of the Brahmani that a monk of the Advaita (non-Dualist) school arrived at the temple, and is said to have initiated Ramakrishna not merely into Advaita *sādhana*, but also secretly into the monastic Order of Sankaracarya, to which he belonged. Despite this, Ramakrishna continued to keep his wife and other family members by his side and to wear not the ochre robes of the ordained *saṃnyāsin*, but the ordinary clothes of a householder. This was followed by a short period during which Ramakrishna came under the influence of a Vaisnava monk, who taught him the worship of the god Rama.

Ramakrishna is reputed to have achieved non-Dualist realisation within a day of his initiation into Advaita, that is, he lost all feeling of his own being and was immersed in Pure Being or Brahman, as it is called. The monk departed, but not before Ramakrishna had convinced him of the reality of Kali, the Divine Mother. Apparently, Ramakrishna remained in a state of non-Dualist consciousness for six months, and only returned to normal consciousness due to dysentery. According to one source, he was cared for by a monk during the period of absorption in *nirvikalpa samādhi* (as the state is called), otherwise he would have died (*Abridged GSR*:55).

It was not long after his recovery that Ramakrishna now met a Hindu who had become a Sufi, and under his guidance performed

Muslim devotions. After three days, he is claimed to have 'realised the goal of that form of devotion' (*LSR*:175), which meant that he had a vision of a man with a long beard, whom we are to assume was either Muhammad or the Semitic God. This person is said to have merged into Brahman, proving to Ramakrishna that he was also but an aspect of the Being whom the Hindus call Brahman.

It was now 1867, and Ramakrishna had not fully recovered from dysentery, so he returned to his native village in the company of the Brahmani, and remained there for six or seven months. His wife, Sarada Devi, who he had not seen since she was seven years old, came to join him from her own village, but met with the stern disapproval of the Brahmani, who was soon forced to leave Ramakrishna after quarrelling with his relatives. Ramakrishna did not see her again.

Ramakrishna as Guru

Between 1868–72 we have not much information on Ramakrishna's life, except that he went on two pilgrimages, and that in 1871 his major benefactor, Mathur, died. This period also marked the beginning of Ramakrishna's transition from a lonely spiritual seeker to a teacher (*guru*) of others. For, it was during the last years of Mathur's life that he began to accept invitations to visit well-known personalities, such as Devendranath Tagore, an ex-classmate of Mathur's from their Hindu College days. It was by this means that Ramakrishna gradually became known to well-educated Calcutta Hindus, many of whom were active members of the Brahmo Samaj.

In 1872 Sarada Devi came to Dakshineswar, to find out whether reports reaching her concerning her husband's insanity were true. She was now eighteen, and had to endure a great deal of gossip, since her husband had not sent for her to join him in Calcutta. She stayed for twenty months with Ramakrishna, looking after him as best she could. At first she stayed in his room, but later moved to the tiny concert tower, where she occupied the small ground floor room. The concert tower was not far from Ramakrishna's room, and she would cook his food and bring it to him daily.[7] Ramakrishna used to entertain visitors in his room, and at these times Sarada Devi would quickly leave, drawing her saree over her face to hide it from view, as was the custom among Brahmin Bengali women.

After Sarada Devi returned to her village once more, Ramakrishna became friendly with Shambhu Mallik who had a garden house near the temple. On his frequent visits, Ramakrishna became interested in Christianity, for Shambhu (though a Hindu) used to read the

Bible to him. After the death of Mathur, Shambhu became the main provider of Ramakrishna's modest needs, and his main companion until Sarada Devi's return in 1874. He even built a simple hut for Sarada Devi and her mother-in-law, which they occupied until Sarada returned to her village in 1875, with severe dysentery. Soon after her departure, both Shambhu's and Ramakrishna's mothers died, within a short time of each other. Hriday, the son of one of Ramakrishna's cousins, now became his main companion and helper, a position which was to increasingly cause annoyance to visitors, who first had to pass Hriday's scrutiny before being admitted to Ramakrishna's room. Eventually by 1881 Hriday had become such a nuisance that he was ordered from the temple premises, and told never to set foot there again.

The year 1875 was important for Ramakrishna, for it was then that he first met Keshab Chandra Sen, leader of the Brahmo Samaj of India. As I have already stated, Keshab was then facing a crisis within his organisation, centering on the controversial marriage of his daughter. He also needed to work out a cohesive doctrine for his Samaj, with which to challenge the breakaway branch.

Ramakrishna and Keshab first met at a private home, where Keshab and some of his followers were staying at the time. Keshab, who had a devotional nature, was drawn to Ramakrishna, who spoke on that occasion of how individuals regard God in differing ways, all of which are valid (*LSR*:226). Not only did Keshab become a periodic visitor to Dakshineswar, but Ramakrishna also visited Keshab from time to time. Keshab also wrote about Ramakrishna in the journal of his Samaj, recommending that his followers visit him for themselves. It was thus through Keshab that Ramakrishna's young educated disciples were eventually recruited. For, nearly all of them were College students, and members of or acquainted with, the Brahmo Samaj.

Historians differ in their appraisal of Ramakrishna's influence on Keshab's thought, and thus in the direction his Samaj was to take. Bose (1969) joins the majority which sees the meeting as a definite watershed, after which Keshab ceased to concern himself with social reform and moved towards a devotional attitude, which culminated in the announcement of the Navavidhan in 1880.

The Navavidhan is translated as New Dispensation, which was a declaration by Keshab of the unity of the teachings of 'all the prophets and saints' (as quoted in Bose 1969:141). A logo was created featuring symbols of each of the major religions known to India, including Christianity, but yet Keshab publicly made a statement acknowledging the supremacy of the power of Christ (1969:141). The notion of Navavidhan ultimately became refined and transformed under the banner of the Ramakrishna Movement, in a manner in which Ramakrishna could not possibly have dreamed. But I do not believe it is possible to ascertain whether Ramakrishna was *directly responsible* for Keshab's notion of religious unity. Historians may have been led astray in this matter, by relying on works by the Ramakrishna Movement, which may well over-emphasise Ramakrishna's influence on Keshab.

In 1879 Sarada Devi returned once more to Dakshineswar, where she was to remain (apart from periodic visits to her own village) until Ramakrishna's final illness. From this time on she was busy day and night catering for Ramakrishna's many visitors, while residing once more in the tiny concert tower. By now, some of Ramakrishna's visitors had come to regard themselves as devotees, and Ramakrishna even gave *mantra*[8] initiation to a selected few, and thus they became the small band of actual disciples. Gradually now, Ramakrishna attracted a nucleus of educated youth, most of whom were to become monks after his death.

On weekends and public holidays in particular, Ramakrishna's room was alive with discussion, and the singing of religious *bhajan*. Many of Calcutta's most illustrious men were among the frequent visitors, including not only Keshab, but Girish Chandra Ghosh the dramatist and Pundit Ishwar Chandra Vidyasagar, a renowned scholar. The impression of Ramakrishna obtained by reading the *Gospel* is that the Conversations between him and his highly placed devotees, reveal him as an astute, perceptive and frequently witty man. He taught often by the use of parables, and was quick to retort to comments by even the most famous of men.

The life of Ramakrishna was brought to an abrupt halt, however, in his fiftieth year, when he developed cancer of the throat. He died in 1886, in a garden house by the Ganges in Calcutta, where he had been moved for medical treatment, leaving behind a childless widow and a staunch band of close disciples and devotees.

Ramakrishna was a colourful figure in his day, but he left behind no organisation, nor doctrine to follow. He more than likely would have passed into Bengali history only as an influence on Keshab Chandra Sen, if it were not for the efforts of his beloved disciple, Naren. It is even questionable as to whether Ramakrishna would have been remembered for his influence on the Brahmo Samaj, for the Samaj was already beginning to decline, making way for a new period in Bengali history: the Hindu Revival, a period characterised by the emergence of Nationalist and patriotic consciousness. Ramakrishna was to become the direct link, through the posthumous emergence of the Ramakrishna Movement, between the Bengali Renaissance and the Hindu Revival.

Chapter 2

The Ramakrishna Movement

From Religious Renaissance to Nationalist Aspiration

Ramakrishna's final days were spent in a garden house in Calcutta, tended by his young disciples. He died on the 16th August, 1886. After this, the devotees who had been paying for the lease and upkeep of the house expected the young disciples to return to their homes, and to discontinue the lease. But, the disciples refused to go home, declaring that they would henceforth lead a life of renunciation. Eventually Surendra (who had paid the actual rent of the garden house) agreed to provide a small house for them, and within a few months, sixteen disciples had gathered there, all males. An entry in the *Gospel*, dated 21st February 1887 notes that Naren, the beloved disciple of Ramakrishna, was wearing the ochre robes of a Hindu ascetic when visited by the author.

The Foundation of the Ramakrishna Order

The alleged process by which the group of Ramakrishna's disciples embraced *saṃyāsa* is clouded with doubts for the enquirer. In the *History of the Ramakrishna Math and Mission* (1957), by Swami Gambhirananda, the General Secretary of the Order, the official description of the events is as follows.

About four months after Ramakrishna's death, a young disciple visited his own village home in the company of eight other disciples, with whom he was then living, in the then embryonic 'monastery'. One night, they lit a fire in the grounds and sat around it to meditate. Then, one of their number, Naren, began to speak of Christ and his disciples, and of how St Paul carried Christ's message to the far ends of the earth (Gambhirananda 1957:50). So moved were the companions that 'they arose up in a body, with the blazing fire in front and the shining stars above as their witness, to pledge themselves to a life of renunciation' (1957:50). They later realised that the night was Christmas Eve. The disciples later returned to Calcutta where in January 1887 they formally took the vows of *saṃnyāsa.*

One of the disciples returned to the 'monastery' in January after wandering in North India on a pilgrimage. During his travels he had found a monk of the same branch of the Dasanami Order[1] as Ramakrishna's own Advaita *guru,* Totapuri, and had copied down the *saṃnyāsa mantras* from him. On a certain day in January, the eleven residents of the 'monastery' gathered before a sacrificial fire, and with Naren acting as officiant, took the vows of *saṃnyāsa* together (Gambhirananda 1957:65–7), adopting monastic names and ochre robes. These disciples became the first *saṃnyāsins* of the later established Ramakrishna Order.

As far as the Ramakrishna Order is concerned, the above description suffices. Some of the first monks in turn initiated their own disciples into *saṃnyāsa,* and so the Order continued, until the present day. However, the bona fides of the Ramakrishna Order have been called to question by orthodox *saṃnyāsins* and laymen since its inception, and some refuse to recognise its members as *saṃnyāsins.* The objections to the *saṃnyāsins* of the Ramakrishna Order are based on two main reasons.

Firstly, the actual *saṃnyāsa* rites taken by the first disciples are void, as far as the orthodox are concerned, as they were not administered by an initiate. Ramakrishna died without initiating his young disciples into *saṃnyāsa* with due rites, even though it is claimed he symbolically admitted them to the monastic brotherhood by the presentation of ochre robes. But, without the rites having been performed by Ramakrishna, there is a break in the all-important *paramparа,* the chain of *guru*-disciple going back to Samkaracarya. The first disciples in effect gave themselves *saṃnyāsa,* as there was no initiated *saṃnyāsin* present to officiate at the ceremony. Therefore, the monks of the Ramakrishna Order have severed their links with the Dasanami Order. The second objection is that the Ramakrishna Order admits Sudras and even Harijans, while neither is 'Twice Born', and thus neither is entitled to have access to the texts on which the discipline of the Order is based. Actually, certain sections of the Dasanami Order have admitted Sudras in the past, as fighting *saṃnyāsins,* but not the branch to which Totapuri belonged. Indeed, Naren, who later as Swami Vivekananda became a national hero, still had to deal with detractors who raised their voices in protest that he, a Sudra, dared to wear the garb of a *saṃnyāsin* (see *LSV* Vol.I: 246 and 266).

It appears that the author of the *History of the Ramakrishna Math and Mission* has caused more doubts about the bona fides of the Order than he has solved. It would probably have been more satisfactory had he taken the lead offered by the author of the *Gospel*, who, in a summary of events after Ramakrishna's death, adds that the young disciples:

> . . . had not yet formally renounced the world. For a short while they kept their family names. But Sri Ramakrishna had made them renounce the world mentally. He himself *had initiated several of them into monastic life*, giving them the ochre cloths of *sannyasis* (*Abridged Gospel*, p. 523).

By adding a mere eight words, the problem of the legitimation of the Order has been solved: Ramakrishna *did* administer the robes with appropriate rites, so presumably, one of those duly initiated, later initiated his fellow disciples. If Gambhirananda would have followed this line of argument, the debate over the legitimacy of the Order could have been quashed once and for all.

In the *Gospel* entry for January 1886 it is stated that Ramakrishna gave sets of ochre robes and rosaries to eleven of his young disciples, and one set to Girish, the playwright. The mere act of giving ochre cloth by a *guru* is sufficient to make the disciple a *saṃnyāsin*, but not sufficient to make the disciple a member of the Dasanami Order. For this, certain rites must be performed, during which the *mantras* and instructions common to the particular branch of the Order are transmitted. By this reasoning, the disciples may have been made *saṃnyāsins*, but it is very dubious that Ramakrishna performed the elaborate rites which would have admitted them to the Dasanami Order. Therefore, it still appears to remain a fact that the rites were only performed after Ramakrishna's death, but *not* administered by an initiate. Thus they remain, for the orthodox, invalid.

The compiled *Life of Swami Vivekananda* dismisses the matter of the first *saṃnyāsa* in one brief sentence. Although it describes the resolve of the young disciples, taken around the fire on Christmas Eve as the evening on which they decided to renounce the world, one of the participants is quoted as saying:

> As a matter of fact, our resolve to become organized first became firm at Antpur. *The Master had already made us sannyasis.*[3] That attitude was strenghtened at Antpur (Fifth Edition 1981:196–7).

Whatever the facts surrounding the *saṃnyāsa* of the first members of the original monastery started in the name of Ramakrishna, the inmates certainly initially drew a great deal of adverse attention. They were young men of middle-class families, and many had not yet completed their College degrees. They had moved to a tumbledown house which was reputed to be haunted. They had barely enough food, and insufficient clothing. Yet, the lay disciples of Ramakrishna, some of them famous men, visited from time to time, showing deference to the young '*saṃnyāsins*', even though some were from Sudra families, including the self-appointed leader, Naren. Since the later formation of the Ramakrishna Order and the Ramakrishna Mission were largely his creations, I shall now trace Naren's path from the obscurity of the Calcutta monastery to that of a well-respected national figure.

The Triumph of Vivekananda

The members of the monastery used it as a base for pilgrimages, some lasting four or five years at a time. Naren set out in 1890, seeking the blessings of Sarada Devi, Ramakrishna's widow, before doing so. He wandered for three years in all, at first in the company of a brother monk, and then alone, visiting North India, then travelling west and eventually down the south coast. Naren met many scholars on his travels, as he knew both Sanskrit, the language of *pāndits,* as well as English, the language of the Western educated. He was confident and poised, quite unlike the majority of orthodox *saṃnyāsins.*

Naren was made welcome by some of India's most influential rulers, and also by countless poverty-stricken peasant families in wayside villages which he passed when travelling on foot. Finally, in the last week of December 1892, he reached Kanya Kumari, a temple on India's southernmost tip. There, swimming to a large offshore rock, he mused on all he had seen. Deeply affected by the wretchedness of village life, he envisaged a way by which *saṃnyāsins* could assist in the uplift of the masses of Indian peasants. As he later wrote to a brother monk:

> Sitting on the last bit of Indian rock, I hit upon a plan: We are so many *sannyasis* wandering about, and teaching the people metaphysics – it is all madness. Did not our Master used to say, 'An empty stomach is no good for religion?[11] That those poor people are leading the life of brutes, is simply due to ignorance. We have for all ages been sucking their blood and trampling them underfoot . . .
>
> Suppose some disinterested *sannyasis,* bent on doing good to

others, go from village to village, disseminating education and seeking in various ways to better the condition of all down to the Chandala (outcaste), through oral teaching, and by means of maps, cameras, globes, and such other accessories – can't that bring forth good in time? . . .

We have to give back to the nation its lost individuality and *raise the masses* . . . Again, the force to raise them must come from inside, that is, from the orthodox Hindus. In every country the evils exist not with, but against, religion. Religion, therefore, is not to blame, but men. To effect this, the first thing we need is men, and the next is funds. Through the grace of our guru I was sure to get from ten to fifteen men in every town. I next travelled in search of funds: but do you think the people of India were going to spend money! (Quoted in Gambhirananda 1957:74).

During his travels, Naren (who called himself by various names until finally becoming known as Swami Vivekananda) had heard that a Parliament of Religions was being held in Chicago in September, 1893, as part of the World's Fair. Representatives of the world's major religions had been invited to participate, and Vivekananda was urged to attend on behalf of Hinduism by various influential people whom he had met. Exactly who paid for his expenses (which included the steamer ticket, a wardrobe of clothes and some spending money) is difficult to ascertain, but some of the funds were collected by devotees in Madras, to whom Vivekananda later refers (Gambhirananda 1957:76).

No official delegate had been chosen to represent Hinduism, since it was not an organised religion with a monolithic structure. It was more a cluster of various sects, each owing allegiance to different deities and *gurus*. Yet, Vivekananda saw his chance: if he could impress the assembly at the Parliament, perhaps he could find enough financial support in the United States to return to India and complete his work.

Vivekananda in America

Many legends have been built up around Vivekananda's success in America. Gambhirananda has him dreaming before his departure of 'Ramakrishna walking over the sea and beckoning him to follow' (1957:76), and we last hear of him facing Indian shores from the deck of the steamer saying 'Verily, from the land of renunciation I go to the land of enjoyment' (1957:77).

Initially, Vivekananda had difficulty in persuading the officials of the Parliament of Religions that he was qualified to speak on behalf of Hinduism. There was nobody to authorise him to do so, until he eventually succeeded in impressing a Professor of Greek from Harvard University, who wrote him a letter of recommendation, praising his scholarship in glowing terms: 'Here is a man who is more learned than all our learned professors put together' (*LSV* Vol.I:406).

Vivekananda was a resounding success at the Parliament, stressing at the opening session the Hindu view that all paths to God are valid, and that there was no place for bigotry or dissent among fellow seekers (*LSV* Vol.1, Ch.22). His striking appearance and excellent command of English soon made him the most popular religious figure, and the Chairman made him the final speaker of his sessions, thereby ensuring a packed hall until closing time. Newspapers, in reporting the Parliament, noted that Vivekananda's impact on the audience was profound, and large posters of his portrait were hung in Chicago streets. By the end of the Parliament, a number of Christian missionaries were decidedly nervous about Vivekananda's success, especially after the following observation was published in the *New York Herald*: 'After hearing him we feel how foolish it is to send missionaries to this learned nation' (quoted in *LSV* Vol.I:428).

The Slayton Lecture Bureau booked Vivekananda to undertake a tour of their lecture circuit soon after the Parliament ended. Through newspaper and other sources we know that he visited at least sixteen cities, earning between thirty and eighty dollars per lecture: a large sum in those days. He spoke on a wide range of topics, on both religious and social themes. Women in particular flocked to hear him, and he became, as the *Detroit Journal* observed, 'The social lion of the day' (14th February 1894). He was the centre of attention at receptions and dinners, and in various cities prominent citizens offered to accommodate him for the duration of his stay. To have Vivekananda as a house guest became a distinct social advantage.

Eventually, Vivekananda became disillusioned with his role. As he wrote to friends in Chicago, the Hale sisters, on 15th March 1894: 'Well, I do not care for lecturing any more. It is too disgusting, this attempt to bring me to suit anybody's or any audience's fads . . . .' (*LSV* Vol.I:469). In the meantime, a fellow Indian, Pratap Chandra Mazoomdar, who had represented the Brahmo Samaj at the Parliament, had been busily informing the interested public that Vivekananda was a fraud, and was not even a monk as he claimed.

This information was filtered through to the Convenor of the Parliament, and to the Harvard Professor who had written his reference. Vivekananda was sorely embarrassed, and hastened to write and assure them that the statements of Mazoomdar were untrue.

By this time, Mazoombar had returned to India and there published an article on Vivekananda in a Brahmo Journal, *Unity and the Minister*, claiming that Vivekananda was a Brahmo, who represented nothing but himself.[4] He also informed his Indian readers that Vivekananda had transgressed many of the rules of orthodoxy, had eaten forbidden foods and in American 'used to smoke endless cigars' (*LSV* Vol.I:496). A copy of this article was forwarded to the *Boston Daily Advertiser*, which quoted it on the 16th May 1894, since Vivekananda had been particularly well-received in that city.

In sorrow, on the 18th March of that year, Vivekananda had written to the Hale sisters that he had news from India that Mazoomdar was accusing him of 'unchastity'. He was particularly hurt that it was the same Mazoomdar who as successor to Keshab Chandra Sen had once sat at the feet of Ramakrishna, and sought his advice. Indeed, we read in the *Gospel* that Ramakrishna had spoken to him about 'Naren' (*LSV* Vol.I:410). Vivekananda had succeeded in counteracting much of the missionary propaganda against his country,[5] and winning thereby respect for his religion and people, only to see a fellow countryman try to tear him down. He prepared to return home to India. He wrote on the 28th June 1894 to one of his staunch followers in Madras that although they all knew the calumny spread about him by Mazoomdar, none had raised a voice of protest on his behalf. They had assured him that most of the Indian press was behind him, but not one clipping in support of him had reached either him or the American press. He regretted their inertia (see *LSV* Vol.I:492–3).

Vivekananda had misjudged his supporters. For, on the 10th April the *Indian Mirror* had published an Editorial deploring the disloyalty of some of Vivekananda's detractors, and affirming confidence, support and gratitude to Vivekananda, and to the American people for their acceptance of him. The editor finally called for the readers to arrange public meetings 'in all parts of the country' to demonstrate their support for Vivekananda.

It was a most illustrious assembly which met in Madras in response to the Editorial, on 28th April 1894. Those present agreed to forward a resolution of support for Vivekananda to the President of the

Parliament of Religions, who had been much dismayed by the controversy over Hinduism's representative. A representative of Buddhism from Calcutta who had also been a delegate at the Parliament delivered an address in which he praised Vivekananda's contribution to the Parliament, and attributed its success largely to the latter's personality.

Other meetings followed in major cities in India, and between May and August press clippings concerning them, as well as news via letters reached Vivekananda. Copies of the proceedings of the meetings were sent by the organisers to the major American newspapers, and key people concerned in the controversy. Finally, Vivekananda wrote a letter pleading with his Indian followers to stop inundating him with press clippings. He wrote to Mrs Hale, mother of the Hale sisters, on the 23rd August 1894 that:

> Every ounce of fame can only be bought at the cost of a pound of peace and holiness. I never thought of that before. I have become entirely disgusted with this blazoning. I am disgusted with myself (*LSV* Vol.I:508).

By now Vivekananda had gathered around him a small band of devotees, and he decided to remain in America for a while to consolidate his work, with the idea of holding regular classes, using New York as his base. At the end of 1894 he set up the Vedanta Society, Vedanta meaning the 'end of the Vedas' or, in other words the *Upanisads*, on which his teachings were largely based. During summer, at a retreat with some followers at Thousand Island Park, he initiated two followers into *saṃnyāsa*, a man of Russian-Jewish descent and a French woman.[6] He was eager to leave behind him capable teachers of Vedanta in the West who could themselves pass on the *paraṃpara*, the *guru*-disciple succession. He also initiated five women into *brahmacārya*, the vows of celibacy. The remaining participants received *mantra* initiation, which can be taken by lay people with no monastic intentions. Thus, all present, having received one type or another of initiation became Vivekananda's disciples, and he their *guru*.

In August 1895 Vivekananda sailed for Paris and London, at the invitation of a woman whom he had met at the Parliament, and another gentleman with whom he had corresponded for some time. He held many classes in England before sailing once more for America in November of that year, promising his English devotees that he would try to send them a *saṃnyāsin* from Calcutta, to continue his work.

Back in America once more, Vivekananda continued to consolidate his work, and delivered numerous lectures, many of which have been collected and published under the title *The Complete Works of Swami Vivekananda,* along with his essays, poems and letters. During this second visit he initiated more followers into *brahmacārya,* and one into *saṃnyāsa.* He was invited to speak at the Graduate Philosophical Club at Harvard, and offered a Chair in Philosophy at Columbia University, which he declined. He taught in America until his departure for India via London in April, 1896.

In London, Vivekananda was reunited with a brother monk for the first time in three years, for Saradanada from the Calcutta monastery was already there, holding classes. Vivekananda arranged a series of classes also, and with a brief visit to Europe in between, continued to teach until he sailed once more for India in December, in the company of three Western disciples.

After an absence of seven years, Vivekananda was returning to his home town and to his brother monks. According to one of his disciples, foremost in his thoughts was the need to build a monastery in Calcutta for the training of monks, and already he had brought with him some substantial donations from the West for this purpose (*LSV* Vol.II:166).

Homecoming

The welcome afforded Vivekananda from the moment when he stepped on to the shores of Ceylon, and later South India, was tumultuous. Vast crowds welcomed him as a hero, and he spoke at numerous receptions as he made his way to Madras, en route to Calcutta. The newspapers took up the progress of his homecoming, so that by the time he reached Calcutta, huge preparations had been made to receive him, including a decorated route and triumphal arch on the road from the station, where he arrived from the coastal steamer's terminus, by special train. That day, the 19th February 1897, marked the beginning of Vivekananda's work in India, though he had been in correspondence with his brother monks during the last three years, expressing some of his hopes and plans.

The Ramakrishna Mission

On the 1st May 1897, a meeting was called in Calcutta of all followers of Ramakrishna, both lay and monastic, and an organisation to be known as the Ramakrishna Mission founded. At the meeting held four days later, certain resolutions were adopted, including two concerned with its objectives and the means for carrying them out. The objectives of the Mission were to disseminate the teachings of Ramakrishna and to help people to put them into practice, and to encourage fellowship between religions, which are all paths to Truth. The method of work was to train teachers for improving both the spiritual and temporal welfare of the people, by establishing centres in India for the training of personnel, and in the West for preaching Vedanta. Vivekananda was appointed the President of the Mission, and any sympathisers, lay or monastic, could apply for membership. The Mission was to be free, however, from any political ties (Gambhirananda 1957:119–20).

Vivekananda's brother monks were dubious about his plans at first, for Ramakrishna had exhorted them to renounce the world, not to embark on teaching and other work, as Vivekananda wanted them to do. But, Vivekananda went ahead, purchasing a plot of land on the bank of the Hooghly, a tributary of the Ganges, for a permanent monastery. The money was donated by one Western woman disciple, and another paid for immediate alterations and additions to the existing buildings. The new premises, known as Belur Math (monastery), were dedicated in December 1898. The relics of Ramakrishna were carried to the new site and worshipped by Vivekananda, who prophesised that the Math would become a world centre of religious harmony (*LSV* Vol.II:399).

Vivekananda remained in India until June 1899, by which time his health had broken down almost completely. In the meantime, monks of the Ramakrishna Order had undertaken, under the auspices of the Mission, famine relief in the eastern states and also to inaugurate an orphanage. During the Calcutta plague of 1898, they organised the cleaning of infected areas, and an education programme on sanitation and hygiene among the poor. A monk had been sent to Madras to conduct classes, and another was working in New York.

In 1896 a journal *Prabuddha Bharata* (*Awakened India*) was started by devotees, but moved to Almora in the Himalayas two years later, where a monastery for the practice of Advaita had been set up. There were to be no devotional practices allowed there, only the study of Advaita texts and meditation on the formless Brahman. This monastery has been a major publishing centre of the Order since its inception. In 1899 *Udbodhan*, the Bengali journal of the Order was founded by the monks in Calcutta. By summer of that year, Vivekananda was satisfied that his plans were proceeding well, and so he departed once more for America, taking with him another monk, to work on the west coast.

There was a shock awaiting Vivekananda in London. His most faithful disciples had changed their minds about him, and there was no longer even a nucleus of interested people for whom to hold classes. He therefore left after a brief stay, for the United States, after receiving an invitation from a group of disciples. In New York he gave classes at the new permanent rooms of the Vedanta Society, before going to the west coast, where he held classes in Los Angeles, San Francisco and other smaller towns where he had a following. He left for Europe in July 1900, satisfied with the work, and with the monks he had left behind. After a short tour of Europe with some disciples, he arrived back in India (unexpectedly) in December 1900.

In January 1901 a Trust Deed was executed, which placed the Belur Math in the hands of a Board of Trustees, all *saṃnyāsins* of the Ramakrishna Order, but not necessarily residing at the Math, which by now had become the Headquarters of the Order. Other Maths and Mission centres were growing up at the same time, and *saṃnyāsins* from Belur Math despatched there as required. New recruits to the Order were received both at branch centres and Headquarters, and lay devotees were drawn into the Ramakrishna Movement (as it came to be called) by receiving *mantra* initiation, given by senior *saṃnyāsins* to those who sought it.

Vivekananda remained in India until his sudden death on the 4th July 1902, some six months before he would have reached his fortieth birthday. Although as founder of the Order and the almost unchallenged architect of the Movement, he left it with both a solid financial and structural framework, his death left a vacuum which proved difficult for one person to fill. Gradually though, a new spiritual leader emerged, in perhaps the most unlikely yet apt person. To understand how this occurred, it is necessary to step back a little in time, in order to discuss the emerging doctrines of the Ramakrishna Movement, known loosely as the Ramakrishna Mission, since the Movement's relief and welfare work is far more widely known than the Order's purely religious aspect.

Ramakrishna, Incarnation of the Age

Until Vivekananda's triumphant return from the West, his brother monks in their Calcutta monastery lived humbly and quietly, receiving as visitors mainly the lay devotees of Ramakrishna, who found comfort in visiting the shrine.

In the West, Vivekananda had attempted to show that 'Hinduism', far from being an amorphous mass of conflicting doctrines and practices, was in fact a coherent thought system, based on Vedic scriptures. There were four major paths which could be followed in order to reach the aim of life according to Hinduism, which was the realisation of the Godhead, leading to liberation from rebirth. Each sect merely offered an alternate means to the same end. The four paths were known as *yogas* or Paths to Union (with the Godhead) and were *karma yoga* (Union through work correctly performed), *raja* (Union through certain mental and physical disciplines), *jnāna yoga* (Union through the study of philosophical texts resulting in true Knowledge), and *bhakti yoga* (Union through devotional practices).[7]

Vivekananda gave a series of lectures on each of the four *yogas*, and later published four volumes based on these, as well as lectures with such titles as 'The Ideal of a Universal Religion' (*Selections from Swami Vivekananda* pp. 178–203), in which he stressed that India has alone understood that no set of beliefs and practices can satisfy all people. It is for this reason that Hinduism provides different paths to the same goal.

The four *yogas* were presented to Western audiences as if they existed as separate entities, from which each Hindu could choose the one best suited to his/her temperament. For example, a philanthropic person could choose *karma yoga*, while the mystically inclined person may choose *raja* or perhaps *bhakti yoga*. While this approach was helpful for his Western followers, who had only to choose one of the *yogas*, this in no way even faintly approximated the manner in which Hinduism was organised in India. The overwhelming majority of Hindus in Vivekananda's time followed the same religious tradition as the rest of the family, since change frequently entailed a change of diet, dress and association, all of which were well-nigh impossible in the Hindu joint family. Even followers of modern movements such as the Brahmo Samaj had often to sever family connections once they joined the Brahmo fold. Moreover, in various regions of India, sects were either community based or in direct conflict with one another for doctrinal reasons, and there was sometimes minimal contact between their various adherents.

Vivekananda in his later years was fired with the conviction that religion alone could raise and unite India, and for this he envisaged that his *saṃnyāsins* would play a leading role. Educated youth would join the Movement, either as *saṃnyāsins* or lay workers, bringing education, medical skills and relief in time of crisis. In the evenings, Mission workers would preach the religion of the *Upanisads*, the Oneness of Brahman, and thus the validity of all sects and religions. Just as audiences cheered his broad views in America, so did

Vivekananda envisage that the diverse peoples of India would accept his plans for the unification of the country through religion. Ramakrishna had practised the *sādhanas* of all the major religions and sects, and realised the Truth through each. Thus he demonstrated the foolishness of sectarian quarrels. Vivekananda put forward a simple solution to India's complex problems, so that a rejuvenated India would become a light to the rest of the world.

Whilst in the West, Vivekananda referred to Ramakrishna on only very few occasions, and initiated his disciples into various *mantras*, according to their inclinations. He presented himself as a philosopher-monk who had come to share the riches of Vedanta with all who cared to hear. India was painted as a country where spiritually reigned supreme, where saints and *yogis* abounded. Vivekananda's India was far removed from the benighted land of the Christian missionaries' tales, and he openly accused Christians in America of believing that they themselves were above criticism, while other cultures were not. Thus, they felt free to heap abuse on adherents of other faiths and ways of life (*LSV* Vol.I:462–3).

Yet, on the other hand, in the early days of his success in America, Vivekananda wrote to his brother monks a sharp letter of rebuke, for having built a cult around Ramakrishna's memory, and for creating legends that: 'Ramakrishna was such and such – and cock-and-bull stories – stories having neither head nor tail. . . .' Instead, he suggested:

> If you want any good to come, just throw your ceremonials overboard and worship the living God, the Man-God – every being that wears a human form – God in His universal as well as individual aspect. The universal aspect of God means this world, and worshipping it means serving it – this indeed is work, not indulging in ceremonials. . . . (*CW* Vol.VII:278).

Back in India, while Vivekananda preached to large crowds his plan for the regeneration of India, he was also obliged, once back in Calcutta, to relate this to the teachings of his *guru*, Ramakrishna, with whom he was very much linked in the eyes of local devotees. In bewilderment, his brother monks questioned him as to how his ideas on social service could be reconciled with Ramakrishna's emphasis on the renunciation of duties. Was this not the reason that they had embraced *saṃnyāsa*? Such doubts were aired at the monastery soon after the Ramakrishna Mission was established (Gambhirananda 1957:123–4), and on that occasion Vivekananda is said to have been reduced to tears in an attempt to persuade the other monks that he had not deviated from Ramakrishna's teachings, and that Ramakrishna himself had inspired him to engage in selfless work.

In an entry in the *Gospel* dated Saturday the 6th December 1884, there is recorded a conversation between Ramakrishna and the highly esteemed Bengali literary figure Bankim Chandra Chatterji, on the subject of charity and helping the poor. Ramakrishna is quoted as saying:

> If a householder gives in charity in the spirit of detachment, he is really doing good to himself and not to others. It is God alone that he serves – God, who dwells in all beings. . . . This is called karma-yoga. This too is a way to realize God. But it is very difficult, and not suited to the Kaliyuga[8] (*Abridged Gospel*, p. 365).

Since at the time of this conversation there were no *saṃnyāsins* present, Ramakrishna did not discuss whether *saṃnyāsins* should undertake work, for in any case, it was not customary for *saṃnyāsins* to do so, and thus the question did not arise. Though it is not stated if Vivekananda was present on this occasion, according to the author of the *Great Master*, Ramakrishna said on one occasion, when he *was* present:

> Take of compassion for beings! Insignificant creatures that you are, how can you show compassion to beings? Who are you to show compassion? You wretch, who are you to bestow it? No, no; it is not compassion to Jivas but service to them as Siva.[9]
>
> It was Narendranath alone who, coming out of the room at the end of the master's ecstasy, said, 'Ah what a wonderful light have I got today from the Master's words! What a new and attractive Gospel have we received today through these sweet words of this, wherein a synthesis has been effected of sweet devotion to the Lord with Vedantic knowledge, which is generally regarded as dry, austere and lacking in sympathy with the sufferings of others. . . .' (pp. 939–40).

It should be noted that this exchange does not appear in the *Gospel*, which is a collection of conversations with Ramakrishna, recorded at the time they occurred. The words of Vivekananda appear in quotation marks in the *Great Master*, but their syrupy style appears quite out of character with the personality of Vivekananda, while at the same time very much in the style of the author, Swami Saradananda, a man of fervent, devotional nature. It was Saradananda, I suggest, who was the main creator also of the legends surrounding Ramakrishna, Incarnation of God, and

Vivekananda's mission on his behalf.

Saradananda was recalled from America, to become the first Secretary of the Ramakrishna Math and Mission (Satprakashananda 1978:129), and after the death of Vivekananda, its main policy maker during the Movement's first crucial stage of consolidation and expansion, both in India and overseas. As Vivekananda once said to Mrs John B. Lyon, his hostess during the Parliament of Religions, he faced his greatest temptation whilst in America.

> 'Who is she, Swami?' He burst out laughing and said, 'Oh, it is not a lady, it is Organization!' He explained how the followers of Ramakrishna had all gone out alone and when they reached a village, would just quietly sit under a tree and wait for those in trouble to come to consult them. But in the States he saw how much could be accomplished by organizing work (*LSV* Vol.I:144).

After Vivekananda's success in the West, people who came to the Belur Math were no longer necessarily devotees of Ramakrishna seeking solace, but a whole new generation fired with enthusiasm by Vivekananda's rousing public addresses, which were widely available also in printed form. The essence of Vivekananda's message in India was that the masses were poor and downtrodden, and that the country had sunken into a stupor by closing its doors to outside ideas. While the West had succeeded in reaching prosperity through political and social reform, this was not India's way. India's way was to rise through religion, which at present had slumped into a period of decay. Quoting the words of Krishna in the *Bhagavad Gita*, one of Hinduism's most revered texts:

> Whenever there is a decline of *dharma* (righteous living) and an increase in *adharma* (unrighteous living), I incarnate myself. For the protection of the good and the destruction of the wicked, and to re-establish *dharma* I am reborn in every age (IV:7–8).

Ramakrishna was the manifestation of this promise for the present age, the Kali Yuga. His was the name behind which the forces of Hinduism must rally. Vivekananda appealed to the young and educated in Calcutta in particular, with the Upanisadic catch cry: 'Arise, wake, and stop not till the goal is reached'. He asked them to have faith in themselves and in their ability to bring about a change in the whole of India, and painted a verbal picture of an India thus rejuvenated, and restored to her ancient glory (see, for example, *Reply to the Calcutta Address*, of 28th February 1897, in response to his official welcome home to Calcutta from the West [Vol.II:221]). It was in this Address that Vivekananda first linked his mission with the Divine Plan of an Incarnation of God, his *guru*, Ramakrishna.

The creation of an Incarnation of God out of the basic material of a saintly life is not without precedent: either in India or for that matter, the biblical tradition. The way in which this was achieved in the case of Ramakrishna was quite simple. For the original disciples of Ramakrishna, he was the *guru*, the spiritual teacher through whom God manifests himself. In this respect, each *guru* is to be regarded as God by his disciples and, as the 'matchmaker' who introduces the devotee to God, is worthy of worship. It was in this spirit that the young monks set up a shrine room to the memory of Ramakrishna, in their monastery. However, at first, before the shrine they sang the praises of the god Siva, Lord of ascetics, as the *ārati*[10] was performed. One of their number, Ramakrishnanada took charge of the shrine room from the outset, and made food offerings before the relics and photograph of Ramakrishna daily (see *LSV* Vol.I:198). At that stage, Ramakrishna was still a *guru*-god, their own *guru*, and thus divine only in the eyes of his disciples.

The earliest devotees to be initiated by the young monks were given *mantras* of one or other of the Hindu deities, and Ramakrishna received their homage as *paraṃguru*, the *guru* of the *guru* who initiated them. However, at one critical stage, this policy ceased, and devotees who came to the monastery (or, later to other branch monasteries also) were given the *mantra* of Ramakrishna. According to the Preface to the *Workship of Sri Ramakrishna*, the official manual of instructions for performing his daily ritual worship, the *mantras* for Ramakrishna worship were composed by Ramakrishnananda. Since he was sent to work among the Madras devotees in the year 1897, and the *mantras* were first used in worship in Calcutta, they must have been composed between the year in which he joined the monastery (1866) and the year 1897.

It can be deducted that worship of Ramakrishna as Avatara (Incarnation) was promoted, perhaps at first without formal *mantras*, during the lifetime of Vivekananda, for it was he who composed two hymns to Ramakrishna for use at dusk in each of the Movement's centres. In these, Ramakrishna is hailed as the Lord. It was also Vivekananda who, on dedicating a private shrine room to Ramakrishna in 1898, composed the following *mantra*:

> Salutations to Thee, O Ramakrishna, the Reinstator of Religion, the Embodiment of all Religions, *The Greatest of all Incarnations*![11] (*LSV* Vol.II:307)

And, what was the meaning of this? Ramakrishna had, according to Vivekananda:

> . . . reincarnated himself in India, to demonstrate what the true religion of the Aryan race is; to show where amidst all its many divisions and offshoots, scattered over the land in the course of its immortal history, lies the true unity of the Hindu religion . . . (*CW Vol. VI:183*)

But, this was not merely Vivekananda's personal opinion. A disciple once asked him:

> Did Shri[12] Ramakrishna out of his own lips ever say that he was God, the all-perfect Brahman?
>
> Swamiji: Yes, he did so many times. And he said this to all of us. One day while he was staying at the Cossipore garden . . . by the side of his bed I was saying in my mind, 'Well, now if you can declare that you are God, then only will I believe that you are really God Himself.' It was only two days before he passed away. Immediately, he looked up towards me all of a sudden and said, 'He who was Rama, He who was Krishna, verily is now Ramakrishna in this body. And not merely from the standpoint of your Vedanta!'[13] (*Selections from Swami Vivekananda*, 1963:434).

Later, after his return from the West, Vivekananda declared that not only was Ramakrishna an Incarnation who came to reconcile all sects of Hinduism, but also all religions. How did he do this? In the *Gospel*, Ramakrishna is said to have practised Christian and Muslim religious disciplines, each for three days, and through the visions of Christ and the Prophet merging in him, proved that each was but an aspect of the one Being, who was Ramakrishna in this life (*LSR*:175).

As Islam and Christianity were the other major religions of which Ramakrishna was aware, it was declared in retrospect that Ramakrishna was the founder of the doctrine of the harmony of Religions, that all religions were paths to God: *Jatho math, tatho path*[14] as Ramakrishna would say, in Bengali. A disciple, Surendranath Mitra had had a painting commissioned to express this ideal during Ramakrishna's lifetime, in which a temple, church and mosque appear in a row, with the Hindu saint Gauranga dancing in ecstasy with Jesus, while other religious figures look on, and Ramakrishna points out to Keshab the 'synthesis of all faiths' (*LSR*:260). A copy of the painting was sent to Keshab, who was deeply influenced by Ramakrishna's teachings, and whose New

Dispensation of religious synthesis was announced shortly after he came into close contact with Ramakrishna (*LSR*:260). It was only after Ramakrishna's death, however, that the Ramakrishna Movement evolved a cohesive set of doctrines concerning the 'meaning' of Ramakrishna's life. And, this development was largely due to the efforts of Swami Saradananda.

In 1909, when he completed a Calcutta house for the use of Sarada Devi, Saradananda embarked on his *magnum opus*: the comprehensive interpretative biography in Bengali of Ramakrishna.[15] The last few crucial months of Ramakrishna's life are not in this work, as Saradananda ceased writing after 1920, the year in which Sarada Devi, known as the Holy Mother, died. Originally, the biography appeared in the Bengali journal *Udbodhan*, in serial form, but was edited for publication in five volumes between 1911–18 (Appendix I, *SRGM*, Vol.II:1039–40). It is this work that finally put together the pieces of Ramakrishna's life, so far only randomly discussed in the *Gospel* and the writings of Vivekananda.[16]

New Realities

The monks of the Ramakrishna Order enjoyed increasing popularity after the demise of Vivekananda, for now the Ramakrishna Mission embarked on a programme of expansion which reached the far corners of India, and beyond. The Western educated and middle class were the major patrons of Mission activities, both in attending classes and in supporting the Mission branches financially. Whilst Mission workers went among the poor and illiterate, opening schools, dispensaries and providing relief in times of emergencies, lay supporters of the Movement saw an opportunity to build up some *punya* (religious merit) by making donations in cash or kind. Many became devotees, and sought *mantra* initiation. No matter which deity their family usually worshipped, those who were brought into the Ramakrishna fold were taught that he (Ramakrishna) embodied that deity. He was its most recent and complete manifestation. All gods and goddesses existed in him. He was, from the Mission's standpoint, the Universal God.

Swami Saradananda and Swami Ramakrishnananda, his cousin, had been educated at St. Xavier's College, Calcutta. They had become deeply inspired by the New Testament, an attitude fostered at that time by the Brahmo Samaj, of which they were both members. Between them they were later to create the props for Ramakrishna's Incarnationhood, as preached by Vivekananda earlier.

Saradananda, in the *Great Master*, sets the stage for Ramakrishna's Incarnationhood by reminding the reader of Krishna's promise in the *Bhagavad Gita*, and painting a picture of how the time was ripe for God to reappear in the mid-nineteenth century, in Bengal. Ramakrishna was conceived and born among miracles which rival those of the Christian Gospels, and his youth was marked by visions, ecstasies, and wise judgements similar to those of Jesus in the Temple. His life after arriving in Calcutta thus becomes a neat progression of spiritual practices, which commence with Dualism and culminate in the Non-Dualist experience of *nirvikalpa samādhi*, or realisation of the formless Brahman. After this, he meets his future disciples, and during his final illness, reveals himself as an Incarnation of God to his dearest disciple Naren, to whom he transfers his power, before passing away.[17]

Ramakrishna's life was certainly extraordinary, and his conversations, as recorded in the *Gospel*, reveal him as a man of sharp wit. Yet, this was deemed insufficient for Saradananda, who goes to great lengths to supernaturalise every aspect of his life. From beginning to end, it is part of a Divine Plan. As Berger and Luckmann have pointed out, in writing religious biographies of such personalities as Incarnations, the gap must be bridged between their mundane existence, and the Divine reality behind it (1966:177–82). Often, the everyday details of their lives and the lives of those closely connected with them have to be reinterpreted. Thus, Saul became St. Paul on the Damascus Road, and Naren became Ramakrishna's heir and apostle at the touch of the Master. By careful use of the pen, 'awkward' details are smoothed over, so that they no longer provide either a problem or paradox.

An example of this is in the 'problem' of Ramakrishna's wife, who remained by his side, despite the fact that he is said to have taken the vows of *saṃnyāsa*. The 'answer' is that Ramakrishna, as Incarnation of God,[18] brought with him his Sakti or Female Consort. Sarada Devi was not merely his wife. Indeed, it is claimed that the marriage was never consummated. She was Ramakrishna's Power, and as in the case of other Incarnations, he brought her with him for the duration of his present birth. So, Sarada Devi's life had later to be reinterpreted in the light of this revelation, a process which did not fully reach completion until after his death.

The *Great Master* became the official biography of Ramakrishna, to which all later Mission publications refer and defer. Just as the doctrine of Jesus as the Son of God became 'true' through the authority of the Gospels, so Ramakrishna became God through the authority of the *Great Master* for the following generations, not only of devotees, but of scholars.

Consolidation

By the first decade of the twentieth century, the Ramakrishna Movement had established itself firmly in Bengal and neighbouring states, undertaking major Relief projects in particular (Gambhirananda 1957:175–6). It had also succeeded in attracting devotees in South India, especially in major cities such as Madras, Bangalore, Mysore, Trivandrum and in Malabar.

Once it became strong in its own right in a locality, the Movement did not have to justify its existence. Branches tended to attract well-known and educated citizens, many of whom were inspired by Vivekananda's call for the uplift of India through an understanding of its ancient heritage. Monks of the Order were a 'new breed': instead of the wandering *saṃnyāsin* with soiled robes and matted hair, the Ramakrishna Order monks were usually clean shaven, and their ochre robes well laundered. They looked, in fact, middle class. Moreover, most of the monks were college educated and spoke good English. They represented the modern India with whom the middle class could identify, while at the same time they spoke in the idiom of the ancient sages.

Ramakrishna Mission centres and Maths were well-ordered, quiet and peaceful, in marked contrast to the noisy, run down precincts of many an existing Hindu institution. Indeed, many centres were landscaped with lawns and flower gardens, as were the homes of the wealthiest and most Westernised of families. Monks used modern business methods in running their centres, and special programmes were announced on dignified personalised printed invitations. And, perhaps more importantly, Vivekananda's stirring lectures and writings on the need for India to arise from its inertia, tied in well with a new force that was emerging at this time: Indian Nationalism.

Indeed, it may be said that Vivekananda acted as a catalyst, as a bridge between the social concerns of the Brahmo Samaj and the political Nationalism of the early twentieth century. In fact, the British saw a direct link between Vivekananda and the growing tide of Nationalist feelings, in Bengal particularly, resulting in the Belur Math and its branches being under constant police scrutiny. The keenness shown by overseas devotees to support the Movement was regarded with suspicion, and the Headquarter's activities were monitored by 'watching its workers in silence and opening foreign letters that reached the Belur Math' (Gambhirananda 1957:211). It was perhaps ironical that at the same time, the Movement was condemned by many Nationalists for not supporting the Swadeshi movement,[19] which came into being in 1906, and later the Independence Movement, which reached a crescendo during the Second World War (1957:211). Yet, the Ramakrishna Movement's official policy remained steadfastly as Vivekananda had stated: non-involvement in political issues.

By the time that India was granted Independence from Britain, the Movement was poised on the brink of further expansion, as many who had espoused the cause of political freedom now sought a new 'cause' to take up. As a result, recruitment to the Order increased, and new centres were opened. The Indian Government declared donations to both Math and Mission to be exempt from Income Tax, and generous grants were made available for the Mission to carry out vital relief, medical and educational work. The Ramakrishna Movement became a highly respectable organisation, which in the India of today is comparable to the International Red Cross in the scale of its relief projects in times of crisis and disaster.

The Movement comprises some 150 centres, with numerous smaller unaffiliated centres and groups also operating, both in India and abroad. It also helped to establish a parallel though autonomous Order for women, which came into being in 1953. It is a branch of this Order in South India, firmly grounded in the Ramakrishna Movement tradition, that is the actual focus and location of the fieldwork on which this study is based. I shall now discuss how the Movement came to Kerala in South India, and how a Womens Math was eventually established there.

Chapter 3

The Ramakrishna Movement in Kerala

I have provided the background which led up to the establishment of the Ramakrishna Order in Calcutta and the spread of the Ramakrishna Movement far beyond the boundaries of Bengal. I now wish to describe how the Movement came to the south west coast of India,[1] and how the Movement was instrumental in bringing about some of the most far-reaching social changes in the former States of Travancore and Cochin and British Malabar. Against this background I shall trace the development of a branch of the Ramakrishna Order in Cochin State, located in a remote village some eight kilometres from the rural town of Trichur, proudly known as 'the Cultural capital of Kerala'.

The first contact between the followers of Ramakrishna and the people of the Malabar Coast[2] was made during the visit of Vivekananda prior to his departure for the United States to attend the Parliament of Religions. He arrived in the region in December 1892, after staying for a few days in Bangalore with a physician by the name of Dr Palpu, a native of Travancore.

Dr Palpu belonged to the Izhava Community,[3] which was classed as *caṇḍāla* or *avarṇa* (Outcaste), that is though Hindu, Izhavas (along with other communities) were considered too lowly to belong to any of the four Vedic *varṇas*. Their main occupation was toddy tapping, considered degrading, as intoxicants were shunned by higher ranking communities – at least publicly. Those who did not engage in toddy preparation were usually labourers in paddy fields and estates owned by caste Hindus or in the coir industry. They were considered polluting by caste Hindus and according to a sliding scale could not come within a certain distance of them: the higher the individual's communal status, the further an Izhava had to keep away. Consequently, when Western education first came to the region, Izhavas could not share in many of its benefits because caste

Hindus refused to associate with them. Dr Palpu studied in an English school run by a European Christian who had no time for caste rules, and who helped him to reach Matriculation level. Despite passing the College entrance for Medicine, he was denied a place, due to objections of the caste Hindu students. He therefore left his home and studied in Madras. Dr Palpu was sent to Europe by the Government of Mysore, in whose service he worked after graduation. He reached a high position in Mysore, but knew he could never practice medicine in Travancore, due to the rigours of caste observance.

When Dr Palpu met Vivekananda he poured his heart out to him about the indignities which he and his fellow Izhavas had to suffer in Travancore, and sought his advice as to how to overcome this. Vivekananda advised him to find a leader among Izhavas and to make him their rallying force, stressing that they must raise themselves, and not look to others for justice (Siddhinathananda 1978:82–3 and Sanoo 1978:72). It is significant that this incident is mentioned both in accounts by a Swami of the Ramakrishna Order and also by an eminent Izhava scholar. Dr Palpu already knew of such a person, the saintly Izhava ascetic who became known as Sri Narayana Guru. In 1896 Dr Palpu came to Travancore on leave and travelled throughout the state collecting 13,000 signatures for a petition to the Maharajah. It expressed the sentiment that despite the availability of education and Government Service, both these and other benefits enjoyed by other subjects were denied Izhavas, condemning them to even further backwardness (Sanoo 1978:71). Eventually Dr Palpu sent an emissary to London to meet a disciple of Vivekananda, Sister Nivedita.[4] Through her connections, she had the matter of the injustices suffered by Izhavas raised in British Parliament. This resulted in an enquiry and precipitated the gradual breakdown of the more blatant forms of discrimination against them (1978:73), for in British Malabar to the north, Izhavas were eligible for all positions open to 'natives' (1978:71).

In 1903 Dr Palpu helped to form the Shri Narayana Dharma Paripalana Yogam, a registered organisation which grew out of the nucleus of the experimental Izhava Mahajana Sabha started in 1896, during his home leave. The by-laws of the Yogam, composed by the famous poet and social reformer Kumaran Asan, an Izhava, started with a quotation from Vivekananda in which he said it is religion that can raise India or degrade it. I shall pick up the threads of the campaign by Izhavas to raise the community much later, and in a different context. But, in the meantime I shall return to Vivekananda's sojourn on the Malabar Coast.

Vivekananda was profoundly shocked by his visit, to which he referred on his return from the West in 1897, during a public address in Madras. He said:

> Was there ever a sillier thing before in the world than what I saw in Malabar? The poor Pariah[5] is not allowed to pass through the same street as the high-caste man, but if he changes his name to hodge-podge English name, it is alright. What inference would you draw except that these Malabaris are all lunatics, their homes so many lunatic asylums, and they are to be treated with derision by every race [sic] in India until they mend their manners and know better. Shame upon them that such wicked and diabolical customs are allowed (*CW* Vol.III:294–5).

In Travancore Vivekananda had stayed with a Tamil Brahmin professor, who had introduced him to many of the State's prominent citizens. But, it was only after Vivekananda's triumphant return from the West that a formal following of Ramakrishna-Vivekananda emerged.

As a result of Vivekananda's visit to Madras in 1897, a group of followers began to meet regularly, to discuss how to translate his message into practice. After reaching Calcutta, Vivekananda sent Swami Ramakrishnananda to Madras to guide and inspire the group there. Knowing the group to be largely from orthodox Brahmin families, Ramakrishnananda, the most orthodox of the young monks, and fluent in English, was the obvious choice.[6]

In 1904 a Bengali gentleman posted to Trivandrum invited Ramakrishnananda to visit him. He had actually visited Ramakrishna during his lifetime, and so had looked up Ramakrishnananda while on a visit to Madras. The Swami accepted the invitation, and stayed with the gentleman, Babu Kalipada Ghosh, for a few months. By the end of the Swami's visit a number of small groups were formed in Travancore, including one in Haripad, in Central Travancore. As was the case in Bengal and elsewhere, it was the Western educated who took the initiative.

The Haripad Association of devotees of Ramakrishna invited the Swami to visit during the celebrations of Ramakrishna's birthday in 1911, through the President, Padmanabhan Tampi, who knew the Swami from Madras. But, the Swami was very occupied with classes and so sent Swami Nirmalananda (who had come from the Calcutta monastery to assist him) instead. So great was the local response that

Nirmalananda remained after the celebrations and in 1913 the first Ramakrishna Asrama in the state known today as Kerala was established, in Haripad.

During the opening celebrations of the new Asrama there was some comment by the orthodox over the policy that no caste restrictions would apply to devotees, and they would all be treated alike. The following year, during the birthday celebrations, all were invited to share the offered food, after the worship was over. Since there was insufficient space for all to sit, after the first group had completed their meal, the servants were requested to remove the leaf plates, so that the floor could be wiped[7] and another set of places prepared for those waiting to eat. The servants, having seen the communal conglomeration, refused, on the grounds that they could not touch plates polluted by those of lowly birth. Whereupon, the Swami briskly picked up the plates himself, saying: 'They are all devotees of Bhagavan.[8] I am their servant. I have no Caste. But you should all maintain yours' (Siddhinathananda 1978:84). The devotees were aghast that the monk should touch the plates, for it was for lay devotees to serve monks, not vice-versa: the caste (communal) question quite apart. There was a rush to remove the rest of the offending plates.

This incident must have had a profound effect on the Asrama officials, all of whom would have been from 'respectable' caste Hindu families. Already they had been forced to compromise their own scruples in order to attend school or College, or whilst travelling by train, or in their work. Now they were being asked to do so in temple precincts: quite a daring request, since it was not until 1936 that the first public temple in Travancore was opened to non-caste Hindus, midst prolonged protests and demonstrations on both sides. The Ramakrishna Asrama Haripad was thus far beyond its time in insisting on full access and equality of treatment for all who came to the Asrama, whether to participate in worship, to attend classes or to visit the Swami.

From Haripad the Swami extended his work to Trivandrum and Tiruvalla in Travancore, and also into the state of Cochin to the North, and then even further into British Malabar. Though all three regions of the Malabar Coast spoke the same language, Malayalam, there was little contact between them, as pollution restrictions prevented travel beyond certain well-defined boundaries. Swami Nirmalananda encouraged devotees from all three regions to visit the other Asramas, assuring them that devotees of Ramakrishna formed a separate community, and could freely mix with each other without fear of pollution. Many devotees, after taking *mantra* initiation from the Swami believed that this was so.

In 1916 Swami Nirmalananda brought Swami Brahmananda, the President of the Ramakrishna Order, to the Malabar Coast on his way to Kanya Kumari. On that occasion he laid the foundation of the Asrama seven miles from Trivandrum on a hill overlooking the town, and initiated many lay devotees. Four or five of the College educated young men who had become close devotees through contact with Swami Nirmalananda later joined the Order, gaining extra conviction through meeting its President, a man of extraordinary presence and personality. One of these, Swami Tyagisananda was the founder of an Asrama in Trichur District, in the state of Cochin, on the 30th May, 1927.

Sri Ramakrishna Asrama, Trichur

While the Ramakrishna Movement was growing in Travancore, further north in Trichur town admirers of Vivekananda had started a high school under the auspices of the Vivekodayam Samajam (Association), in 1915. The school was under the patronage of His Highness Rama Varma Appan Tampuran, a senior Prince of the Cochin royal family, a famous literary figure of his time, and a man of great sensitivity. The Headmaster was Krishna Menon, an advocate in Ernakulam, Cochin's main port and town. The aim of the school was primarily to provide a modern education for the children of well-known families, mainly of the Nayar community to which Krishna Menon belonged. Alongside teaching the usual syllabus, the school had as its policy to 'propagate the life-giving, man-making ideas of Swami Vivekananda, to awaken real *viveka*[9] in our boys and girls and to make them fully conscious of our rich cultural heritage' (Menon A.S. 1978:70).

In 1915 Gandhi had coined the word 'Harijan' or 'Children of God' which he applied to Outcaste Hindus, and Gandhi's plea for caste Hindus to help in their uplift was readily taken up by some of the dedicated followers of Vivekananda who had created the Ramakrishna Mission largely for this purpose, almost two decades earlier. In 1927 Krishna Menon took over a tiny elementary co-educational school that was being run in a thatched shed in a predominantly Harijan village, eight kilometres from Trichur town. It is unclear who was the original teacher, but as soon as Krishna Menon took over the premises, he opened a hostel for Harijan boys, where they could live whilst studying, receiving free board and food.

Krishna Menon stayed at night in the hostel with the boys, appointing a teacher to actually run the school at first as he continued to be Headmaster of the Vivekodayam school in Trichur. He walked daily to Trichur and back, despite the blazing sun in summer and the rain and floods of the monsoon season, which left the low-lying paddy fields between the village and town hazardous to cross. In the village he cooked for the boys and helped tend the kitchen garden, in addition to concerning himself with the problems of the Harijan villagers, who worked as labourers in the fields of local landlords.

The Harijan work in the village of Puranattukara caused Krishna Menon to be the object of abuse by local caste Hindus, and he was sometimes stoned as he entered or left the school premises.[10] Soon after coming to live in the village, he decided to apply for membership of the Ramakrishna Order, and was accepted as a *brahmacāri*.[11] It was only after receiving the vows of *saṃnyāsa* that Krishna Menon, now known as Swami Tyagisananda, resigned his position as Headmaster and concentrated his energy wholly on building up the village project. The school and hostel became a branch of the Ramakrishna Math in 1927, and H.H. Rama Varma Appan Tampuran, at that time the Manager of the Vivekodayam School, agreed to assume the responsibility of management, resigning his position at Vivekodayam even before Krishna Menon.

The resignation of the two key leaders of the Vivekodayam School must have caused a sensation. The High School had been started for the education of children from aristocratic families, many of whom had built a town home in Trichur purely for the higher education of the younger generation. The Vivekodayam, with a qualified advocate as Headmaster and senior member of the royal family as Manager had inspired the confidence of even conservative family heads. So high was their reputation that modern education did not seem suspect, in their hands. For them now to give this up, and to live and work with Harijans, who by local law were obliged to keep at a distance from caste Hindus, was at first for many inexplicable, and for some, remained so. In order to expand further why the steps taken by the Tampuran (Prince) and Krishna Menon were so daring, I shall now fill in the background of Trichur society of which they were a part, before returning to the foundation of the Ramakrishna Asrama, Trichur.

Trichur in the Early Decades of the Nineteenth Century

Trichur has been since the time of Sankaracarya, founder of the Dasanami Order of *saṃnyāsins*, the stronghold of learning and orthodoxy and consequently conservatism on the Malabar Coast. Sankaracarya's four chief disciple set up four Maths (monasteries) in Trichur[12] for the study of Advaita, and the teaching of Brahmin youth, who attended as boarders, free of charge. Around these centres of learning, powerful Brahmin families have lived for generations, sending their sons to a particular Math, which they supported also with gifts and endowments (Menon A.S. 1978:167).

The Brahmin community of Kerala appears to have settled there, probably from the east coast, in about the eighth century,[13] and believes itself to be of Aryan origin, descendants of the invaders who entered India from the north west, but became powerful only during the aftermath of the Chola-Chera Wars of the eleventh century. As the indigenous people were engaged in fighting, the Brahmins, who became known as Nambudiris, consolidated their position. The temples which they had built and their surrounding lands were both spared the ravages of the wars and exempt from tax. Consequently some local chiefs transferred their land to the temples in order to spare them from the enemy, possibly in return for protection. Nambudiri families eventually took large portions of temple lands for their own use, to be worked by dispossessed and/or impoverished local people. By the thirteenth century the Malabar Coast was a feudal society, ruled over by landowning chiefs, some of the wealthiest of whom were Nambudiris. In turn, groups of chiefs were allied to one or other of the more powerful rulers, whose fortunes and areas of control changed frequently over the centuries, as local and outside wars continued. The local inhabitants of the Malabar Coast could be called up at various levels, up to full mobilisation, at the behest of their chief. And, this caused havoc with society. Large numbers of men were killed in battle, especially *chavers*, suicide squads who died to uphold the prestige of their chief, in the face of defeat.

Since the fourteenth century, European travellers to the shores of the Malabar Coast have testified to the fact that women there had multiple sexual partners (Fuller 1976:2–3). What they were referring to was actually the system of *marumakkathāyam*.

Leaving aside the debate concerning its origins, *marumakkathāyam* appears to have developed after the Chola-Chera wars. It is a system of matrilineal descent rules which link together the Nambudiri community, royalty, temple personnel and upper sections of the community known as Nayar, in a complex network.

As I have explained, members of the Nambudiri community accumulated great wealth in the form of agricultural land, which they managed to keep intact, despite invasions and constantly changing political boundaries. In order to do so they devised a system whereby only the eldest son in a family could marry a Nambudiri spouse, who would then come and live with him. In turn only the eldest son of this marriage would marry, and so on, the other sons remaining unmarried for life, in the family home. In this way the family property did not have to be shared by more and more members, each successive generation. The younger sons (denied the right to marry) formed *sambandham* unions, a form of concubinage, with women of royal houses, or of the Nayar community. They chose women usually only of wealthy families which generally obtained Nambudiri *sambandham* visiting partners. These families became an aristocracy, adopting many Brahmin customs and attitudes. Children of these unions remained with their mother and her matrilineal kinsfolk, the father having no legal rights or duties towards them. The authority figure for the children was the eldest uncle of the entire family, who was known as the *kāraṇavan.* He held control of the property, which remained indivisible, each member of the family receiving clothes and other necessities, and food being provided for all in the large dining halls. Such families – known as *taravāds* – grew very large, and some comprised many hundreds of members, all under one roof. Eventually a woman and her children would break away and form a new *taravād,* but only in certain specified circumstances, which need not concern us here.

The advantages of this system were shared by both Nambudiri and Nayar alike. For those Nayar *taravāds* involved it gave prestige, for Nayars belong to the Sudra category, that is the lowest of the four *varṇas.* Those *taravāds* which took Nambudiri *sambandham* partners became a 'cut above' other Nayars, and over the generations their appearance became markedly different from those Nayar *taravāds* whose women took Nayar *sambandham* partners. As is the case in other parts of India, fairness of skin and fineness of features are highly regarded, as associated with high caste or 'Aryan blood'. The indigenous people of the Malabar Coast are Dravidian, a dark skinned people, and so the Nayar aristocracy, through *sambandham* unions has developed quite distinctive features, midway between Nayar and Nambudiri. Unfortunately, those children (especially daughters) who are dark in complexion in such *taravāds* were and are extremely disadvantaged, whilst those who are fair (and thus more Nambudiri looking) greatly favoured and sought after. Therefore, for the Nayar *taravāds* involved, the Nambudiri *sambandham* unions gave them an opportunity to associate with Brahmins and to absorb many of their characteristics, thereby distinguishing themselves from *taravāds* not able to do so. For the Nambudiris, the advantages were mainly in their property remaining intact over many generations, and the freedom of their menfolk to form liaisons with Nayar women more or less at will, and free from obligations. The losers in the whole system were women of the Nambudiri community, many of whom were denied all opportunity of marriage, due to a shortage of 'eldest sons'. Some were married late in life as second or third wives, and some even on their deathbed, so that the scriptural injunctions that a woman should be married would be fulfilled. In order to ensure that unmarried women did not stray, and thus upset the whole system (by producing sons who could claim a share of the property) women of the community were kept in complete seclusion, rigorously enforced on the pain of banishment with loss of caste, or death.

Nambudiris were concentrated in certain areas of the Malabar Coast and, as I have already mentioned, Trichur was a centre of Nambudiri learning and also economic dominance. Associated with the great Nambudiri *manas* and *illams* (as their residences were called) were the *taravāds* of the aristocratic Nayars, who were linked to the local Nambudiris by *sambandham* ties. Between these groups were a few exclusive communities of temple personnel, and the royal lineages. These in turn were linked to both Nayar *taravāds* and Nambudiri *illams* and *manas*.

In the first two decades of the twentieth century three major community-based organisations were inaugurated on the Malabar Coast, the earliest being the SNDP Yogam under the guidance of Dr Palpu, for the uplift of Izhavas. This was followed by the Yogakshema Sabha of the Nambudiris, which sought to change the rules of primogeniture, so that all sons could marry Nambudiri spouses, with equal rights to a portion of the property, and the end of seclusion for women. The Nayar Service Society (NSS) was not founded until 1914, and it sought the total reform of the *marumakkathāyam* system as its major goal.

The leaders of the NSS were for the most part educated youth who were not content to sit at home after completing their studies. Opportunities were growing in the towns for work in government offices and private businesses, in the professions and various other new occupations. Whilst a Christian man could take his wife and property share and move to the town of his employ, a Nayar was hampered, with the *marumakkathāyam* system. The family property was corporate. No individual could claim a share and leave. Neither did he have a wife whom he could take to the town. His responsibility was of course to his sister's children, and to the entire *taravād*, to which he owed many ritual obligations also. Many young men, influenced by Gandhi's campaign against Untouchability, began to view the whole feudal structure of Nayar society (with its exploitation of hapless Harijans) as outmoded, unjust and against the interest of ambitious forward-looking individuals, indeed for a free united India.

The southern state of Travancore was the first to enact laws which acknowledged the needs of employed Nayars, and the rights of the individual *taravād* members. In 1912 the First Nair Act was passed, giving males the right to give half of their self-acquired property to their sons and the other half to their nephews. The state of Cochin in 1919–20 enacted the Cochin Nair Regulation which limited the power of the *kāraṇavan*, the powerful *taravād* head, and legalised *sambandham* unions as 'marriage' while at the same time prohibiting polygamy. Men were now obliged to maintain wife and children, and so corresponding legislation had to be prepared, making way for the *taravād* property to be partitioned into individual shares.

As far as I can ascertain, no scholarly work has captured the confusion and anguish caused by these so-called 'progressive' legislative measures. The legislation requiring a man to support his children and to legalise his marital status cut directly across the main feature of the *sambandham* system, which bound a man's loyalty to his sisters and their children rather than to his offspring. Furthermore, among the higher levels of the Nayar community, hypergamy operated, in which *sambandham* partners were of different status levels, the male partner always being of higher status than the female. I have already stated that a system of unapproachability existed in the region, and this applied also to Nambudiri-Nayar contact. Thus, a Nambudiri male would become ritually polluted by touching any Nayar, including his own *sambandham* partner. This is why men used to only visit their partners at night, after the supper was over, for once they had touched their Nayar *sambandham* partner they remained ritually polluted until they bathed fully. Hence the rule that male nocturnal visitors should depart well before dawn, so that they could return to their own homes, after bathing first in the family bathing tank. For at dawn, ritual duties had to be performed, and by this time a male should be cleansed of the night's ritual pollution.

The new legislation required a man to support his wife and children, but this became very difficult, because Nayar men still felt an obligation towards their sister's children. Nambudiri 'younger brothers' who up to now were not officially allowed to marry felt no obligation at all to their Nayar *sambandham* partners. Obviously, if a man had to support his wife and children, he had to have access to a personal income, and this meant the inevitable campaign for the division of the corporate joint family property into individual shares. Few men were in paid employment: virtually only those in the professions such as teaching, or in government service.

One other major difficulty existed concerning the legislation. Among the higher ranking Nayar *taravāds* in which hypergamy was practised, how could a man be expected to feel responsible for a wife and children of lower status? Even if the legislation made them legally his family and heirs, how could he accept them as such when he was forbidden to even take a glass of water from their hands or touch them without immediately incurring ritual pollution? In 1981 I visited a house in Trichur in which a Nambudiri husband, then in his eighties, had come to live in the house owned by his wife, during the period of the new legislation. Since that time he had maintained his own prayer room for the performance of his daily rituals, and cooked and ate alone, out of sight of his wife. His daughter had married a Prince, who also lived in the house. The Prince also ate alone, for he was a *kṣatriya*, too low to eat with his father-in-law, but too high ranking to eat with his wife. His wife, mother-in-law and his children ate together but when his wife's brother visited, the question of dining became even more complicated. He had, following the rules of hypergamy, married a woman of a lower-ranking Nayar family, so although the brother could eat with his sister and her children, his own Nayar wife and children, being of lower rank, were not really welcome to eat with anyone in the house. At this stage, the system of ranking gave way to modern pressures, and in fact the brother's wife did eat with her sister-in-law, but there was tension involved, especially between the cousins: the sister's children ranking higher than those of the brother.

Finally, what transpired was this: Nambudiris pressed for the right for all brothers to marry within their community, so that they would not have to give their family property to and live with Nayar wife and children. The first legislation granting equal rights to property and to marry within the community was passed in British Malabar in 1933. Similarly, the royal houses preferred to marry between each other, rather than to allow their members, whether male or female to marry Nayars and thus pass their inheritance to commoners. The Nayar aristocracy, thus denied royal or Nambudiri spouses for their women, began to marry among itself: ancient feuding families now uniting in marriage alliances for their own survival. And, further down the line of ranking, Nayars of lesser status began to marry among themselves, looking for sound education, and employment as well as lineage when seeking husbands for their daughters.

All in all, the reforms caused a great deal of social upheaval on the whole of the Malabar Coast, for each of the three regions enacted similar legislations. The great Nayar and royal *taravāds* found themselves losing their former prestige, as Nambudiri men were not interested in legally eligible Nayar young women, now that the *sambandham* system was officially illegal. Without the boast of their Brahmin connections as the main source of aristocratic prestige, Nayar families and royalty were ready to turn their quest for prestige elsewhere, when the opportunity arose.[14]

The First Trichur Recruits to the Ramakrishna Order

The reaction to *Krishna Menon*'s resignation from the position of Headmaster of the Vivekodayam School was mixed. Some could not understand why a young man with such a promising future would give it up, especially as he had attained the most coveted position: he had an independent salaried income. He could have found a wife easily, and yet he chose to 'bury' himself in a village with Harijans, thereby severing all social contact with caste Hindus.

On the other hand, some of the other educated young men from Trichur could understand Krishna Menon's motivation. They had read Vivekananda and Gandhi, and were convinced that for India to become a modern nation, first the masses must be educated and their lot in life improved. Krishna Menon became a hero for them, and after he became a *saṃnyāsin*, some spoke of him as a saint.[15]

After the village School and Hostel in Puranattukara became a branch of the Belur Math in 1927, six young educated men who had been associated with Krishna Menon came to the village to join the work, and also to enter the Ramakrishna Order. Out of the six new *saṃnyāsins* none was a Brahmin but one was high ranking, belonging to a tiny community of *ambalavāsi* temple personnel, two were Nayar (from the same family) one an Ezhuttachan (a small community of teachers and builders,[16] considered low caste but not Untouchable), and one an Izhava. The communal status of the sixth *saṃnyāsin* I could not ascertain, as he was no longer alive in 1981, and I did not know any of his relatives, from whose names I could have worked out a communal status. To have asked directly the communal status of any of the members of the Order would have been highly offensive, not only because *saṃnyāsins* 'have no family' and hence communal affiliation, but because the lowly origin of some of the *saṃnyāsins* is considered best 'forgotten'. As far as the Order is officially concerned, its *saṃnyāsins* are all (as are lay devotees) 'children of Ramakrishna', and there the discussion ends.

Mathru Mandir

In 1927, two small orphaned Harijan girls were brought to the Asrama and the first published Report of the Asrama (1933–5) notes that though there were women in the town who were willing to help support a village Hostel for girls, so far no Warden could be found, that is a woman who would be prepared to live on the premises with them. In the meantime, the girls were growing year by year, causing some adverse comments by local people, since the Swamis were looking after them, and according to the orthodox view, a *saṃnyāsin* should not even look at a woman, no matter how young.

The Asrama Report for 1935–6 announced with relief that a Warden had been found for a Harijan Hostel for girls, orphaned and destitute after a local epidemic, and that a 'local sympathiser' had given a house rent free for the girls (who now numbered 11) and the staff. The Warden's name was given as Srimathi A.A. Bhavani *Amma.* She was actually a relative of one of the young *saṃnyāsins* of the Asrama, and of Izhava origin. The courtesy title '*amma*' added to her name in the Report was one used only for women of the Nayar community.[17] This may give us the clue as to why an Izhava woman would choose to live and thus become identified with Harijans – who were even lower on the scale of communal hierarchy. By 1935 the campaign against the practice of Untouchability by Gandhi had gained wide respectability, and had been taken up as a cause by many educated caste Hindus. By becoming Warden of the Harijan Hostel an Izhava such as Bhavani would have been associated with not so much of the Harijans, but with those who employed her: namely, Swami Tyagisananda and the Tampuran. She did not lose status, but gained: she was now not simply *Bhavani,* as caste Hindus would have called her, but 'Srimathi A.A. Bhavani Amma', and accorded courtesy if not respect by visitors to the Asrama.

By this time some caste Hindu boys also had sought admission in the Gurukul, as the Boys Hostel was called,[18] mainly at first relatives of the *saṃnyāsins,* who lived far from a school. The Report declared that children of all communities in the Gurukul lived together:

> . . . without any invidious distinctions of high and low. The atmosphere of the institution has become so natural and healthy that visitors from outside even belonging to orthodox families feel no objection whatsoever to share the common life and mess of the Gurukul (*Report* 1933–5, p. 9).

However, the courtesy extended to Bhavani in the Report of 1933–5 may have met with some objections from supporters of the Asrama, as in the next available Report (1939–40) she is no longer referred to as 'Bhavani Amma', but as 'Sister Bhavani' this being an English translation of *chechi,* the Malayalam word for elder sister.[19] Most likely the children in the Hostel addressed her in this way, and it became her usual form of address, *chechi* being common to both the majority of Nayar and Izhava families in the region.

In the community-conscious town of Trichur and its environs, the small but expanding Ramakrishna Asrama was certainly a pioneer in the field of inter-communal integration, and tactful compromises, as can be understood by the choice of a dignified title for Bhavani. Indeed, the Asrama was one of the earliest fully integrated Hindu residential institutions of the whole of India: quite a remarkable accomplishment in view of Trichur's ultra-conservative, Nambudiri dominated reputation.

It should be mentioned at this juncture that it was only in 1935 that, following a long and bitter campaign, the Travancore Maharajah issued a Proclamation opening temples in his kingdom for the first time to *avarṇa* Hindus. It had been only in 1928 that the roads adjacent to temples in Travancore had been opened to all, following a non-violent protest, supported by Mahatma Gandhi. In Cochin, however, an independent kingdom, temples were only opened to all Hindus in 1947, that is following Indian Independence, when Untouchability was made a punishable offence throughout India (Menon A.S. 1978:228).

Despite the shortages of commodities experienced during the Second World War, the Asrama built a High School (*Report* 1939–40), some of the funds being raised in Malaya and Singapore, where many from the Malabar Coast were employed. The same Report announces that 30 small dwellings for Harijans had been built in a housing Colony, not far from the Asrama, and that a small printing press had been set up, for the publication of the Malayalam journal of the Order, *Prabuddha Keralam.*

In the *Report* of 1943, a worried President of the Asrama writes that food prices had risen 'three to four times the pre-war days' (p. 3), and that although the Cochin Government contributed Rs 100 annually towards the cost of feeding the poor students, the actual outlay was now Rs 360 and rapidly escalating. Not only that, the cloth ration for students had been cut by 50%, so that children in the School received only one set of clothes each school year. It was feared that children would not be willing or able to continue their schooling, for in the rainy season their clothes would become soaked almost daily, and without a second set, they would not be able to come to school, since in the humid climate clothes take two days to dry. In the midst of these problems, the village experienced a cholera epidemic, and the Asrama found itself, despite a desperate shortage of funds, supporting twelve poor families left without even one earning member. The following year, it opened a Charitable Dispensary in the village, where 'allopathic' or Western medicine was freely available, under qualified direction.

Meanwhile, the Girls Hostel was being consolidated. In 1948 it was given its own compound and buildings, opposite the Asrama Boys School, Hostel and monastery. The two compounds were separated by the main village thoroughfare, an unsealed road which linked the town of Trichur with the pilgrimage centre of Guruvayur. Bhavani had been assisted by two helpers since 1939–40, one of whom was a young Nayar woman, the sister of one of the Asrama School masters who had worked with Swami Tyagisananda since the early days of the Institution. Although this new assistant had only completed high school, she was asked to teach 6th and 7th standards of the School. Later, she passed her Bachelor of Arts privately and was sent to Trivandrum to complete a Bachelor of Education.

Bhavani and her assistant teacher both brought female relatives to the Hostel to complete their schooling, she bringing a cousin and her assistant a niece. Their respective families, being familiar with the ideals of the Asrama, must have weighed the possible stigma of a child living with Harijans against the rising general support of Gandhian ideals, and the longterm benefits of a sound education. The Asrama Hostel offered girls an opportunity to absorb the spirit of the Nationalist Movement which had reached a crescendo after the War. Though maintaining a neutral stand on political issues, the Order supported the Gandhian campaign for the revival of village-based industry, and worked towards it. Hostel girls and teachers joined villagers in spinning, and the new Industrial School run by the Asrama wove cloth on its 19 handlooms. The Hostel staff wore the cloth (which I have been told, was coarse, rough, heavy and the wrong dimensions for the traditional womens' garb) without complaint.

Bhavani eventually left the Hostel, which had moved to its own premises, now was known as Sarada Mandiram. Her assistant went on to become Warden. Bhavani's cousin was sent to College to complete a Bachelor of Arts. The new Warden's niece and one of the Harijan Hostel girls underwent Teachers Training in Trichur, which qualified them to teach at primary level.

By 1950 Sarada Mandiram had four young qualified female teachers living on the premises, since all the newly trained teachers returned there after their studies. A fifth young and highly intelligent woman, the daughter of a *sambandham* relationship between a Nayar woman and a powerful local Namburidi landowner, began to take interest in the Asrama at this time, and became an honorary Hindi teacher in the School.[20] She went on to complete a Bachelor of Science and a Bachelor of Education, and despite great opposition from both mother's and father's families, she joined in other resident teachers at Sarada Mandiram in 1952.

The reason why the Hindi teacher had decided to risk the wrath of her relatives and live at Sarada Mandiram was because news had reached the President of the Asrama that the Trustees of Belur Math were seriously considering starting a Math for women in time for the Birth Centenary of Sarada Devi, the Holy Mother, in 1953. In 1951 two Dedicated Women Workers (as lay women living in Institutions run by the Order were now officially known) had come on a visit from one of the Order's largest Institutions, a Calcutta Girls School. They had been sent by the Belur Math to look over the possibility of starting a Womens Math eventually in Trichur, out of the nucleus of Sarada Mandiram. Already the two groups of women had met, when two of the teachers from Trichur had gone to Calcutta for *mantra* initiation in 1949. The Calcutta women were delighted with the rural setting of Sarada Mandiram, and with the teachers there, who were well educated, yet living an austere and simple life. The following year, two of the other teachers went to Calcutta for initiation, and the fifth received hers during a visit of the President of the Order to Madras in 1952. The President of the Trichur Asrama since 1942 was Swami Iswarananda, who was particularly supportive of a Womens Math. Swami Tyagisananda had been transferred to Bangalore to recover his shattered health and a brief interregnum had followed, before the Asrama had once again found firm leadership. Swami Tyagisananda's successor had actually resigned, and eventually left the Order altogether.

The growing support for a Womens Math was coming from branches of the Order all over India, but Trichur and Calcutta already had Institutions which could readily supply the first members if the Trustees voted for the Motion, to be put before its meeting on 29th May 1952. The Motion requested that steps be taken to make way for the admission of women into the Ramakrishna Order, an idea first mooted by Swami Vivekananda in a letter dated 1893 (*Letters* 1960 ed. p. 216) and enshrined in the original Rules and Regulations of the Belur Math framed by the Swami himself.

Chapter 4

The Foundation of a Monastic Order for Women

Vivekananda's Plans for a Womens Math

Vivekananda wrote to one of his fellow monks as early as 1894, during his first visit to the United States:

> Why is it that our country is the weakest and the most backward of all countries? – Because Shakti is held in dishonour there. Mother[1] has been born to revive that wonderful Shakti in India; and making her the nucleus, once more will Gargis and Maitreyis be born into the world. Dear brother, you understand little now, but by degrees you will come to know it all. Hence it is her Math that I want first. . . . First Mother and Mother's daughters, then Father and Father's sons – can you understand this? . . . To me, Mother's grace is a hundred thousand times more valuable than Father's. . . . (*CW* Vol.III:474–5).

From the beginning of his stay in the United States, Vivekananda met many educated and capable women. And, he lamented over the sorry plight of women in India in comparison with the women in America:

> And how pure and chaste they are here! Few women are married before twenty or twenty-five, and they are as free as the birds in the air. They go to market, school and college, earn money, and do all kinds of work. Those who are well-to-do devote themselves to doing good to the poor. And what are we doing? We are very regular in marrying our girls at eleven years of age lest they should become corrupt and immoral. . . . Can you better the condition of your women? Then there will be hope for your well-being. Otherwise you remain as backward as you are now (*Life of Swami Vivekananda* Vol.I:531).

Through his letters and conversations, we can see how Vivekananda's plan for a Math for women encompassed two problems with which he was preoccupied: finding a suitable home for Sarada Devi and also a means of persuading Hindu women to raise themselves, through education. But, with his personal success on returning from the West, the plan for 'Mother's Math' was set aside whilst the Ramakrishna Mission and Belur Math took shape, as it was men, not women, who came to hear him speak, and men who read his works and volunteered their services. From the distance of the United States it would appear that Vivekananda had forgotten just how conservative his own society was. When he returned to India, he was questioned as to how he could expect a Womens Math to take shape. When he raised the topic at the Belur Math, as recorded in a diary entry of a disciple in 1901, doubts were expressed as to the very wisdom of the project. The conversation is recorded as follows:

> With the Holy Mother [Sarada Devi] as the centre of inspiration, a Math will be established on the eastern bank of the Ganges. As Brahmacharins and Sadhus[2] will be trained in this Math here, so in the other Math also, Brahmacharinis and Sadhvis[3] will be trained.
>
> *Disciple*: Sir, history does not tell us of any Maths for women in India in ancient times. Only during the Buddhistic period one hears of Maths for women; but from it in the course of time many corruptions arose. The whole country was overrun by great evil practices.
>
> *Swamiji*: It is very difficult to understand why in this country so much difference is made between men and women, whereas the Vedanta declares that one and the same conscious Self is present in all beings. . . . If you do not raise the women, who are the living embodiment of the Divine Mother, don't think that you have any other way to rise.
>
> *Disciple*: Women are a bondage and a snare to men. By their Maya they cover the knowledge and dispassion of men. It is for this, I suppose, that scriptural writers hint that knowledge and devotion are difficult to attainment to them.
>
> *Swamiji*: In what scriptures do you find statements that women are not competent for knowledge and devotion? In the period of degradation, when the priests made the other castes incompetent for the study of the Vedas, they deprived the women also of all their rights. Otherwise you will find that in the Vedic or Upanishadic age Maitreyi, Gargi, and other ladies of revered memory have taken the places of Rishis[4] through their skills in

discussing about Brahman. When such ideal women are entitled to spiritual knowledge, then why shall not the women have the same privilege now? What has happened once can certainly happen again. . . . Manu said, 'Where women are respected, there the gods delight; and where they are not, there all works and efforts come to naught' (III:56). There is no hope of rise for that family or country where there is no estimation of women, where they live in sadness. For this reason, they have to be raised first; and an ideal Math has to be started for them (*CW* Vol.III:214–5).

In this conversation, which was with a Brahmin, was conveyed most of the common conservative attitudes of the day regarding women. That is, those which echoed the lawgiver Manu, which was coupled with a 'protective' attitude. This was born of the notion that women suffered from the inherent inability to be chaste, and that to allow them independence of action was therefore against the interest of society.

Early betrothal was offered as the solution to the problem of women's character preservation, followed by consummation of the marriage by puberty. In view of this, the disciple asked: 'With the present hard restrictions of society, who will permit the ladies of their household to join your Math?' (*CW* Vol.III:216).

The Swami replied that widowed devotees of Ramakrishna already existed, and that together with Holy Mother they could found a Math. Daughters of devotees would be sent there, and from this beginning, it would spread to the general public. He then went on to outline his plan in detail, which included a school with boarding facilities, in which girls would learn both academic and domestic subjects, together with religious instruction. At the completion of their courses, the students could either marry, or remain at *brahmacārinis*, eventually taking the vows of celibacy. The latter category of students would then become teachers, and as the project grew, they would open branches all over the countryside, for the education of other women and girls. Even those students who chose to marry would nevertheless 'inspire their husbands with noble ideals and be the mothers of heroic sons' (*CV* Vol.VII:218).

The disciple expressed the view that those women who had received a modern education were simply becoming Westernised, and that there was no evidence that their characters were benefitting at all. To this the Swami replied that education must be based on religious values rather than secular, and that even the development of one great woman would inspire countless others. Only if women were uplifted would India be restored to its former glory, for only then would 'culture, knowledge, power and devotion awaken in the land' (*CV* Vol.VII:220). For Vivekananda, the education of women would awaken their innate *Sakti* (Power), and by this power, the only Power that existed, would the country arise.

Vivekananda's conviction that it was imperative to educate women was no doubt rooted in his early days in the Brahmo Samaj. However, his reasons for the education of women were somewhat different from those of the Samaj. His plan was not to produce a generation of well-read, modern wives, who would support their husband's careers, but rather to foster women of renunciation and high spiritual attainment, who would raise a new generation according to Vedic traditions. And, for Vivekananda, education was the key (*CW* Vol.V:28–32).

The reason for Vivekananda's original plan for a Math for the Holy Mother as an urgent priority was because when he had taken leave of her before his Indian pilgrimage, he had found her to be living in most unsatisfactory circumstances. At that time she was commuting between Kamarpukur (Ramakrishna's village) where she had a small home, and Calcutta, where she stayed with close devotees of her late husband.

In Kamarpukur, Holy Mother was lonely and unhappy, barely managing to keep herself alive, as her in-laws were 'indifferent' towards her. She was a childless Brahmin widow, and as an inauspicious person, Ramakrishna's impoverished relatives did not feel responsible for her welfare. In any case, they looked to Ramakrishna's devotees – wealthy Calcutta people – to maintain her. After all, she was their *guru*'s wife. But, the Calcutta devotees had no idea of Holy Mother's sufferings at Kamarpukur, for when she visited them, she never said a word about her financial or other problems. Nevertheless, in 1890 Vivekananda had realised that Holy Mother needed a place to live when in Calcutta, so that she could be near the devotees, and yet be independent. He therefore thought of building a small Math where she and other female companions from Dakshineswar could live in peace and dignity. It was this that remained uppermost in Vivekananda's mind during his subsequent travels in the USA and elsewhere.

However, in Vivekananda's absence, Holy Mother's position had changed, as he was to find out on his return. So miserable was she in Kamarpukur that her own relatives suggested that she return to her own native village, where (as I have explained) she had lived for some years after her marriage, since her 'mad' husband seemed to have abandoned her. But once she arrived back at her childhood home, she found that her brothers had an ulterior motive in inviting her to stay. Their mother was elderly, and their wives too young to shoulder the responsibilities of running the household. Moreover, they were short of money, and expected that she could help them out, through her Calcutta contacts.

Holy Mother's only source of satisfaction was her youngest brother, who did not share the attitudes of the rest of her family. He was studying to be a physician, but suddenly contracted cholera and died in 1899, leaving behind a young pregnant widow. It soon became clear that the shock proved too much for her sister-in-law. She became mentally unbalanced, and remained so, for life. When the child was born, Holy Mother assumed responsibility for both mother and child, and the remainder of her life was focussed on their welfare.[5]

Slowly, Vivekananda was to realise that what Holy Mother needed was not a Math in Calcutta, but a home where she could live with her relatives, and at the same time receive visitors. Thus, eventually Vivekananda was forced to look elsewhere for a nucleus for his work among women. It was seven years after Vivekananda's death that a Calcutta house was finally built for Holy Mother, where she remained until her death.

Nivedita

In 1895, whilst on a visit to England, Vivekananda gave a talk in a private drawing room to a small and select audience, all friends of Lady Isabel Margesson. Among those present was a young Irish lady, Margaret Noble. None of those present was immediately impressed by the subject of the talk, but the personality of the speaker was so attractive that some decided to go along to his current series of public lectures, being held in London.

Margaret attended two lectures, and when the Swami departed once more for America, she realised that there was something in the man which she found deeply moving. Thus, when he returned to London the following spring, she eagerly sought him out, and attended his classes and lectures.

It was during one of his classes that Vivekananda challenged the audience to join him in his work, leaving all security behind. In an official biography of Margaret Noble (who later became Sister Nivedita) we read that:

> . . . the Swami suddenly rose and thundered: 'What the world wants to-day, is twenty men and women who can dare to stand in the street yonder, and say that they possess nothing but God. Who will go? If it is true, what else could matter? *If it is not true, what do our lives matter*?' (Atmaprana 1961:16).

Margaret sat down and wrote a letter to the Swami after the lecture, asking him exactly what his own plans were, and what for those who were prepared to follow him. Swiftly came the reply, in a stirring letter in which he said, among other things, that:

> What the world wants is character. The world is in need of those whose life is one burning love, selfless. . . . I am sure, you have the making in you of a world-mover, and others will also come. Bold words and bolder deeds are what we want (Atmaprana 1961:17).

The letter did not tell Nivedita what was required of her, but he later gave an indication, in the broadcast of terms:

> I have plans for the women of my own country in which you, I think, could be of great help to me (Atmaprana 1961:17).

One of the reasons why Vivekananda saw in Margaret a potential helpmate for his Indian work was because she already had made a name for herself in London, in educational spheres. She was a journalist of repute, and the Headmistress of an innovative school in Wimbledon, based on the educational philosophies of Froebel and Pestalozzi. Her social circle and influential contacts were broadly based, as were her interests. At the age of 28 she was mixing in the most sophisticated company, including membership of the Sesame Club, where she had come to know Bernard Shaw, T.H. Huxley and Yeats among others (Foxe 1975:16–7).

Vivekananda had recognised at once Margaret's independent and fiery nature, which made her strike out and seek new ways, if those time honoured by society did not suit her. Yet, he did not try to persuade her to follow him, when three of his disciples decided to leave with him for India, and two others to follow later. Margaret was thinking carefully as to whether to broach the subject, but merely mentioned it in passing to a friend, who mentioned this in turn to Vivekananda. He let the subject be for a time, so that when he returned to India during December, the topic was left in suspension. The next move was to be Margaret's.

Margaret and Vivekananda corresponded during the following year. He had tried to motivate an educated Indian woman to join him in his plans for the education of women, but had failed. Now his attention turned to Margaret. A Report of the new Ramakrishna Mission was forwarded to her, outlining the relief work it had undertaken. Here was something which could appeal to the English devotees, placing his philosophy far beyond esoteric speculation, into the field of social action. In July 1897 Vivekananda invited her to come to India, warning her of all the difficulties which lay ahead. She sailed for India during winter, and arrived in Calcutta in January 1898 (Atmaprana 1961:28–30).

Vivekananda was mindful of the cultural backgrounds of his Western disciples in India. On St Patrick's Day he took Margaret on a very significant visit. Holy Mother had arrived in Calcutta from her village, and Margaret was now to meet her. Holy Mother, an orthodox, conservative rustic Brahmin woman, not only welcomed Margaret and her two other Western companions, but sat and ate with them. This totally unexpected and broadminded act delighted all concerned, and went a long way to smoothing Margaret's transition into Calcutta orthodoxy. The following week, on the Feast of the Annunciation, Vivekananda initiated Margaret into the vows of *bramacārya*, that is, lifelong celibacy, renaming her *Nivedita*, the Dedicated (Atmaprana 1961:35–6).

After travelling in the Himalaya region with a party of Western disciples led by Vivekananda, Margaret (henceforth called *Nivedita*) settled in a house in Calcutta, in the same lane in which Holy Mother was then residing. She spent her time studying Vedanta and Bengali, the local language, and planning to found a girls school, which she knew would be experimental at first. On Kali Puja Day, the festival of the goddess Kali, Holy Mother opened her school, and the following day, a servant was sent to nearby houses to collect the first few students. Out of school hours, Nivedita gave public lectures, and taught history at the American Missionary School. She also gave teachers training for local Brahmo women, the most *avant garde* at the time, mainly women from prominent, educated families. She also personally supervised plague relief that year, nursing dying patients in the slums, evacuating premises, disinfecting huts and teaching hygiene.

By December Nivedita had thirty students on her roll, but as summer drew near she became disheartened, as one by one they had left the marry, or through lack of encouragement. She realised that teaching reading and writing, painting and sewing in her lane was hardly enough to accomplish the Swami's great plan for the establishment of a Math. She could not envisage a team of dedicated women emerging from her low-key school at all. She discussed the matter with the Swami, and they agreed that the school should admit widows and orphans: girls who could not readily be given in marriage, and who were unlikely to be happy in their present circumstances. She was persuaded to return to the West during the heat of the summer, to collect funds for a Womens Home. Nivedita sailed for England in the company of Vivekananda in June 1899, to this end.

Nivedita was in for a shock on her arrival. In London, some of the Swami's staunchest supporters had turned against him. After less than a month he decided to sail for America, and Nivedita followed soon afterwards. She had expected that the female disciples of the Swami in America would enthusiastically help her to raise funds, but instead, she received a very, very cold shoulder. Perhaps this reception was due to jealousy, or perhaps to her abrasive personality, but Nivedita stayed on, giving public lectures whenever she could, on life in India in its various aspects, in order to raise public interest and hopefully, funds. By February 1900, Nivedita had aroused enough interest to publish a booklet on 'The Project of the Ramakrishna School for Girls' (Atmaprana 1961:105). In January 1902, she made her way back to India, via Europe and England, where she spent a year and a half altogether.

Nivedita started her school again, in the same locality, this time with the assistance of another of Vivekananda's Western disciples, Christine, who had come to Calcutta from America. They called themselves Sisters, and dressed in garb which would be readily identified as 'religious'. They hung out a plate saying 'The House of Sisters' at the front of the house, suggesting thereby that the house was a convent of Western women living as Hindu *brahmacārinis.*

Nivedita looked forward to receiving *saṃnyāsa* and had approached Vivekananda about this as early as 1899, after meeting a woman disciple who had been given *saṃnyāsa* in the United States.[6] The Swami is said to have replied, 'You just keep as you are' (Atmaprana 1961:84), that is, as a *brahmacārini*, who had taken the vows of celibacy, but had not severed worldly ties and commitments. Vivekananda had detected in Nivedita not only an independence of will, which did not necessarily go against membership of the Order as a *saṃnyāsini*, but also a growing interest in the Nationalist Movement: awakening an interest which had been evident from her childhood. Nivedita's father and grandfather, both ministers of the Church, were enthusiastic supporters of the Home Rule Movement in Ireland. Nivedita showed signs of not merely wishing to confine her activities to a sedate school, but to help harness the leaders of Bengal into a similar movement, to rid India of British Rule also.

There is controversy surrounding the rest of Nivedita's life, but it need not concern us unduly, except that suddenly in 1904, after the death of Vivekananda, she announced that after the period of mourning, she would no longer be formally associated with the Ramakrishna Order.[7] The parting was amicable however, and she remained on cordial terms with the monks and devotees for life. But, she knew that her desire to identify with the cause of Indian Nationalism was against the Rules of the Order, and of the Ramakrishna Mission, which expressly required members to eschew political involvement. Nivedita had realised that her priorities had altered. It was only Vivekananda's continued presence that had restrained her from taking this serious step earlier.

Nivedita and Christine continued to expand their school, which was loosely referred to as 'Nivedita's School', despite the fact that Nivedita was absent on speaking and other engagements almost continuously. She wrote in many journals (including those of the Mission), combining religion with political and Nationalist sentiments. Some accounts of Nivedita's life depict her henceforth as a dedicated revolutionary, a glamorous behind-the-scenes leader who was closely connected with extremist elements (see, for example, Roy Choudhury 1956:326, Raymond 1953, Burman 1968 and Chatterjee 1968). This is sternly denied by the author of the biography published under the Ramakrishna Movement's auspices (Atmaprana 1961) and by Foxe (1975), an English devotee.

Christine took charge of the school, employing a Bengali woman, Sudhir, to assist her, whilst Nivedita went on an extended overseas visit, between 1907–9. On her return, relations between the volatile Nivedita and the placid Christine became strained, and remained so until Nivedita contracted dysentery and died unexpectedly, in Darjeeling in 1911.

Just before Nivedita left for Darjeeling, Christine announced that she was going to leave the school, to work in the Brahmo Girls School instead. Sudhir left soon after, much to Nivedita's distress. However, after Nivedita's death Sudhir returned to Nivedita's school, and kept it running until it was officially incorporated as a branch of the Ramakrishna Mission in 1918, as the Sister Nivedita Girls School. Christine looked after the School's management until 1914, when she returned to the USA due to illness. The War years intervened, and Christine returned to India only in 1924, for a brief visit. In the meantime, Sudhir became the Headmistress, and under her leadership the School purchased permanent premises in 1917, adding the Matri Mandir, a boarding section for students and the women who lived and worked with them, now known as 'Dedicated Women Workers'. Holy Mother performed the dedication ceremony of the new premises.

After the School's affiliation with the Ramakrishna Mission its stability was ensured, and it continued to grow and prosper. Its Industrial Section (started in Nivedita's lifetime) expanded, so that its trainees were able to earn their own living after learning a craft. Though under the management of the Ramakrishna Mission, the School became run more and more as time went on, by the Dedicated Women Workers themselves, especially after a traumatic period when the School almost foundered, under the management of a certain *brahmacāri* Ganendra.

The years of the Second World War saw the Nivedita School barely survive, but as soon as the War ended, once more it began to prosper, as one of the well-known institutions of Calcutta. By the late 1940s, a nucleus of six unmarried Dedicated Women Workers was living at the School, in circumstances similar to those of the Sarada Mandiram, Trichur. The two groups came into contact in 1949, as I mentioned previously, and discussed the hope that before the end of the Centenary Celebrations of the birth of Holy Mother, a Math for women would be formed and, that after years of unpaid service to the Order, they would all be received into it as monastic members.

A Math for Women

The Trustees of the Belur Math had been considering the establishment of a Womens Math in time for the Centenary Celebrations, but some had serious reservations. Nevertheless, the Rules and Regulations of the Belur Math as founded by Swami Vivekananda clearly stated that:

1 . . . for women too there will be started a similar Math.
2 The Womens Math will be conducted on exactly the same principles as that for men. There will be this restriction that in the Womens Math there will be no connection with men, and in that of the men no connection with women.
3 Two such Maths will be started in some suitable places in the Himalayas and conducted on similar principles.
4 The Womens Math will be managed by the men from a distance, so long as competent women are not available for the task. After that they will themselves manage all their affairs (Gambhirananda 1957:135).

During the Nationalist Movement and the subsequent granting of Independence, many educated Indian women came forward to assume public duties, some of them defying family opinion and refusing to marry. Gandhi had glorified the ancient Hindu practice of *brahmacārya* or celibacy, as the main source of strength for India's leaders. Energy expended in sexual activity was energy lost, so that a sexually active person would become physically and mentally debilitated. Moreover, any physical attachment to a particular human being prevented the individual from being available for service to wider Indian society. Thus, the Dedicated Women Workers of the Ramakrishna Mission found their status generally enhanced, a growing number of devotees and parents of school children regarding them as selfless and noble, rather than as unfortunate and unfulfilled.

As the Centenary year drew near, the Trustees of the Belur Math called a meeting for the 29th May, 1952, at which four recommendations made at the recent Monks Conference of the Order were placed before them. I cite them in full, in view of their historical significance:

> As this Conference is of the opinion that it is high time to go forward to realise Swamiji's idea that women should be put in a position to work out their destinies independent of men, it recommends:
>
> i) that women aspirants in the highest spiritual life who have renounced their homes and joined our Math and Mission work with the approval of the Headquarters and who are designated as dedicated women workers to be helped through reasonable stages to form as early as possible an independent organisation of their own;
> ii) that as a first step in this process, a central body of such dedicated women workers be formed, and that the existing women's institutions and sections of our Math and Mission be placed one after another under its management;
> iii) that at the end of ten years or earlier, if this central body of dedicated women workers is found competent by the Math and Mission authorities as the case may be, it should be legally registered and the relevant Math or Mission institutions for women be legally transferred to it;
> iv) that the interim arrangements should be inaugurated on the occasion of Holy Mother's Birth Centenary by providing this

> central body of dedicated workers with a suitable Home, so that when this body will be finally separated and registered, this Home may develop by the time of Swamiji's Birth Centenary into an independent Math for women as laid down by Swamiji in the Belur Math Rules.

Since women aspirants have been initiated into formal Brahmacharya by Swamiji, Swami Brahmanandaji and Swami Shivanandaji, this Conference recommends that this initiation be given, during the interim period but not afterwards, by the President of our Order to the dedicated women aspirants who are found fit by the President and Trustees for the time being.

Having regard for the fact that Swamiji, in his writings and utterances and specially in his Math Rules, had strongly advocated Sannyasa for women, this Conference recommends that, at the time of the complete separation of this body of dedicated women workers as an independent organisation, if any of them already formally initiated into Brahmacharya should make a request for Sannyasa and be found fit by the President and Trustees for the time being, the President will ordain them as Sannyasinis but thereafter there will be no such ordination of women by our President (Gambhirananda 1957:407–9).

There was some opposition from certain monks who reminded the assembly that Buddha had stated that his *Sangha*[8] would decline after women were admitted, and that this is indeed what had transpired. Also, the public would not accept *saṃnyāsinis*, and so their existence would open up a whole series of troubles for the now-respected Ramakrishna Order. And, there was the doubt concerning the wisdom of allowing women to remain without male custody.

Nevertheless, the meeting could hardly reject the proposal, since Swami Vivekananda had said that such a Math *would come into being*. He could not have been wrong. And, the approaching Birth Centenary was obviously the auspicious time for its inauguration. The recommendations were accepted, but not without some mixed feelings.[9]

Initially, the whole idea of celebrating Holy Mother's Birth Centenary on a large scale was greeted with hesitancy by some of the more conservative monks. As the *History of the Ramakrishna Math and Mission* records:

> Even her children[10] felt diffident at first . . . and to many of them it seemed a little indecent to talk so loudly of one who shunned publicity (Gambhirananda 1957:409).

The Centenary celebrations were inaugurated on the hundredth Birth Anniversary, that is the 27th December, 1953 of the civil calendar. On that day, without any publicity, the first group of five Dedicated Women Workers underwent the ceremony of *brahmacārya*, the candidates being driven to the Belur Math by the private car of trusted devotees of the Order. The first *brahamacārinis* were all from Calcutta, except one, the Warden of the Trichur Sarada Mandiram. A house was allocated to the Calcutta *brahmacārinis*, until the new permanent Math premises were ready for occupation. The new Math for women was dedicated as the finale to the Centenary Celebrations, on the 2nd December 1954 (the day on which Holy Mother's birthday fell that year, according to the Bengali calendar). It was, as Vivekananda had prophesised, 'on the eastern side of the Ganges', in fact just north of the Dakshineswar Kali temple, the site of Ramakrishna's *leela* (play on earth of a deity). Vivekananda has also said that Holy Mother would be 'the centre of inspiration', but as she had died in 1920, a suitable senior woman had been sought by the Trustees of the Belur Math, to assume responsibility of President of the new Womens Math.

Sarala

The Trustees wished the Sarada Math to be linked as far as was possible with the traditions of the Ramakrishna Order, and so the ideal President would be a woman who had had a long association with it. They knew of such a woman. She had been living in Varanasi for twenty years, practising austerities. Her name was Sarala. (*See: Pravrajika Bharatiprana* 1973)

Sarala was enrolled by Nivedita in 1902 in her new School. She was then eight years old. She was a local Brahmin girl, and was already married. One night in 1911, she ran away from home, and went straight to Sudhir, who was then in charge of the School. Sarala became a disciple of Holy Mother, and briefly became Matron of the Brahmo Girls School, before being suggested as Supervisor of the Womens Section of the Ramakrishna Mission Home of Service, Varanasi, an institution run by monks of the Ramakrishna Order. In order to carry out her duties in a professional manner, Sudhir arranged for Sarala to be admitted at the Lady Dufferin Hospital, where she studied general nursing and administration for three years, in preparation for later Mission work among women. In those days (and even today) it was quite a scandal for a Brahmin girl of good family to take up nursing, especially in a Christian hospital.

Surprisingly, Holy Mother greatly encouraged her, and also silenced the protests of others concerned for Sarala's welfare. After completing her nursing training, Sarala stayed with Holy Mother, nursing her during her final illness, to which she succumbed in 1920. Later in the year, while on a pilgrimage with Sudhir and other staff of the Nivedita School, Sudhir fell from a train, and died of her injuries the following day. Sarala returned to Calcutta in a state of severe depression and shock, having lost two of her closest benefactors and companions.

Swami Saradananda, General Secretary of the Ramakrishna Math and Mission became the guardian of Sarala from this time on. It was he who had built a house for Holy Mother in Calcutta in 1909, some of the funds being met from the proceeds of his book, *Sri Ramakrishna the Great Master.* For the next seven years Sarala taught in a school, then took over the nursing of two of Holy Mother's closest companions: the same ones who had strenuously objected to her studying nursing. In 1927, Swami Saradananda also died, but not before advising her to spend her days henceforth in practising austerities in the holy city of Varanasi. The monks of the Order watched over her welfare from a distance, arranging at one stage for her to come to Calcutta for an eye operation, which saved her vision. In 1952 she accepted an invitation to attend the Golden Jubilee of her old school, the Nivedita Girls School of which she was a foundation student. The visit was to cause a great change in her life.

According to an oft-repeated story, told by members of Sarada Math, part of Swami Saradananda's instructions to Sarala were that she was to 'Wait in Varanasi' until called. She should inform each successive President of Belur Math that she had been given *saṃnyāsa* secretly by Saradananda, and renamed *Bharati,* and that she was staying in Varanasi until called. Six Presidents later, Swami Shankarananda was to call Sarala back to Calcutta, during her visit in 1952.

The Trustees agreed that Sarala was the obvious choice for the future President of Sarada Math, and she was the one whom fate had ordained. Though Sarada Math was to become legally independent of the Belur Math, the two Orders, the Ramakrishna Order of *Saṃnyāsins,* and the future Ramakrishna Order of *Saṃnyāsinis* should be run on parallel lines. The latter should draw on all the tradition and experience of the former, to establish itself. While the Ramakrishna Order *Saṃnyāsins* could link itself directly to Ramakrishna through the chain of discipleship, so Sarala was linked with Ramakrishna through Holy Mother, her *mantra* guru, and with

Ramakrishna through her *saṃnyāsa* guru, Swami Saradananda. Moreover, she had met Vivekananda when he visited Nivedita's School in 1902, and also at Belur Math, during a School outing. She had been the personal attendant of Holy Mother, the Divine Consort of Ramakrishna, and educated by Nivedita, founder of the worthy institution from which some of the first *brahmacārinis* of the Ramakrishna Order had been recruited. She had lived a long life of self denial, service and austerity, and was of the respectable age of 58–60 by the time she was to assume to Presidency of Sarada Math.

Against the conservative voices among the Trustees who objected to a woman receiving *saṃnyāsa* at all, stood the undeniable fact that Swami Vivekananda had ordained Marie Louise in the United States, and now it was revealed that Sarala – Bharati – had also received *saṃnyāsa* from Swami Saradananda, the first Secretary of the Math and Mission. The vows of *brahmacārya* had already been administered to women by Vivekananda, and Swamis Brahmananda and Sivananda, the first and second Presidents of the Ramakrishna Order. In Hollywood, USA, a monk of the Ramakrishna Order had been given permission to initiate a Western disciple into *brahmacārya* in 1947. In the same year a Womens Math, Sarada Math was opened in Santa Barbara, for a group of female disciples of the Hollywood Swami, who had been living for some years as a community attached to the Vedanta Society of Southern California.

Though diffident at first about assuming responsibility for the *brahmacārinis*, Sarala eventually agreed to take up the position of President of Sarada Math. In 1959 she and seven *brahmacārinis* were initiated into *saṃnyāsa* with full rites, as practised by the Ramakrishna Order. They all received the title *Pravrajika* (female ascetic) plus a name ending in *prāna* (life force). Bharati thus became Pravrajika Bharatiprana. As the President of Sarada Math she would be called in future not only to give *mantra* initiation, but *brahmacārya* and *saṃnyāsa* initiation also to female candidates of the Ramakrishna Order of *saṃnyāsinis*. In view of the controversy surrounding the circumstances of the status of the *saṃnyāsa* of the direct disciples of Ramakrishna, it is not difficult to ascertain why Sarala was requested to undergo the rites of *saṃnyāsa* for a second time: this time *officially and openly*.

In August 1959, some of the new *saṃnyāsinis* became the first Trustees of the Sri Sarada Math, as a result of a Trust Deed executed by the President of the Belur Math, and in 1960 the Ramakrishna Sarada Mission was registered, to carry out work similar to that of the Ramakrishna Mission:

> Thus the Sri Sarada Math and the Ramakrishna Sarada Mission, though legally separate, are basically one with the Ramakrishna Math and Mission, being their counterpart (*The General Report of the Sri Sarada Math and Ramakrishna Sarada Mission 1968–70*).

All remained in Calcutta for the time being, except the new *saṃnyāsini* from Trichur, the only one from outside Bengal. She returned to Sarada Mandiram, Trichur, her clothes now dyed in ochre, as worn by many Hindu ascetics, including those of the Dasanami tradition. Her new status raised hopes for the four *brahmacārinis* that in due course Sarada Mandiram would become an independent Womens Math also.

Sarada Mandiram Gains Independent Status

By 1968, all the original five *brahamcārinis* had received *saṃnyāsa,* and were back in Trichur teaching in the School. Their mode of life had not changed greatly at first since none had stayed long in Calcutta, until the last three of the original Dedicated Women Workers spent a year at Sarada Math in 1961. Until then, they did not realise how little they knew about the daily routine for monastic members of the Ramakrishna Order. Life could not have been very easy for the first three to undergo training at Sarada Math, since two of them were Sudras (Nayar) and one a Harijan, whilst their Bengali counterparts were overwhelmingly Brahmin. Moreover, there was a great deal of difference in custom between the two regions. The Kerala *brahmacārinis* were not given duties concerned with shrine or kitchen at Sarada Math, and as I overhead one say, concerning this continuing problem, the Bengalis, *South Indians upare, viswas ne* ('They have no trust in South Indians'), meaning not as people, but in their ability to observe the minute rules of ritual purity as practised at Sarada Math. The real problem, it seems to me, is that the two regions have conflicting notions of purity in many crucial respects, but that the Bengali members of the Order simply assume that South Indians (a very sweeping category, I might add) do not know the 'correct' way. I cite examples in due course.

In 1962, the Trichur Asrama opened a separate School, Sri Sarada Girls High School, in the compound adjacent to Sarada Mandiram, and the Asrama High School now became a Boys High School. The seniormost *saṃnyāsini* became the School Headmistress, and the Hostel management was handed over to the next senior, Bhavani's cousin, who also taught in the High School, with one other *saṃnyāsini.* The other two *saṃnyāsinis* continued to teach in the Asrama School, as they were only trained for primary work, which remained with the Asrama. As soon as the Upper Primary School was divided and the Girls School transferred to the care of the *saṃnyāsinis,* no female monastic members of the Order taught in either mixed or boys Schools. But still, despite the foundation of an independent Sarada Math in Madras in 1965, Sarada Mandiram remained for the time being officially under the Ramakrishna Asrama.

The Headquarters at Belur Math had been planning to hand Sarada Mandiram over to Sarada Math Calcutta, but had run into a problem regarding property. It had been agreed between Belur Math and Sarada Math that no Womens Math or Mission should be allowed within five kilometres of a Ramakrishna Math or Mission. The exception was in Calcutta where Sarada Math and the Ramakrishna Sarada Mission had taken over such existing institutions as the Nivedita School and Matribhavan maternity hospital, which were not to be moved. But, Sarada Mandiram was only across the village road from the Ramakrishna Asrama, and also its next door neighbour, as the Asrama had playing fields and a hospital adjacent to Sarada Mandiram. The Belur Math Trustees wanted Sarada Mandiram to find premises elsewhere, as its monastic membership was growing, and they did not want *saṃnyāsins* and *saṃnyāsinis* living at such close quarters in an isolated village.

However, Kerala Land Reforms and the partition of the joint family property had assured that there were no sizeable holdings available as an alternative site for a Math. The land which Sarada Mandiram presently occupied was a plot of over seven acres, with possible room for further expansion on two sides. Moreover, it was highly convenient for the growing number of well-to-do parents who had admitted their children to the two Hostels, to be able to visit both sons and daughters at the same time. It became the practice for such well-to-do mothers, if coming from a distance, to dine at Sarada Mandiram, and rest before returning home, whilst the menfolk ate and rested at the Asrama. The same applied to visiting devotees. Also, on Saturday afternoons, Asrama Hostel boys were permitted to visit their sisters at Sarada Mandiram Hostel. It seemed that everyone was pleased with the arrangement except the Belur Math Trustees, who sent a senior South Indian monk to investigate, whilst on a scheduled visit to the region.

I was told that the Swami paced the distance between the two Institutions, all the while declaring that a solution must be found.

Finally, an answer dawned on him: why not make the entrance to Sarada Mandiram on the opposite side of the compound? Then, it would be in a different village altogether, and the gates of the two Institutions would be more than five kilometres apart! Finally, commonsense prevailed, and the Trustees decided that Sarada Mandiram would remain where it was. The Ramakrishna Movement values continuity, and especially significant events which link a centre with Ramakrishna, Sarada Devi, Vivekananda or one of the other direct disciples. Sarada Mandiram, like the Sister Nivedita Girls School had such a link, enabling the Institution to become independent of the Asrama in 1968.

How Holy Mother Came to Stay at Sarada Mandiram

Those associated with Sarada Mandiram do not believe it was an accident that a Womens Math was to be established in that particular village, for Holy Mother Herself had chosen to come and reside there. This is how it happened, according to a story, as told to me by a late senior monk of the Order, who was present during the events of 1926 described below:

The second President of the Ramakrishna Order, Swami Sivananda visited the Nilgiris (a hill station in South India) in 1926, for the opening of a new Asrama there. A member of the Cochin royal family came to see the Swami at the new Asrama for spiritual advice, and before he left the premises, the Swami presented him with a most sacred relic, much to the astonishment of his attendant (who told me the story). The relic was a piece of cloth on which the footprints of Holy Mother had been imprinted, with red resin.[11] According to the story, Holy Mother had 'appeared' to the Swami, and instructed him to give the footprints to the Prince. He had felt very upset at these instructions, as he used to carry them with him and worship them every day. Nevertheless, he complied, wondering why the Prince should receive this special blessing. As soon as the Prince accepted the footprints, he at once placed them on his head and danced around the room crying out, 'Jai Ma, jai Ma!' – Hail to the Mother, Hail to the Mother! Then the Swami knew that he had given the footprints to a worthy person, for the Prince was in a state of ecstasy. The Prince took the footprints with him, and they became a special object of daily worship for his family. The family in turn felt that it had the special grace of Holy Mother, Divine Mother in human form.

However, finally the Prince died, and the family property

underwent partition (as did all joint families), and its members scattered. There was anxiety that nobody would be able to continue the worship of the footprints, or be fit to inherit them. Members of the family thus wrote to the Prince's son, who was a monk of the Ramakrishna Order, serving overseas at the time. He suggested that the footprints be kept at Sarada Mandiram, where Holy Mother was worshipped daily, in the shrine room. Since the inmates had dedicated their lives to Holy Mother, they were the fit persons to inherit her relics. Only, on each anniversary of the Prince's death, the footprints should be taken by members of his family, for worship. One year, this was not done, and the same year 'the Swami met an untimely death in Paris'.

I could not ascertain the year in which the relics came to Sarada Mandiram for certain, but as Swami died in 1957, it must have been some time between 1948 (when Sarada Mandiram was built) and 1957. As the relics were taken home 'each year', it would have been given some years before 1957. As the first Dedicated Women Worker received *brahmacārya* in 1953, giving some permanency to the Institution, I strongly suspect that the relics were given in that, the Centenary year. This would have been a good omen and a fitting gesture by the Swami towards the future of the Womens Order and its Trichur members in particular, for his relatives in Trichur were the main supporters of Sarada Mandiram.

After the demise of the Swami, the surviving members of his (matrilineal) family arranged that every year a special *pūjā* (worship) should be performed on the death anniversary of the Prince, at Sarada Mandiram, but paid for by them. The footprints have been placed on the actual shrine (on which the photos of Ramakrishna, Holy Mother and Vivekananda are kept), but not openly displayed.[12] Very few know of their existence.

The Swami who was the attendant of Swami Sivananda when the footprints were given, later became the President of the Trichur Ramakrishna Asrama, and officially received them on behalf of Sarada Mandiram some twenty five years later. It was also he who decided to encourage the Dedicated Women Workers to remain, even during the discouraging War years, and who built Sarada Mandiram. Towards the Birth Centenary year the same Swami recommended all five Workers as suitable candidates for the Order. It was therefore logical for those concerned for the future of Sri Sarada Mandiram to see the 'hand of Holy Mother' in all the events described above. In 1968 Sarada Mandiram became a branch of Sarada Math, retaining its name as Sri Sarada Mandiram. The entire

Math with adjoining Hostel, and the School and its compound were transferred by the Ramakrishna Asrama, the latter thereby losing almost half of its property, and its most vital asset: its best groundwater supply.

Just as the Nivedita School was grounded in the traditions of the Ramakrishna Movement through its links with the Holy Mother, Vivekananda, Nivedita and Sarala, so Trichur Sarada Mandiram had similar links, through the relics, which linked Holy Mother to the Institution through Swami Sivananda and his disciple, who became the President of the Ramakrishna Asrama, Trichur. The story had a particularly Kerala flavour, through the association of the Prince, from the ruling house of Cochin. The same family had produced H.H. Appan Tampuran, the Prince who had been the Manager of the Vivekodayam School, and later the Manager of the small village school which in turn became the Trichur Ramakrishna Asrama.

Interim Developments in Kerala

In 1957 the Malayalam speaking regions of the Malabar Coast merged to form the state of Kerala. After this time, rapid progress was made in respect of land reforms and the partition of joint families, causing a great change in the financial status of the landowning families. The Agrarian Relations Act of 1961, limited landholdings to fifteen acres of double crop paddy, and the Kerala Land Reforms Act of 1969 limited the holdings of single persons to five acres, and families with five or less members to ten acres. The main exemptions to these provisions were for certain plantation and forest estates, non-agricultural lands and *religious and educational institutions* (Menon A.S. 1978: 234–5). The latter Act also gave full ownership of the lands which they cultivated to present tenants, under a complicated system of land tenure operating in the state. Overnight, large landowners found themselves bereft of their main source of prestige and income: land.

Successive Acts of Parliament had also been passed confirming the rights of individual members to their share of family property. This had occurred as early as 1937–8 but now, combined with the All-India Hindu Succession Act of 1956, both men and women had equal claim to inherit from both parents: fathers as well as mothers. At the same time, each of the great *taravāds, illams* and *manas* was partitioned, the family members challenging each other in court, as property was portioned out. Most families (in a number of cases) found that by the time their legal settlement was obtained, it was the tenants on the land concerned who had become the legal owners. Later still, the former landowning families were to discover that the compensation due to them by their former tenants was to be largely ignored, and that courts were so choked with claims, that it was all but useless to try to take action against them.

Within a short space of time, the large landowner's homes, which once dominated the landscape, became empty shells surrounded by hostile ex-tenants, against whom claims were pending. Individual members of the former great families abandoned their ancestral homes one by one, to seek their fortunes in the towns and cities, both in Kerala and beyond. Without the security of the corporate family property, individual Nambudiri and Nayar men in particular found it hard to compete with other communities for places in the workforce, especially with Christians and Izhavas.

Christians belonging to the Syrian rite of the Catholic church also had landholdings, but were not hampered by the joint family system as were their Hindu counterparts. They were therefore spared the trauma of family partition. Moreover, Christians were among the first to seek a Western education and to enter the workforce with newly gained skills and qualifications (Nair 1976:10). Hindus lagged behind through conservatism mainly born of a reluctance to break those rules which restricted interaction between individuals of not only different communities, but also of disparate status within their own community.

To add to their economic woes, Nayars of aristocratic *taravāds* found they faced a great problem in finding husbands for their daughters. Families which had never in living memory taken *sambandham* partners of Nayar status, found that Nambudiri men were not available, as they were choosing to marry within their own community, now that restraints against younger sons doing so had been lifted. It was only when nieces and daughters reached well into their thirties that in many cases mother's brothers and fathers of women (who both felt concerned for their unwed state) agreed to marry them to fellow Nayars.

Devoid of landed property and ill equipped to earn a living, many Nayars were subject to strains and pressures undreamed of by the previous generation. It was unknown for a man to have to be legally committed to support a wife and children for life, and to have to earn an income, for their maintenance. Though dowry payment was not practised among Nayars, slowly families sought not only bridegrooms but brides with either some property, education or secure employment. Members of aristocratic families, whose very names formerly commanded respect, now found that the younger generation was deleting the *taravād* name and even titles which signified aristocratic status from their signatures. There was no family status left of which to boast.

It was these changing circumstances which, I suggest, encouraged members of the now *former* aristocracy to patronise the Ramakrishna Asramas in Kerala, including the Trichur Asrama. Firstly, a large part of their former prestige was derived from their close association with Nambudiris, and aristocratic families had adopted many Nambudiri customs and attitudes by virtue of this. Deprived of association with Nambudiris by the abolition of the *sambandham* system, aristocratic Nayars found compensation by association with the *saṃnyāsins* and *saṃnyāsinis* of the Ramakrishna Order who, although of non-Brahmin origin, had unashamedly adopted Brahmin modes of behaviour. At the Trichur Asrama (and other branches of the Order in Kerala[13]) devotees could attend classes on the *Upanisads*, works of Sankaracarya, and on other Sanskrit texts to which formerly only the 'twice born' had access.[14] And, secondly, I feel that it was the collapse of the religious beliefs of educated Nayars which also turned their attention towards the Ramakrishna Asramas.

Nayar religious reliefs were bound to the *taravād*, and larger *taravāds* had their own network of rituals centered on its various shrines. An 'old' family, as well respected *taravāds* were called, would have within its walls a shrine dedicated to ancestor worship, in which deceased *kāraṇavans* (family heads) were honoured and propitiated. In the compound was the *serpu kavu* (serpent grove), where the family serpents (cobras) received offerings, and usually an outdoor Devi shrine dedicated to a goddess. The family temple precincts (which consisted mainly of a shrine dedicated to one of the main Hindu deities) was marked off by courtyards and walls from the *taravād* compound. It was under the direction of a Brahmin priest employed by the *taravād*. *Taravād* members, being non-Brahmin, could not enter the shrine, but stood in the inner courtyard to witness the daily worship, subject to ensuring that they were in a state of ritual purity. *Taravāds* also often had a small temple or temples dedicated to indigenous local deities, which were propitiated by low caste priests. Members of the *taravād* did not visit these, due to the inferior status of the priests, nor partake of the offerings, as was the case with the Brahmin-run temples. All the various forms of cults combined to ensure the welfare of the *taravād* property, and of its members: each deity, spirit or ancestor responsible for a particular facet of this. A Nayar informant assured me that in this setting, individual members of the *taravād* felt no need to perform austerities for their own welfare or ultimate liberation. 'We have Brahmins to look after all that.'

Once the first generation of educated Hindu men (who were of mostly Nayar or higher communal status) left their *taravād* and moved to the towns, the religion of the *taravād* became less and less meaningful, as it was orientated towards the corporate *taravād*, and not towards the individual. Later, when *taravāds* were forced into partition, the property was portioned out not to the members, but to former tenants, there was a final dissolution of the *taravād*-associated beliefs and practices. In this vacuum some Nayars turned to Communism and avowed atheism, whilst others sought a new religious affiliation within the general framework of neo-Hinduism, such as expressed by the Ramakrishna Movement.

During fieldwork, I met family after family in Trichur which, having lost its land-based prestige, had sought to rationalise its decline in fortunes in terms of family *karma*. In other words, they blamed their ancestors for having mistreated 'the poor' and believed that they were now paying the price. Some had felt genuine regret, especially the educated youth of the nineteen forties, who tried to make amends by espousing the cause of the poor, turning to one or other of the available groups which were working among them. The writings of Marx, Vivekananda and the actions of Gandhi inspired many, and within families it was not unusual for some members to become Marxists, some Gandhians, and some followers of the Ramakrishna Movement. In many cases, Ramakrishna Movement devotees who had become staunch Gandhians during the thirties and forties, returned to become supporters of the Ramakrishna Movement again after Independence. The Trichur Asrama was all along seen to be in accord with the teachings of Gandhi, as it was a pioneer in work among Harijans, and joined in the less overtly political aspects of the Gandhian Movement, such as the revival of cottage industries.

The Ramakrishna Movement then, built up its following on two fronts: the religious, which offered a form of neo-Hinduism to those whose traditional beliefs were no longer relevant to their new lifestyle, and that of social action, for those who regretted the inequities of Kerala Hindu society. This 'package', designed by Vivekananda at the turn of the century was peculiarly suitable for the Nayar community of Kerala in particular, during the time when its entire social system was undergoing extremely rapid change. Some tried desperately to cling to the past; some sought an alternate belief system, one which unlike that of the *taravād*, was geared to the needs of the individual, his or her fears and aspirations. To both of these, the Ramakrishna Movement appealed: at least well into the sixties, when new forces in Kerala society became evident, altering the aspirations of caste Hindus in quite a different direction.

Right up to the time of Sarada Mandiram's separation from the Asrama, the twin Institutions became and remained a place of solace, a place where members of the declining 'old' families were still treated with respect. They were well appreciated for the way in which children in the Hostels were trained in the old ways of the *taravād*, emphasising co-operation, modesty, and respect for seniors. With this went a Spartan lifestyle, characterised by simplicity of dress and diet, early bathing[15] and faithful adherence to the annual ritual cycle of rites and observances. In the Ramakrishna Movement Institutions, prayers and chanting took the place of radio and cinema. Though other boarding schools[16] were more prestigious, conservative families tended to have more confidence in the Asrama and Sarada Mandiram. The Trichur Asrama School became a favourite place for Kerala Hindus overseas to send their children for their education. It came to represent the last vestige of all the good things remembered of the old way of life, though paradoxically, only the external trappings of Kerala custom were observed there. The cult of Ramakrishna was far different to those of the Nayars, or for that matter of the Nambudiris, yet it was not recognised as such. In the nineteen fifties and sixties the Asrama and Sarada Mandiram prospered, perhaps oblivious to gathering social and economic forces which were to cause their present crisis, to which I shall return to in due course.

Chapter 5

The Ramakrishna Order of Samnyasinis and its Trichur Branch

I have brought the narrative of the foundation of the Ramakrishna Order of *saṃnyāsinis* up to the separation of Sarada Mandiram from the Ramakrishna Asrama Trichur, in 1968. I now wish to examine the structure of the Sri Sarada Math and the Ramakrishna Sarada Mission, as a background to understanding the internal organisation of Sarada Mandiram, which is now a branch of Sri Sarada Math, Dakshineswar.

In 1981, Sri Sarada Math had five branches, and the Ramakrishna Sarada Mission ten branches, if the Headquarters is included as a branch centre of both Math and Mission, which it is. In addition there were two retreat centres for monastic members of the Order, one in the holy city of Varanasi, and the other in Haridwar, Himalayas. The Mission included five schools, one maternity hospital, one degree College, three students hostels (apart from boarding sections of three Mission schools), and various kindergartens and training programmes for women and children. In addition, Sarada Mandiram ran a Typing School for women and a Parallel College, where students could prepare to sit for College examinations as private candidates.

In January 1981 there were 160 members of Sri Sarada Math, of which 87 were *saṃnyāsinis* and the remaining 73 *brahmacārinis.*[1] Pre-Probationers and Probationers are not included in these figures, although Probationers are usually referred to as 'members', as they have formally completed a written application, and been accepted by the Trustees as potential candidates for *brahmacārya.* The Ramakrishna Sarada Mission had 121 members in total in 1981, 67 of whom were monastic and the rest, all lay women devotees.

Sri Sarada Math Branches

Branches of the Sri Sarada Math are under the direction of a President, who is appointed by the Trustees of the Order. The Trustees are ten in number and consist of senior *saṃnyāsinis* from Calcutta and major branch centres. The President of Sarada Mandiram is a Trustee of the Order. Local Presidents serve in a branch centre for as long as the Trustees deem fit, as with the other members of the Order, and can be transferred to another centre if necessary. There is no provision for monastic inmates[2] to automatically 'rise in the ranks' or for members of a centre to appoint or elect their own President. There are no other office bearers in Math centres.

Sri Sarada Math, Dakeshineswar, is the Headquarters of the Order and the largest Math, as each candidate for *brahmacārya* must spend two years there during the Probationary period. In January 1981, there were 26 trainees at the Math, and 45 inmates altogether, at least six of whom were involved in the administration of the Order, from the combined Math and Mission office. Trichur is the second largest Math centre, with 21 monastic inmates residing there in January 1981. Other Math centres have on average only five monastic inmates, as were not involved in 'Mission' type activities, necessitating a large number of monastic personnel.

Ramakrishna Sarada Mission

The monastic inmates of Mission centres are usually more numerous than those of Maths, as all Mission centres undertake educational and/or welfare work, in which monastic members (and Probationers) actively participate as honorary workers. Each Mission has a Managing Committee comprised of a lay President and a monastic Secretary, and roughly ten other lay members. The Treasurer is also chosen from monastic inmates, if there is a suitable candidate available. In this way, correspondence and accounts are in monastic hands, whilst the President's powers are limited by lack of access to Headquarters. The Committee is appointed by the Governing Body of the Mission (the same personnel as the Trustees of the Math) on the advice of the local Secretary. There are no elections or manoeuvres for places on the Managing Committees: possible candidates are quietly approached by the Secretary, and equally quietly accept or reject the offer. Very few devotees or inmates of the Mission centres know who Committee members are, unless they notice who attends the monthly Committee meetings, or take careful note of the Annual Report of their Mission centre, in which the Committee members are listed.

The Mission Managing Committee has very little real decision-making capacity: all major policy decisions, including the opening of new branches of work or the undertaking of construction must be ratified by the Governing Body. All correspondence is undertaken by the Secretary, so that decisions become in effect her recommendations, subject to approval by Headquarters. Since only women may attend classes and other religious activities at Mission centres,[3] Committee membership excludes men. Most of the members, however, are well known in their own right, as either professional women, or from well known families. A few, however, may be the wives of prominent men. The eleven members of the Managing Committee of the Trivandrum Mission branch for 1980 comprised seven graduates, and all but one were Nayar.

It may be noticed that although the Mission has ten branches, the total membership of all centres combined in 1981 was only 121. Although in theory any devotee of a Mission centre is eligible for membership as a lay member, in practice few know this is possible. The Ramakrishna Sarada Mission has relied in this matter on the experience of the older Ramakrishna Mission, which underwent a crisis in 1929. At that time, a certain faction within the Order tried to gain control of a difficult situation by recruiting large numbers of lay supporters, each with voting rights (Gambhirananda 1957:316–7). Since the Ramakrishna Sarada Mission has only 87 *saṃnyāsinis* in all, and only two-thirds or so reside in Mission centres at any one time, it can provide a maximum of 67 monastic Mission members at present. By keeping the number of lay members low, lay members are less likely to control voting at the Annual Meeting. Moreover, any-monastic member who steps out of line, can have her Mission membership revoked at once by the Governing Body, for this becomes a matter of internal discipline within the Order.

The Administrative Organisation of the Order

Both Math and Mission centres are financially independent of the Headquarters, and each centre is responsible for its own funding. In establishing a new centre, there has first to be demonstrated to the Headquarters sufficient local interest to maintain a branch if it is sanctioned. Usually this is achieved by a nucleus of women already attending the local Ramakrishna Math or Mission inviting a *saṃnyāsini* to visit them for a lecture or even a retreat. From this, gradual interest may build up over several years, usually under the auspices of a Sarada Sangham. The Sangham (Association) consists of lay female devotees of Holy Mother who usually meet regularly in certain large towns and cities, for *bhajan* and either a short talk, or readings from a scriptural text or on an aspect of Holy Mother's life. Meetings are held in private homes, before decorated photos of Ramakrishna, Holy Mother and Vivekananda. The Sarada Sangham was founded as part of the Centenary Celebrations of Holy Mother, and was seen as an eventual source of staunch lay devotees who would work towards the establishment of Maths for women in their locality. Once a group of women devotees decides to try to have a branch of the Math or Mission established, they write to the Headquarters, under the guidance of whatever *saṃnyāsini* (or *saṃnyāsin*) they have consulted, outlining pledges of regular financial support, endowments and perhaps even an offer of a suitable property. Then, negotiations begin as to the type of work which could be established, if it is to be a Mission branch, and the personnel at Headquarters[4] start seeking a potential Head of Centre.

The main difference in funding for Math and Mission centres is that Mission centres have a system of Monthly Donations, whereby a number of devotees pledge to give a set sum of money each month for the recurring expenses of running the centre. These amounts may be quite small, the largest usually being a donation direct from the local Sarada Sangham (whose members may also donate as individuals).[5] Math centres do not have this form of security, as it is considered out of keeping with a *saṃnyāsin[i]'s* 'reliance on the Lord'. Mission centres are permitted to rely on Monthly Donations, as the maintenance of lay people is in their hands also, in the form of students, Hostel girls, patients etc. Mission workers who are monastic candidates for *saṃnyāsa* are not permitted to accept a wage for their work (or fees for lectures), and are officially designated as Honorary Workers. However, not all Honorary Workers are monastic candidates. There are some women who work in Mission centres in return for board and keep, but are not candidates for monastic life.

Mission centres receive Government Grants (from both State and Central Governments) for many of their activities, including the running of kindergartens, the maintenance of orphans and/or Harijans in their hostels, school building grants, and special grants for the promotion of the Sanskrit language. Other agencies may augment these grants, such as CARE which provided food for free distribution to poor children. Other international Service Organisations and Clubs, including the Red Cross and Rotary, also support the Mission's work.

Most Mission work is in part financed by fees paid by those (or some of those) who use its service. Parents pay for their children's education at Mission schools and hostels in most centres, although each institution reserves places for those who are unable to pay or for those for whom they receive grants or scholarships. For any specific purpose, both Math and Mission centres can raise donations by public subscriptions. Buildings in particular are paid for by publishing of a 'Souvenir' magazine, which is a combination of articles and advertising, or by selling books or coupons, each for a set amount. Devotees and lay personnel associated with a centre assist in this task, as do children of the branch's institutions. Increasingly also, benefit performances, in the format of a concert or dance programme are favoured as a means of raising funds, and some famous artists have been included, making functions a highly desirable social event.

There is a long tradition among Hindus that *punya* (religious merit) is gained by giving donations in cash or kind to religious institutions or 'holy men'. It is therefore becoming a tradition among devotees to make offerings to centres or to their representatives during visits or on special occasions, such as festivals. To celebrate the attainment of a milestone (such as a sixtieth or seventy-fifth birthday) or to commemorate a parent or child, more affluent devotees may make an endowment or donate a room or a building or special fixtures, such as ceiling fans. The offering box which is placed before the shrine is also a source of donations, and the individual amounts (though modest) can add up to a sizeable amount. The Sarada Mandiram offering box was the source of Rs 1300 approximately in 1980, the equivalent of a respectable monthly wage for a teacher. However, by comparison, a well-known temple in Kerala collected Rs 125,000,000 in 1980, in addition to 2.5 kilograms of gold, 21 kilograms of silver and 15 tonnes of bronze.[6] But, whereas a centre of the Ramakrishna Sarada Mission or Sarada Math is unlikely to attract more than 150 devotees for even the most major festival, this temple attracted 500,000 pilgrims *per day* during its annual pilgrimage season. The whole Ramakrishna Movement has only succeeded in attracting a small, select following, with a very narrow base. I shall expand this statement in a following chapter.

Each Head of Centre must complete a printed form once a month, on which is entered the names and numbers of monastic inmates, transfers, new recruits and any new work undertaken. Also included is any information relevant to the Consolidated Report of the Math and Mission, published annually, such as the opening of a new building, or the expansion of activities. Once a year, audited accounts for each centre are forwarded to the Headquarters, also for inclusion in the Consolidated Report. Each centre, however, publishes its own Annual Report, which is circulated to all donors for the previous financial year. All donations to the Math and Mission are Tax Deductible,[7] and should be acknowledged with an official receipt. The exceptions are amounts deposited in the offering box, or into the hands of senior *saṃnyāsinis.* The latter category of donations should be immediately taken to the office and a receipt given or, if the donations are made during a visit outside the Math or Mission, a receipt should be forwarded to the donor. This is not always done, especially in the latter case, so that at times substantial amounts remain in the possession of *saṃnyāsinis,* in particular the Heads of Centres. This unaccounted for personal money is entirely against the Rules of the Order. When accumulated in large amounts, such donations can become 'black money', a handy way of purchasing real estate in India. One case of such a transaction came to my attention during fieldwork.

Once every two years the General Secretary or her Assistant should visit each centre. During these visits she will carefully inspect the account books, and meet with new monastic inmates and devotees. She will also strengthen her links with close devotees and employees of the branch during these visits. Each monastic inmate will be closely observed during the stay, and each will be called for a brief chat, if she does not go to see the *saṃnyāsini* of her own accord at one of the times when she is conspicuously free, perhaps with just that purpose in mind. Special objects of her close (but not obvious) attention are monastic candidates who do not meet the regular qualifications but are 'on trial', and those who have been in ill health, or shown signs of being unsuited to the monastic vocation. The visit of the main office-bearers of the Order will usually coincide with a Jubilee, or the inauguration of a new building, and is looked forward to with a mixture of anticipation and trepidation for all concerned: lest any inmate be found not up to expectation. Everyone is on her best behaviour on these visits, even the children of the Institution's Hostels, who sense the frantic preparations and tension before the arrival. Every room is cleaned, and every inmate in her most presentable clothes for such august visitors. The singing at prayer time is at its best: everyone is punctual and careful to appear alert and active at all times. The whole centre heaves a sigh of relief when the taxi taking the visitors to the station (to continue her inspection tour) pulls out of the driveway at last.[8]

The President of the Math and Mission also visits about once every two to three years. Although the most favoured person to open new buildings or centres, her main function during these visits is to initiate new monastic candidates and devotees into the Ramakrishna *mantra*.[9] This initiation brings visitors into the circle of devotees, as all initiates are in direct disciplinic succession to Ramakrishna himself. Devotees of Sarada Math or the Ramakrishna Sarada Mission may, however, seek initiation from the President or Vice President of Belur Math. The former also visits most regions of India each year, and religious aspirants travel to the nearest centre to receive initiation if they are particularly keen. Usually, aspirants who have been attending classes at a centre for at least a year will be asked if they would like to receive initiation, if they do not enquire of their own accord. The process of initiation is so low key that many regular visitors to centres do not know that it is possible. On a visit to the Kerala Mission in 1978, for example, 21 devotees received *mantra* initiation, and this is considered a substantial number, as males are seldom in close contact with the *saṃnyāsinis* in charge of centres. The main exception is when a husband and wife together receive initiation, in which case, this may be done at a Womens Math or Mission. It is considered desirable for both to be initiated together if possible.

Annually, all Heads of Centres are required to attend a meeting at the Headquarters, and all do so. Policy decisions affecting the whole Order are discussed at these meetings, which are timed just after a Trustee Meeting: the only one which the three Trustees who reside outside Bengal can usually all attend. During these visits to Headquarters, Heads of Centres keep their eyes open for bright junior candidates undergoing training, ready to transfer elsewhere once their two years at Sarada Math is completed. Once again, the process is very subtle, and Heads of Centres may discuss their choice with the General Secretary, to seek her opinion, since transfers are permitted only subject to her approval.

Generally, relations between the Headquarters and the branch centres are good, with genuine affection between the Heads of Centres and the main office bearers at Headquarters. The cordiality between Headquarters and its branches is expressed by a system of gift giving, which encompasses the entire Order. Heads of Centres visiting Calcutta bring with them a personal gift for the President of the Order and General Secretary, usually an item of clothing. When a junior is sent to Calcutta or to another branch centre, she will take with her a gift of food items, either made at her own branch centre or a specialty of her region.[10] When office bearers of the Order visit branches, however, they present each and every monastic inmate with a saree, though this is becoming an expensive exercise in the case of a large branch such as Trichur, where membership is steadily increasing, as is the price of cloth.

Heads of Centres and members of the Order departing from Headquarters after a visit from another city, or after receiving vows, are given an article of clothing by the President and/or General Secretary. This is usually a saree or shawl and is sometimes one which is *prasād*, that is, offered in the shrine beforehand. Whether *prasādi* (offered) or not, cloth given by the President or General Secretary is regarded as 'special', not only because it is in most instances of better quality than is routinely issued,[11] but because of its association with the most revered members of the Order. Clothes given in this way are often set aside for use on special occasions, such as festivals, and whenever worn, the recipient will comment, 'President Mataji gave me this saree'. The most precious clothes, however, are those issued and worn for the taking of vows. These are worn rarely afterwards, and thus kept for many years. The gift of cloth and other items such as food is an important means of cementing goodwill, not only between the Headquarters and its branches, but between one centre and another. Similarly, gifts may be made to very close lay devotees, the choice of the two categories of cloth and food being very significant. Both are highly susceptible to absorbing either positive or negative influences of the donor, and transferring these to be recipient.[12]

Local Autonomy and Central Control

Branch centres of the Sarada Math or the Ramakrishna Sarada Mission have seldom given the Headquarters cause for serious anxiety. Routinely, crises are adequately met by the individual Heads of Centres. However, one major mutiny has occurred so far. This was from the Calcutta College, where a Head of Centre gathered a personal following and began to scorn direction from the Headquarters. A series of incidents culminated in her leaving the Order with some followers, to set up her own organisation.[13] Within the Ramakrishna Order, there have been a number of similar cases over the years of *saṃnyāsins* either leaving the Order or being expelled. Some of the institutions set up by these 'rebels' have proved very successful, and one in particular has in recent years opened its own Womens Maths in South India. Although local Heads of centres have a great deal of autonomy (especially those centres far from Calcutta) they are in constant communication with the Headquarters. However, if the need arises, the Head of Centre can be replaced at short notice or even expelled from the Order. In this respect, ultimate control rests with the Trustees/Governing Body.

Yet, although there is continuity in the daily routine followed by all centres, and the training at Headquarters is shared by all, each centre bears to a high degree the stamp of the personality of the Head. The way in which she deals with those in her charge, whether she is 'modern' or orthodox,[14] a good speaker or efficient administrator, whether she has the ability to mix easily with lay devotees, are all major factors in the successful running of a centre.

* * *

A Profile of the village, 1981

The growth of interest in 'community studies' had encouraged anthropologists and other behavioural scientists to concentrate on institutions and discrete geographic areas as isolates. Perhaps in the case of *saṃnyāsis* they are studied outside their wider social context because of the philosophical notion that this is where they properly belong. I wish to demonstrate that this is far from the case.

I have chosen the Trichur Sarada Mandiram to illustrate how a branch of the Ramakrishna Order of *saṃnyāsinis* operates in practice, and how it fits into the wider society, of which it is a part. Perhaps it is the most interesting anthropologically of all the branches, situated as it is in the midst of a rapidly changing society, torn between violently conflicting ideologies. The place and role of Sarada Mandiram in Kerala today will serve to highlight some of the stresses faced by the major Hindu communities in the state, and the possible direction of their resolution.

By 1981 Sri Sarada Mandiram owned approximately 20 acres (8 hectares) of land in a village which is 8 kilometres from Trichur town in the state of Kerala. According to the 1981 Census, then underway, there were 1,431 houses in the village, and a total population of 6,150, which broke down into 3,201 females and 2,949 males. The inbalance in the male/female ratio is to some extent caused by the absence of men for work outside the village.

The 1981 Census figures did not provide statistics on communal status, but in 1971 there were 383 females and 373 males of Scheduled Caste residing in the village. It was, however, estimated by the Village Office that one in four residents of the village was of Scheduled Caste in 1981. The local Roman Catholic priest of the village estimated that just over half of the villagers were Christian. Thus, about one in two Hindus in the village was of Scheduled Caste in 1981. This seems a very high proportion, but in fact the Office was lumping together Scheduled Castes with Other Backward Communities, which included Izhavas, the largest Hindu community. They constituted almost a quarter of the population of the Trichur District.

Village Communities

The village consists of a main thoroughfare which, though potholed, is bitumen coated in the centre. It is along this road that a Government bus runs, linking Trichur town with the pilgrimate centre of Guruvayur. Some private bus services also extend to Guruvayur, but most terminate in nearby villages or townships. At night the main village road is dimly lit by widely spaced electric lights, interspersed with the glow of candles or kerosine lamps, from the houses along the way. Few homes have electricity, but those that do are mostly on the main road. From each side of the road branch narrow lanes, barely visible from the street, and hedged with thornbush. They are surfaced with sharp orange-red laterite pebbles, which are characteristic of this part of Kerala.

A sharp line can be drawn dividing the village road, from north to south. The eastern half consists of Hindu houses, and the western half Christian. The caste Hindus live in the south east section, in the block which contains the village's Krishna temple. Here live two Nambudiri households: not wealthy landlords, but impoverished families. The other occupants of this section of the village are Nayars who constituted roughly 15% of the population. Their houses are mostly two storeyed, and of laterite blocks, with thatched roofs. Nayar houses are sparesely furnished. The more affluent families have red tiled roofs and plastered, whitewashed walls. Many have a well in the garden, but only a few have an electric pump and running water.

A Nayar household would typically consist of a husband and wife and their two to three children, and frequently the woman's widowed mother. Some homes, however, still followed the matrilineal pattern of residence, with a woman being the homeowner, but her married daughters and their children residing there also. Frequently, one or more husbands resided outside the village, and indeed outside the district, as most were in clerical positions, or the military. They returned to their wives and families when on leave. The same applied to the other communities in the village, where often the men were absent, mostly on manual contract work overseas. Most Nayar homes had a small plot at the back, where a kitchen garden was maintained. Each house grew papaya, banana and coconut trees, and the mandatory mango, which was cut down on the death of a family member, to provide the funeral pyre.

Literacy among the Nayars was almost universal, even among the older generation, and many of the younger women worked, mainly in clerical positions, or as teachers. A few were employed in the Asrama or Sarada Mandiram in various capacities, and some were employed in the town. In this part of Kerala, there was no question of women working as shop assistants or in restaurants or other public places, and only the most impoverished caste Hindu woman would resort to labouring to earn a living. Poor Nayar women did, however, work as indoor servants and cooks for more affluent Nayars.

The next Hindu category was Artisans who represented approximately 5% of the village: Ashari (Carpenter), Kallan (Stone cutter), Kollan (Blacksmith), Mushari (Metal Worker) and Thattan (Goldsmith). The village had a few of each category, as well as the Mannan (Thatcher) with their Mannati (Washerwomen) wives, a traditional combination. These Washerwomen only launder ritually polluted clothes for caste Hindus, which are then rewashed by a Nayar Washerman before use. The Artisans lived in a cluster at the junction of the Hindu-Christian division, on both the north and south sides of the road. A few Artisan families lived in the Asrama Housing Colony, along with Izhava and Scheduled Caste families. Most older Artisan men worked at their traditional occupation, though it was becoming increasingly more difficult, as metal vessels gave way to plastic, and cotton clothes to synthetic. Also, it was fashionable to shop in Trichur town, and no longer did the former family patronage of Artisans apply.

Below the Artisans in communal hierarchy were the Izhavas, who constituted roughly 20% of the village population. The overwhelming majority of Izhavas worked as labourers, though some also tapped toddy, their traditional occupation. There were, however, a few well-to-do Izhava families in the village, most of whom had gone overseas (to the Gulf States) on manual contract work, and amassed considerable wealth. These families built modern houses in the latest fashion on the main street. The homes were conspicuous, with flat concrete slab roofs, fancy wrought iron widow grilles, and were well plastered and pastel colour-washed, both inside and out. Such homes boasted modern sofas in the lounge, perhaps a bathroom with a Western style toilet and basin, and a dining table with laminated top and plastic-seated chairs. Most Izhavas worked as daily wage labourers.

The Scheduled Caste Hindus constituted a likely 10% of the village population. Pulayas were represented in this category, as well as Vettuva, who are of tribal origin. Men and women of these communities worked as daily wage labourers also, and both Izhava and Schedules Caste women worked as 'sweepers', cleaners who swept the compounds of Nayar families, and cleaned their bathrooms (which had outside access).

Roughly half the village population was Christian. Most of the Christian villagers were also daily wage labourers, though some ran small shops, or worked in the town as clerks. Their standard of living was similar to that of Nayar or Izhava, depending on family status, and indeed they ranked themselves on a quasi caste basis, as did other Christians, Muslims and Jews in Kerala. Christian girls can and did join Convents as a choice of career, and also favoured nursing, an occupation looked down on by caste Hindus, though sometimes chosen by Izhavas.

There were no doubt one or two families of other communities in the village, but as my access to the village was limited, by the nature of my fieldwork, I can only surmise that Ambalavasis would have been represented; that is, temple personnel. They would have been associated with the Krishna temple. There were no Muslims in the village, though Muslims lived in close proximity, and were a major political force in the Trichur township.

In general the village presents a neat profile. The street and lanes are swept clean daily, and are overhung with tropical trees and vines. Even The Harijan (Schedule Caste) lanes are well kept, unlike other regions of India. All village land is dry, though wetlands (paddy fields) surround the village, providing the inhabitants with seasonal work. The Harijan and other non-caste Hindus live in small huts, on plots not exceeding 10 cents (0.04 hectares). Walls are of unplastered laterite, though very poor families live in huts of plaited palm branches. Roofs are of coconut thatch, and the floors of mud, mixed with charcoal and tamped to a hard surface. A typical hut would be roughly 2.4 metres by 3 metres, with a single room, perhaps with a half partition. A palm leaf extension may provide a kitchen area at the back, and there are no bathing facilities. Inside, the hut would contain some old rolled up bedding in one corner, and a rickety chair or stool. Few have a table, and many not even these basic possessions. An extra set of clothing is either usually kept outside on a clothes line, or hanging on a string within the room. The extra clothes may be used by whoever needs them at the time, since they consist of a simple length of cloth. A small bell metal lamp which burns kerosine may be kept on the window sill, but many families simply puncture the lid of an ink bottle, place a wick of rolled up cloth in the resulting hole, and fill the bottle with kerosine. By this smokey lamp many a child in the village is expected to study, in a room in which weary parents are already asleep soon after dark, after a hard day's work in the fields. Labourers are paid daily wages by plot owners, and work seven days a week if work is available. On their way home the daily rice ration is bought, and perhaps 50 p (a small amount) of fish or vegetable, if there is nothing to pick in the tiny garden on a particular day. A few leaves made into a paste with water, or a paste of a chunk of coconut are often the only accompaniment to the evening rice. Some families have one or two scrawny chickens, in which case an egg or two may be available, and usually eaten by the man of the house. Families typically consist of a husband, wife and children (average three to four) with one or two widowed parents (of either party) in residence if they are otherwise homeless.

There are ten Municipal wells in the village for common use, the well in the Sarada High School grounds being favoured as it is deep, and moreover, the children already mingle socially at School and feel less uncertain about sharing a common water supply than would their caste-conscious parents. Many caste Hindu homes, however, have their own wells.

Within walking distance of the village is a Government Primary Health Centre, Family Planning Clinic and Leprosy Health Assistant's Office. There is also a Veterinary Dispensary where free TB testing is carried out on the cattle, though very few families can afford to own even one cow. Despite the official listing of the above personnel, on numerous occasions I tried to meet the Health and Family Planning officials, who are supposed to be regular visitors to their allotted village rooms, but found that they were not there. However, the lists were always signed to signify that they had in fact attended their session, as required. Local People were amused that I persisted in leaving messages for the officials to contact me or send a messenger when they were in attendance. They were cynical about the conduct of the officials, but blamed their employers (the

Government) for not checking on them. There was a Village Office about a kilometre away which dealt with the Panchayat, that is the group of four villages to which Puranattukara belongs. Within the village is the Block Office, which was the administrative centre for a group of Panchayats: in this case seven. The next largest unit is the Taluk or Revenue District, which includes all the Blocks within a few miles of Trichur, the Administrative centre.

The actual village is further divided into nine Wards, and each house in each Ward has a Ward number painted on its front door post. This is useful for official purposes such as Census, tax and immunisation. Houses are known by a name, the old families of village caste Hindus retaining their traditional name,[15] whilst others choose any modern name which appeals to them such as 'Lakshmi Vilas'. There are no street names or numbers, so that the village postman often has to rely on local gossip to find a newcomer.

Ward number 9 is called Gurukulam, after the Gurukulam or boarding school of the Ramakrishna Asrama. Sarada Mandiram is included in this Ward, along with the Asrama. The Asrama has grown considerably in the post-War years, and at present has a mixed Lower Primary School, and a Boys Upper Primary and High School with a total enrolment of over 1,000. In the Gurukulam Hostel thirteen Harijans were accommodated in 1981 and eighteen orphans and poor students from surrounding villages, as well as paying boarders, mostly from the other districts or overseas, about 60 in number. Lack of water in summer prevents the Hostel numbers from expanding further. In addition the Asrama runs a free dispensary and a well-kept hospital with eighteen beds. Although treatment is free except for a token registration fee of Rs 2 renewable each month, patient numbers have declined dramatically over the last ten years. During my fieldwork, the hospital beds were for most part unoccupied, even though a doctor lives on the premises, and there are basic diagnostic and operating facilities. Even though it would be convenient for patients from the village with fevers or injuries to stay in the hospital, where good clean linen and Asrama food is provided, there is almost a boycott of the Institution. Villagers told me that they just do not have faith in its medical services and resent the modest monthly registration fee demanded by the Asrama. They would prefer to queue and be admitted at the filthy, squalid Municipal Hospital, even sleeping on the floor if necessary. However, sick children from the Gurukulam and Sarada Mandiram use the medical services of the Asrama, and almost daily children from both Institutions are taken there with a variety of minor ailments, injuries, childhood diseases and fevers.

The Asrama runs a printing press from which the Malayalam journal of the Order, *Pradbuddha Keralam*, and numerous books (many of them translations from Bengali, English or Sanskrit) are published. The press has an extremely high standard, and is one of the major presses of Kerala. Some of the more literary-inclined *saṃnyāsins* write, translate and edit publications and also supervise the proof reading. Nine villagers work in the press as printers and compositors, and are trained on the premises, as are the nine women who bind and finish the books and journals.

The Asrama employs in addition about twenty men and women in the fields and for general cleaning and maintenance work, as well as the teachers in the School. However, most teachers come from the town, and the School does not thus directly employ a significant number of villagers, very few of whom hold the necessary qualifications.

The original Harijan Colony built by the Asrama now has 90 houses, and at dusk a small shrine dedicated to Ramakrishna is the focal point of evening devotions. Once a week a *saṃnyāsin* visits the Colony to lead the prayers and to give a simple talk. Two young women from the Colony are paid a stipend by the Asrama to run a creche for mothers who work in the fields, and one of these was sent for training at the Asrama's expense. Every day between 15 and 18 sick or unemployed Harijans are fed, also at the expense of the Asrama. In the early days two of the five Dedicated Women Workers of Sarada Mandiram worked in the Colony but in 1981 Sarada Mandiram personnel had no connection with the Colony at all.

In the Colony the Asrama has in recent times implemented a Savings Scheme in which two paid collectors visit every house each evening and request 50 paise or Rs 1 as the case may be. These amounts are banked and when a target sum is reached, the Asrama contributes an equal amount or some other donation in kind. For example, if the savings are to go towards thatching, the Asrama may help by donating palm leaves. 'The people have faith in us, even despite propaganda', said the President of the Asrama. 'Propaganda' is an oblique reference to the village Communist leaders.

The village has a small post office which exists mainly to deal with the large volume of mail and parcels from the Asrama and Sarada Mandiram, a couple of small general stores, and a ration shop for rice, kerosine and sugar. The stores sell basic goods, such as soap, pens, pencils and cheap exercise books, paper, ink, hair ribbons, combs, plastic buckets (for washing), tiny packets of biscuits, sweets sold from a large jar in ones and twos, and 'fancy' items such as perfumed hair oil, talcum powder and plastic trinkets. A few bolts of cloth in white and coloured cotton and a small pile of wearing cloth completes the stock. One of the shops, in the Christian section, sells veils for use in church and holy pictures also. It is even beginning to cash in on the Christmas trade, keeping a small pile of soiled cards in a rubber band in its little glass showcase. There are also two provision stores for grains, lentils, oil, tea and basic vegetables. Four tea shops and toddy shops complete the main village trade, and these are visited by labourers after work. They are the venue for the exchange of gossip, though wives resent the amount of money spent there. A lone fish vendor on a cycle plies his trade every afternoon, crying *oooh* (fish). Whilst I was in the field, a tailor set up shop in a room above the new Christian general store. Already a young lady near the village church was available to tailor simple articles such as blouses and school uniforms for a modest price 'Rs 2.50 for the poor and Rs 3.50 for the rich', per blouse.

Among traditional occupations, the village had a barber who worked from a 'Saloon', complete with fancy chair, the former ritual functions of the barber today giving way to 'fashion cut'. Indeed, one village barber had secured a contract position in the Gulf States, and was sending home Rs 1,000 per month (which equalled a middle class salary). He formerly used to cut the hair of the senior *saṃnyāsinis* of Sarada Mandiram, and had sent gold paint to coat the top of Sarada Mandiram's temple dome. This was surely a strategy to impress his neighbours, while his sad little children, left behind, were the centre of attraction in their hot, synthetic 'foreign' clothes.

Only barbering and tailoring seemed to be expanding businesses, but even these were limited by the lack of money of their customers. The wealthiest man of the village, however, was reputed to be a Christian bus owner, who plied two bright red buses (with the name 'Jesus' prominently displayed in painted letters beneath a multi-coloured painted-on picture of a mournful Sacred Heart) between the next village and Trichur town. The same man was the owner of a cashew nut grove between the Sarada Mandiram and Christian sector. The villagers said the grove was 3.2 hectares. A group of Harijans had permission to clear the undergrowth. In return they took home twigs and branches for firewood.

The church was a prominent whitewashed, spired building, and had a shrine to a popular saint in Kerala, St Sebastian, near its gates. Virtually every Christian attended Sunday Mass, and every child Sunday School, at which the priest presided, cane in hand. The priest lived in a huge two storey house with a male housekeeper, and had no assistants. He was perhaps in his thirties. For company he conducted a Youth Club, which consisted of a handful of better educated young Christian men of the village, who met for discussion at the church once a week. Members of St Vincent de Paul in Canada had adopted the village and had sent money for the setting up of Christians as tailors, and in other small businesses, a move which the Presidents of the Asrama and Sarada Mandiram condemned. 'Indians must be raised by Indians working and earning Indian money', said the former. 'It is this foreign money coming into the villages that causes prices to go up, and hurts those who can't get hold of such capital. All these small businesses are set up by Christians with foreign money, as Hindus don't have a chance'. Christians are grateful for overseas aid and the female tailor who had received a treadle machine told me that when the Bishop had come recruiting he had 'chosen' two of her sisters to 'go to foreign': one as a trainee nurse in Germany and one as a religious novice in Italy. And, she added, her sister from Italy had visited last year, dressed in a *short* black dress that showed her *legs,* with a veil and looking plump and healthy. The family now had no worries for these two daughters, as both would be taken care of for life, she assured me. She herself was too young at the time to be chosen. Most Christians were poor, working as labourers. However, there was also a well-to-do Christian Section of the village where teachers, business proprietors and government employees resided.

The nearest paddy fields were at least two kilometres away, and the village's labour pool, men and women of Harijan and other Backward Communities such as Izhava, were available to work on whichever plot needed attention. Owners and managers 'call' labourers for work by word of mouth, but work is not constant. It is estimated by villagers that all a labourer can expect is 250 days of work per year. Wages are just sufficient to cover the daily cost of rice, and periodic expenses such as kerosine. Families cannot save, and the 'lean season' is indeed lean: cold, and raining, with hungry families huddled together in leaking huts, afflicted with respiratory infections, rheumatic pains, and the digestive disorders of this miserable time. The Kerala school year begins with the rains[16] but many poor children cannot attend regularly, as they do not have a dry change of clothes. When the harvest is ready, again many poor children are absent from school, as parents expect them to take their place in the fields, where during harvest payment is in grain. Though virtually all young children are enrolled in the village Schools (where a meal is provided for Lower Primary students) parents engaged in 'outdoor' work (as labouring is known) fear that children will be incapable of doing manual work if not trained from a young age. Few see any other future for their children, and as many poor children slip further and further behind in their studies as the years progress, they leave by the end of Primary School, or the beginning of High School. Of those who remain to complete their School Leaving Certificate (at 15), at Sarada Girls High School in 1980 only 62% of candidates passed. At the Asrama High School the percentage was even lower. Although education is not seen as a key to a career by poor villagers, at least most villagers under 45 are literate, a high achievement in India. Only the elderly sign for their wages in an inky thumbprint, and most can write a letter to absent relatives, this being the most vital use of literacy in a milieu in which books are not readily available, and newspapers and magazines beyond the means of all save the middle class.

Politically, the village is divided along quite rigid lines. The Harijan and Backward Community citizens vote solidly for the Communist Party (Marxist), as long as they continue to work for daily wages. However, a few who have white collar occupations vote for the Congress Party. The caste Hindus and most well-to-do Christians also support Congress. But, the village has a clear majority of Marxist voters,[17] who make their presence felt in the form of protests and strikes, usually over the use of non-union labour in town, often forcing both Schools to close. There is solidarity among Marxists, and word of action in the town swiftly brings workers in the village out in sympathy. Both Schools close as soon as threatened, as neither has an insurance policy, and could easily be vandalised or burnt down. The word '*samaram*' or strike is frequently and joyously on the lips of students, as they pour out of the School gates during school hours, day after day. Both Institutions fear the chance of violence if they were to defy strikers' demands, and so it has become a ritual for strikers to approach the Schools and for the Headmaster/mistress to announce their closure forthwith.

Alongside the Congress and Marxists another group was gaining power in Trichur in 1980–1 after being banned during Indira Gandhi's Emergency of the 1970s. This was the Rastriya Swayamsevak Sangha (RSS), a far right Hindu group committed to making India a Hindu nation. An RSS follower was responsible for the assassination of Mahatma Gandhi, for his conciliatory attitude towards Muslims.[18] The RSS in Trichur sees its enemies as both Marxists and Christians, and in Muslim areas, violence between Hindus and Muslims is on occasion incited by the RSS. During my time in the field there were periodic clashes between RSS and Marxists in particular, throughout the Trichur area. In the town, Hindu merchants, supporters of the RSS, clashed frequently with 'Head Load Workers', who are Marxist supporters, over the conditions of loading and unloading goods. This had repercussions in the village, where caste Hindus saw all labourers as troublemakers, and labourers saw all non-workers and bosses as money hungry. Three times during my fieldwork the entire town was brought to a standstill by a General Strike of all unions, representing most of the town's labour force. Caste Hindus and wealthy Christians did not venture onto the streets on these occasions, and few who owned cars dared to use them, lest the vehicles be stoned or burnt. The anger of the striking crowds was always towards manifestations of wealth, of which private cars were the prime example, and symbol.[19]

There were also other subtle stresses and problems in the village regarding relations between workers and owners of property. The most striking example involved the relations between the villagers and a major employer, the President of Sarada Mandiram.

Sarada Mandiram

In 1981 Sarada Mandiram was a large organisation with eleven separate branches of work, which were as follows:

1 Math

The original Math building is still in use with many additions and alterations. It is a square building with an inner courtyard, and rooms on all sides, all opening onto a covered inner square verandah, after the *nalekettu* model of aristocratic Nayar families. The main modification to the traditional design is that the dining hall (which has now been replaced) was originally in the west wing, instead of the north. This was to utilise an already existing deep well. In the south west corner was a shrine room, which could be closed off from the *thekkini*, or open hall, which during prayers was used as a prayer hall to the shrine. Recently, a separate temple has been built.

There were 21 monastic inmates of the Math during the latter period of my fieldwork, although the number fluctuated, due to transfers, and new arrivals. Of these, eight were *saṃnyāsinis*, five *brahmacārinis*, five Probationers, and three Pre Probationers. Six Probationers from Trichur were in Calcutta undergoing training, three of whom had completed one year, and the other three of whom were sent to Calcutta in December 1980, just before two

Probationers returned from Calcutta after training and *brahmacārya*. I shall examine life in the Math in detail in the following chapter.

2 Balika Gurukulam

This is a Hostel for girls attending either the Asrama Primary School or Sri Sarada Girls High School. In 1981 there were 131 girls in the Hostel, 22 of whom were Scheduled Caste and six of whom were orphans. Four girls were of neither category but were accommodated free of charge, and a further two girls received a reduction in fees. Eight of the girls had parents interstate and thirteen had parents overseas, mostly in the Gulf States. Of these families, seven fathers had gone on contract work without their wives.

In regard to the communal status of the boarders, 47 were definitely of Nayar or higher communities, but exactly how many others could not be ascertained.[20] A large number of boarders were Izhavas, daughters of merchants or professionals who wanted their children to grow up with refined 'cultured' Hindu behaviour. About 8–9 children came from an unhappy home environment, where alcohol or divorce was adversely affecting them.

Two female Nayar cooks and one Izhavas helper prepared food for the Hostel, and two outdoor workers cleaned the bathing areas and latrines, as well as laundered the clothes of the younger Hostel girls. Older Hostel girls were responsible for their own laundry, cleaned their dormitories (known as 'halls') and helped with the preparation of vegetables for lunch and supper on a roster basis. Parents paid Rs 120 per month for Hostel fees, which included food, which is vegetarian and of a high standard. Those who request it, may have a tumbler of milk once a day, for which a charge of 50 p a day is levied.

3 Sri Sarada Girls High School (SSGHS)

The School provides classes 6–10, that is, Upper Primary and High School. The final School examination is taken at the age of 14 or 15 in Kerala, after which those who want to pursue tertiary students enrol for two years at a Pre Degree College. There were 1,283 students at the SSGHS in the 1980–1 school year, most of the girls living within walking distance. There is no other school within walking distance of the village, except the Asrama School, and so virtually all children of this and neighbouring villages attend one or other of these Institutions. However, while no monastic inmates teach in the Asrama School, five monastic inmates were teaching at

SSGHS. A further two were on leave, with the intention of retiring, as they were monastic seniors and a lay Headmistress had recently been appointed. They did not wish to serve under her. The rest of the teachers were lay women, and all Hindu. All school tuition is free in Kerala, and School uniform cloth available from a local ration shop at reduced price. Harijan students received an allowance per year of Rs 70 to help defray the cost of books and clothing, and are exempt from the annual 'special fee' of Rs 10, which is levied for the use of School equipment.

4 The Sishu Vihar

Forty-five pre-school children from about the age of 3–5 attend the Sisu Vihar, which is open on school days, and elder brothers or sisters usually leave the children before School, and pick them up on the way home. The children (both boys and girls) are provided with a hot midday meal, some of the ingredients for which are provided by CARE, and the rest by Sarada Mandiram. No charge is made. In 1981, four children in the Sishu Vihar each had a parent working as a teacher in either Sarada Mandiram or Asrama Schools, ten were the children of small plot owners, four had parent[s] in the Gulf States, one was the child of a mechanic, and the rest – children of daily wage earners. Fifteen of the children were Christian (one third), whilst roughly half of the School children were Christian. The Sishu Vihar was run by a trained teacher, and a Pre Probationer (also trained and employed before coming to Sarada Mandiram) was her assistant. The equipment was in a broken-down condition, and the children spent most of their time with their arms folded, sitting at benches reciting numbers and nursery rhymes, whilst the teacher wielded a cane.

5 Charkha

This was a new section, conducted in two very gloomy rooms attached to the Sishu Vivar. Since Gandhi reintroduced the *charkha* or spinning wheel as a means of reviving India's cottage industries, this among all manual occupations has an aura of respectability associated with it. The Khadi (Homespun) Board has given 24 mechanised *charkhas* and string making machines for the use of the spinning section of Sarada Mandiram, and women work them for 8 hours a day, 6 days a week. Experienced spinners can earn Rs 100 or more, about the same as a female daily wage labourer at Sarada Mandiram, but much less than a woman working on a daily basis outside. However, spinning appeals to the poor Nayar or other 'respectable' Hindu female villagers, for whom labouring is not deemed appropriate. Also, it does not involve standing in the hot sun, a practice which is dreaded, as it darkens the skin. Two orphans who grew up in Sarada Mandiram but failed their School final examinations are among those who obtain a living from spinning. These two girls, however, still live at Sarada Mandiram, while other women come daily to the spinning section from their homes.

6 Sri Sarada Typing Institution

This was opened while I was in the field, and is housed in the neat upstairs room of a former dwelling, opposite Sarada Mandiram.[21]

Eleven students were enrolled in the first term of typing, for whom there were two teachers. Students attended for one hour a day at a cost of Rs 8 per month. The Institute owned five typewriters, all very old, and students could only learn on English language machines (Malayalam machines are still rare). Thus, potential students needed to have a fair command of English to succeed. Out of the initial students, two girls had completed pre degree College, one a Master of Science, and one a Bachelor of Commerce. Students supplied their own paper, and ribbons were only placed in the typewriters once they had mastered the keyboard. One of the teachers told me that she had studied for 2½ years to attain a speed of 50 words per minute typing, and 80 words per minute shorthand, but she was now rusty. There were no plans to teach shorthand at the Institute, however.

7 Sri Sarada Hostel for College Girls

Very centrally situated in the town is a Hostel for girls attending the local Colleges. The building was rented from the Ramakrishna Asrama for Rs 350 per month and is extremely overcrowded. Forty five girls were enrolled at the Hostel in 1980–1, five of them former free boarders from Sarada Mandiram. One *saṃnyāsini* was in charge of the Hostel, with a lay assistant, as well as kitchen staff, and a male gatekeeper who assists with much of the shopping and other errands. College Hostel girls come to Sarada Mandiram for the Sunday religious classes on a roster basis, and attendance at morning and evening prayers is compulsory. The girls are also very closely supervised, and are not allowed to leave the premises (except to go to College) without a specific reason, and an escort.

8 Sanskrit Classes

Although Sanskrit is taught as an optional language at Sri Sarada Girls High, extra classes are held outside of School hours for interested students and teachers. Examinations of four levels are held annually, conducted by the Bharatiya Vidya Bhavan of Bombay. The Government of India gives a special grant for the teaching of Sanskrit, the amount being Rs 5,400 in 1980 (as against State grants for the nursery school of Rs 1,000 and Rs 2,030 for the orphanage). Pre Probationers and Probationers at Sarada Mandiram all have to study Ṣanskrit, but classes are held for them separately, though they sit for the same examinations. One hundred and ten candidates (mostly Hostel girls) sat for extra-curricular Sanskrit examinations in 1979, with generally good results, since the girls who sat for these were learning Sanskrit already at School. Two *brahmacārinis* were receiving wages as Sanskrit teachers, but were not in fact teaching.

9 Religious

Pūjā (ritual worship) is held daily at Sarada Mandiram, and morning and evening prayers, attended by monastic inmates and Hostel girls. The temple is open to the female visitors, but not one woman from the village visits regularly. A handful of local Nayar women attend on major festivals, along with 30–40 women from the town. On Sundays a class is held, but often no more than eight or so outside women attend, the audience being made up of inmates of Sarada Mandiram and the College Hostel. Only once a year, during the annual retreat, held in conjunction with the Asrama, a sizeable number of women gather at Sarada Mandiram. Most of these, however, are not from the Trichur vicinity. At the 1980 retreat only 10 out of the 52 retreatants were from Trichur, the others coming from the major towns of Kerala.

Saṃnyāsinis from Sarada Mandiram accept invitations to give lectures outside their Institution, and to conduct religious retreats and classes. At least two or three times a year the President travels interstate by request of devotees of the Ramakrishna Movement, usually taking a junior monastic inmate with her as an attendant. There is no process at Sarada Mandiram for training junior monastic inmates for future preaching, and when accompanying a senior they are expected to remain silent and in the background.

10 Agriculture

Apart from a one acre plot in a nearby village which yields 2,225 kilos of paddy each year, Sarada Mandiram also has an extensive 'compound' of its own, in which produce for daily use is grown. In 1981 on an average nine women and three men were engaged in the gardens daily as labourers, and another two men in the dairy. The gardens produced a wide variety of seasonal vegetables, as well as fodder, fruit, and a small amount of cashew nuts, which were sold for processing. The coconut plantation had 210 trees, which yielded on average 200 nuts per month. Many of the trees were still young, and were not yet producing. Coconut gardens are regarded as a sound investment in Kerala, where every part of the tree as well as the actual coconut is utilised. The dairy had three cows and a she buffalo, which only yielded 13 litres of milk a day in total, despite both fresh and processed fodder. This was insufficient for the daily needs of the Institution, and milk had also to be purchased from outside.[22]

11 Sri Bharati Kalalaym

In 1982 Sarada Mandiram opened a Parallel College in a compound nearby the new Typing Institute. The house and adjacent land were donated by a female devotee. There were 28 girls enrolled during the first year, all of whom paid a fee. The former Headmistress of the SSGHS became the Principal of the College, on her retirement from the School. Parallel Colleges are eagerly sought by students who did not gain admission to regular Colleges. They give tuition, so that students can sit for College examinations as private candidates. Attendance is on a daily basis, and there are many of these institutions now emerging in Kerala. Many of the staff are highly experienced tertiary teachers who had reached the official retirement age. The advantage of such Colleges, is that the management may accept students and staff, free from Reservation criteria, and can charge fees. Many, such as that run by Sarada Mandiram, teach only Arts students, which require little or no equipment, except desks, benches and blackboards. A new building constructed for the College in 1982 collapsed during the August rains, with many people inside, some of whom were seriously injured. Though I had left the field by this time, the villagers, through correspondence, let me know they had no doubt in their minds as to how this occurred: divine retribution for the way in which the senior inmates of Sarada Mandiram treated the villagers.

Sarada Mandiram provides, in conjunction with the Asrama, substantial employment in the village, giving opportunities for a steady income to men and women from all communities and in a wide range of occupations. Even two local carpenters and a builder are almost fully employed by the two Institutions, as are ex free boarders who have no home to which to return. In the circumstances, it could easily be assumed that the relationship between the villagers and the two Institutions would be harmonious, as virtually all of them have spent many years in close association with the Ramakrishna Movement, through its Schools, if not as employees. However, the absence of local people at the religious activities of the Asrama and Sarada Mandiram would indicate that somehow the message of Ramakrishna-Sarada Devi and Vivekananda is not well received in Puranattukara.

Before I discuss the relations of Sarada Mandiram with the villagers, I wish to describe the internal workings of the Institution, so that it will become increasingly clear what its actual role was in Trichur 1981, and why this has changed considerably since its inauguration in 1927.

Chapter 6

The Monastic Inmates

I have already described how the original five inmates of Sarada Mandiram came together to become the first *saṃnyāsinis* of the Ramakrishna Order. Four of the 'pioneer' members were still in Trichur in 1981, while the fifth had been transferred elsewhere in Kerala. Approximately one fifth of the entire Sarada Math had joined in (or through contact with) the Trichur branch. I would now like to discuss how candidates came to hear about, and eventually join the Order from the south west region of India.

There is no planned intake of candidates for the Order. Young women apply for information on their own initiative, either through personal contact with a local Ramakrishna Asrama or Sarada Math, or write to a branch of the Order, frequently finding the address in an Asrama publication, or through a devotee. In the case of a candidate unknown personally to Sarada Mandiram, the President will write and ask her to come and stay for a few days, if she appears to fit the basic qualifications for candidature. There are seven qualifications set out in a brochure published by the Bangalore Ramakrishna Asrama, which I quote below, as there is no similar list published by Sarada Mandiram. The qualifications for female candidates do, however, differ slightly.

1 Acquaintance with the life and teachings of Sri Ramakrishna and Swami Vivekananda, and a relevant and keen desire to follow their ideals.
2 Good health.
3 Readiness to do any work entrusted and at any place where he is posted.
4 Willingness to conform to the discipline of the Asrama.
5 Minimum educational qualification of a pass in the SSLC[1] or its equivalent.

6 Age limit of 18–25 in the case of matriculates. In the case of graduates, the upper limit may be relaxed up to 30.
7 Freedom from family encumbrances.

The eligible candidate is admitted in the first instance as a pre-probationer. After satisfactorily completing a year of pre-probation, he would be accepted as a probationer. The period of probation consists of four years, including two years of training at the Head Quarters (Belur Math) at the end of which, if he is found fit, he would normally be initiated as a Brahmacharin. Again after the four years' training as a Brahmacharin, if he is considered properly qualified, he would be ordained as a Sannyasin, a full-fledged member of the Ramakrishna Order (*Sri R.K. Ashrama Bangalore and its Activities* 1968:8).

For female candidates, the President would normally ask a prospective candidate to come and stay if she meets requirements (5) and (6), though for Sarada Math, the SSLC is considered insufficient education for a candidate. The reason for this was explained to me as follows:

> The Ramakrishna Mission does not insist on post school training for candidates. Because, if a boy is sent home or leaves he can take any job or stay in a hostel if his family won't take him back. Girls in India can't do that. If they get training, they can stand on their own feet if sent back or leave. Our girls are not like in the west where girls stay in a room or live in a house with girls and boys or even all boys. *We* are not like that.

Sarada Math therefore insists that prospective candidates who have not completed College degrees qualify in secretarial work, needlework or other vocationally orientated diploma, before formally applying for admission. Also, as regards age limits, Sarada Math sets 28 as the maximum age for a graduate, and 30 for a post graduate. Questions of health and family encumbrances are also important, but usually health problems only become evident after the candidate has arrived. Any prospective candidate who is the main or sole financial support for her family may not join until suitable arrangements are made to ensure that her departure does not cause hardship. Nobody may be admitted as a candidate while having outstanding debts, nor may he or she resign a job for the purpose. Those with paid employment are cautioned to take leave for as long as they can, and to resign only if and when they (and the authorities) feel that they are suited to monastic life within the Order. As for item

(1), as we shall see, many applicants who come from Kerala know nothing about Ramakrishna or the Order on arrival. Sarada Math places special emphasis on the figure of Holy Mother, and her life is studied and discussed with as much fervour as those of Ramakrishna and Vivekananda.

The Candidates

The first new recruits to join the original five members in the 1960s were already known to Sarada Mandiram when they applied. Two were ex inmates of the Hostel, and one an ex day pupil of the Asrama High School. The fourth candidate was the niece of the *saṃnyāsini* who became President when Sarada Mandiram became independent of the Asrama. One of the other candidates was the niece of a monk of the local Ramakrishna Asrama.

This information tells us how the candidates came into association with Sarada Mandiram, but for answers to the question: 'Why did you join?' a very extensive and delicate probing had to be undertaken. Some candidates were willing to answer the question directly, but others were very wary. This was either because they were afraid of speaking about themselves without the permission of 'seniors', or afraid of the use I would make of their answers.

Those who had defied their parents in order to join were clearly proud of this, and quite willing to talk about it.[2] At the same time, I asked the Heads of the two Kerala centres to describe the backgrounds of the candidates, and how they came to Sarada Mandiram. I found that the Heads were highly inaccurate in answering questions regarding qualifications and family background of candidates from Karnataka. A third source of information was through devotees (who visited during retreats and special functions) and lay inmates of the Sarada Mandiram complex. Finally, candidates often knew something of each other's backgrounds, either having known each other before joining, or through discussion over the years at Sarada Mandiram. Quite often, the information coming from differing sources did not tally with the story given by the candidate. I then tried to ascertain 'the truth' and also why differing versions were given, and by whom. For example, a candidate may tell with pride how she realised that married life was a lower ideal than a life of renunciation, and so she ran away, against great odds. A lay devotee would then tell me that her marriage was being arranged to a man that she did not like, or that there was an unhappy home situation. I would now like to give some examples of backgrounds, and to illustrate how these differing perceptions can be seen as fitting into a single 'Hindu' way of looking at life and its purpose.

There is a clear link between home situations and the decision to join in the case of the four candidates described above, all of whom have now taken *saṃnyāsa.* Two of them are Nayar, and both lost their mothers very soon after their birth. A generation beforehand, the loss of a mother may not have been so traumatic for a Nayar, as the *taravād* organisation ensured that all children of similar age grew up as brothers and sisters, cared for by a generation of 'mothers'. Thus, one of the senior *saṃnyāsinis* told me that after her mother died, her mother's younger sister immediately assumed the role of mother. In the case of the younger *saṃnyāsinis, taravād* partition had already taken place, and once a Nayar woman died leaving young children, there is no longer a core of matrilineal kin who could or would take the responsibility of raising her children. Also, the dead woman's sisters would have themselves gone to reside with their husbands, and although they may have felt responsible for the welfare of their sister's children, their husbands certainly would not. Or, stated another way, the sisters still felt the pull of matrilineal kinship obligations; but while their husbands were legally bound to support them and their children, they considered this sufficient burden, without having the added problem of the wife's nieces and nephews as well. The dead woman's husband would call on his own sisters for help, but they also had their own families to worry about. They moreover felt that their brother's children were not really related to them, but to their late mother's *taravād.* The ambiguous nature of 'who are my kinsfolk' has caused major problems for semi-orphaned Nayar children. Unless or until children come to regard themselves as fully belonging equally to both parents (but it seems, never so far to father's matrilineal kinsfolk) this problem will exist.

One of the two *saṃnyāsinis* who lost her mother, confided in me that her mother had died when she was a baby, and that she was in the care of her father and his mother. Her father used to bring her to Sarada Mandiram, as he was a devotee, and show her the photo of Holy Mother in the prayer hall. In the holidays she used to sometimes stay for a few days, and from the first year of high school asked to attend the School as a boarder in the Hostel. She felt more at home at Sarada Mandiram than she did at her father's home. Her father was a scholar, who had little spare time for her. After completing her degree, she decided to join the Order, staying on there after the annual retreat. Her father tried to make her come home, saying that he was ill, but she refused. Even though he was a devotee, he found it difficult to accept his daughter's decision. He admitted that it was because he was lonely without her, and feared she would be sent far away, where he could never see her.

The second Nayar mentioned above lost not only her mother but her father also, while studying in College. She was orphaned at 19. Her family home was in the village, and already she had become deeply influenced by the President of the local Asrama, who used to give her mangoes every morning before school, in the season. After her degree, one of the Swamis helped her to secure a teaching position in a Ramakrishna Mission School, north of Trichur. She worked there until the Centenary year of the Holy Mother, during which she joined a pilgrimage to Calcutta. Although by this time she was over-age, she requested permission to become a monastic inmate. She said she did this 'because I was already leading a celibate institutionalised life'.

The other two candidates both come from 'Backward Communities', and had problems with their fathers. Both communities follow patrilineal descent rules, wives joining the husband's joint family on marriage. One came from Trichur. She had lost her mother, and her father had remarried. Although she would not discuss her background, I heard from very reliable sources that she had a very unhappy home. In the second case a *saṃnyāsini* from a rural background also refused to discuss her reasons for joining but her widowed mother during a visit, told me: 'No, I am not sorry that my two daughters joined.[3] Married life is so terrible, I suffered so much'. Tears welled up in her eyes as she spoke. She needed money badly, yet allowed both to join, because of her own unhappy experience of married life. Her other children were employed and support her.

The influence of a Swami of the Ramakrishna Order played a significant role in the decision to join by nearly all the candidates who came from Karnataka state, but in Kerala also, this has sometimes been the case. Two candidates were ex-students of a Ramakrishna School in Kalady, birthplace of the philosopher Sankaracarya. Both were from poor Nayar families, one having a widowed mother living in a tiny house near the Asrama, and the other the daughter of a small plot owner. The former told me that:

> At school I was attracted to the picture of Sri Ramakrishna in the shrine. I didn't look at the other ones. Once I said to the Swami (Agamananda), 'I like the colour of your cloth. What shop can I get it at?' He said, 'No, you can't wear it. It is for *saṃnyāsins.* If you come and stay here I will give you this cloth'.

> I used to wear flowers in my hair. I loved them. One day the Swami asked me why. 'To look pretty'. He said, 'Who will see?' I said, 'Everyone'. He replied, 'They will fade soon. Bring one to-morrow to me'. I did, and he led me to the shrine room and placed the flower before Sri Ramakrishna saying, 'Doesn't it look beautiful here? Here it will not fade'. I never wore flowers after that, but I still loved *kavi*[4] cloth. When I came here to join I had with me a saree of that colour. (She laughed). I didn't know that it was silly. The year before I came here my father died. Swami said, 'married life won't bring happiness'. I saw that. It was true. I wrote to Mataji asking permission to come and stay.

Following these two candidates, two sisters from the capital, Trivandrum sought admission, the younger one coming to Sarada Mandiram at 16 to live while attending College. Her mother is a devotee, but in strained circumstances, due to the separation from her husband. The daughters have no contact with their father. They also have a negative evaluation of marriage: from their mother's bitter experience.

After these two sisters joined, a new pattern is observable in candidates who sought admission to the Order from Kerala. Four junior candidates had not been associated with the Ramakrishna Movement before joining, but decided not to marry, and *sought* an institution where they could live and be taken care of in a religious atmosphere. They were all from poor, rural Nayar families, with only a pass in the SSLC, plus a junior certificate in typing or similar very basic course. This brings me to an important question in Kerala today: what happens to a girl who does not want to marry or who cannot find a partner?

In Kerala, education is extremely highly regarded by caste Hindus and their Christian equivalent, and parents go to great lengths to ensure that their children secure a 'seat' in College. A system of 'Reservations' operates in Colleges, whereby a significant number of seats are reserved for children of 'Backward Communities'. Such communities are clearly defined, and membership is confirmed by producing a certificate from the village authorities in a person's native village. A 'community' is a group to which an individual belongs by birth, and formerly in the case of Hindus, distinguishable from other communities by following a separate occupation. Backward Communities are those whose traditional occupations were labouring and other menial or polluting tasks, and formerly subject to severely brutal and repressive behaviour from superior communities. Those deemed Harijans (Untouchables) and members of Tribes receive maximum benefits under the system of Reservation, being given a relaxation of marks necessary to gain admission in College, plus a living allowance. Other less 'Disadvantaged' communities, known as Other Backward Communities (OBC) receive only Reservation of seats without the accompanying financial assistance. Nearly all those to benefit in Kerala are 'Hindu', although certain other religious groups are identified as 'Economically or Educationally Backward' and receive Reservations also.[5] Non-Government Colleges, may, in addition, reserve a percentage of seats for members of the community of the management. Thus, Roman Catholic and Syrian Christians, Nayars, Izhavas, and the Muslim Educational Society all have a network of Colleges, with some seats reserved for their own community. In addition, a small percentage is allotted at the 'discretion of the management'. This leaves about 40% of total seats available for competition on the basis of marks, in private Colleges. The result is that a Nayar student with average marks has little chance of securing admission, unless his or her parents are able to pay a 'donation', as large sums of money given in return for assurance of a seat are called. For professional courses, donations have reached the cost of an expensive modern house. Rural Nayar families, sending their children to indifferent village schools and without the means to pay a donation find that their children cannot attend College. Since Nayar *taravāds* have all undergone partition of property and most *taravād* paddy fields and other agricultural land transferred by law to former tenants or sold, it has become vitally important for Nayar youth to have a means of livelihood. As I have shown, seats in Colleges for professional courses are highly competitive, yet without professional qualifications Nayar youth find it hard to secure alternative employment. They scorn all manual occupations, and with little capital and no business skills, find it well nigh impossible to compete with those communities that already dominate the commercial centres of Kerala. For a youth to find a wife, he must have means of supporting her. For a Nayar girl to secure a marriage with a tertiary educated and employed youth, she herself should ideally also have tertiary education. Therefore, the chances of a rural Nayar girl with minimal education and lacking 'good family' or fair complexion, finding a husband with an assurance of a livelihood (let alone a reasonable income) are not good.

The only candidate of Sarada Mandiram of Nambudiri Brahmin family actually completed a degree in Commerce but could not find employment, as her family was too poor to pay 'donations' or to exert influence in other ways on those in charge of selection. She would therefore have had trouble in finding a husband, as her parents could not provide a dowry, a necessity among Nambudiris. Her uncle is a monk of the Ramakrishna Order, and called on her mother in her village home one night, after missing the last bus to a local Asrama. She did not know that the Womens Asrama existed, until he suggested that she tried joining there. Her father escorted her to Sarada Mandiram on the day before Holy Mother's birthday. Everyone was very busy arranging for the birthday celebrations, and nobody noticed her. She spent the day sitting on a bench outside the office. That night (she told me) that she went to the President's room and told her that she had been ignored, and wanted to go home. 'Then I shall call your father to come and take you', was the reply. She thought, 'Well, since I am here, I may as well give it a try.' She had no idea about life within the Order. She had asked Christian friends what convents are like, and she heard that they were full of 'partiality'. She stayed on at Sarada Mandiram, and has never regretted it. She said that if I would have asked her at the time of arrival why she had come, she would not have known what to say. 'Now', she said, 'if you ask me, I would say to lead a pure life and to try for realisation, if I can.' Her brother later joined the Order, and was educated at its expense. Even though she seemed to be very interested in becoming a bank employee before joining, that did not mean that she was basically worldly. According to Hindu belief, a girl born in a Nambudiri family must have strong *saṃskāras* (tendencies) towards renunciation. These tendencies, latent within her, became fully manifest after becoming an inmate of Sarada Mandiram. It was fully expected that she would be well suited to monastic life. And, she is! Which, by the way, confirms the theory of good *saṃskāras.*

Only two candidates gave 'religious' reasons for joining, rather than 'I did not want to marry'. One is a junior *saṃnyāsini,* from a reasonably well-to-do Nayar family. She was orthodox and religious from childhood, and read Mission publications purchased by her father, a devotee of a rural Ramakrishna Asrama, south of Trichur. She entered and won an essay competition held by the Ramakrishna Asrama in Trichur on 'The Aim of Life'. After that she considered joining, as 'there all will be of one mind, and it is the proper atmosphere for religious practices'. She said the aim of life is 'God realisation', and she did not want the attachment of family. I was interested to find that the Hostel girls almost unanimously declared her to be the 'best' *saṃnyāsini,* i.e. the most austere and sincere.

One of the most recent to arrive was the niece of a famous monk of the Order. She comes from a poor rural Nayar family and did not attend College. She is one of six children. She told me that she had a dream in which Holy Mother appeared and told her to 'go and serve her sisters', meaning at Sarada Mandiram where she had briefly been a boarder during High School. She wrote to her uncle, who blessed her and encouraged her. Her family was upset, but at last her father agreed to let her go (she told me), as her horoscope predicted that she would take to a life of renunciation. There was no use fighting fate. She told me about her uncle many times, and asked me to visit her village. This behaviour struck me as unusual, as it is not customary for candidates to speak of either home or family. She also would have been condemned to a life of poverty.

Finally, there was a recent candidate of local Harijan background from a Colony on the outskirts of Trichur. Her sister was a free boarder in the College Hostel run by Sarada Mandiram. She used to visit her, and in this way came to know that there were *saṃnyāsinis.* Her father is a 'drunkard'. This I heard from others. She did not mention family background as a reason for joining at all, but said she did not want a householder's life. She had only studied the SSLC when she applied to stay at Sarada Mandiram as an inmate. She was sent to study Fine Arts in the town, and passed her diploma, making her eligible to apply to become a monastic candidate.

There has been a pattern in the type of girl applying to join the Order from Kerala. For Nayars, apart from the first four, loss of a mother (three cases) or father (three cases) was a motivating factor to avoid the sorrows of family life. Among those of Backward Communities, four had 'bad' fathers, bringing them to similar conclusions concerning marriage. There has been a shift in the mid to late seventies and afterwards. Improving health care has raised life expectancy and lowered the death rate of women in childbirth. Now the candidates who seek to join are rather the victims of poor life prospects than loss of a parent. Both groups have a highly negative view of married life based on their parents' experiences.

As it may appear that I am endeavouring to 'create' motives, I should point out that all but two answered my direct question 'what made you decide to choose monastic life' by an answer which was a variation on the negative statement 'I didn't want to lead a married life'. I should also point out, that contrary to Western notions of nuns being women 'disappointed in love', this has not been the case for any of the Kerala candidates. Gossip is such an effective source of information in Kerala that if there was any hint of a girl being associated with scandal before joining was made, I would have heard of it. However, since some candidates run away from home to come to Sarada Mandiram, their sudden departure and the subsequent visible distress this often causes their parents, gives rise to speculation among neighbours. Parents are accused of encouraging their daughters to join in order to avoid the expense of a wedding or, in the case of communities with patrilineal descent rules, the payment of dowry. One candidate told me frankly that someone from her village spread the word that she had been seen in Trichur town 'with a big stomach'. It had transpired that this candidate had run away to join, and was seen in the clothes adopted by new candidates: coarse white saree with coloured border worn loosely to cover the entire body, in contrast to the colourful tightly worn sarees of other girls of similar age. Since no religious insignia is worn by candidates, the mistake is understandable, especially as monasticism for Hindu women is so very recent. It is only some three years after being accepted as a monastic candidate that the saree is covered by a large cotton shawl: common enough in Bengal, but not in Kerala. This 'uniform' is slowly becoming recognised in the Trichur area.

One further question remains to be asked. Did the candidates renounce the world to avoid bereavement and/or poverty? It is here that one should be careful not to impose his or her own preconceptions, formulated in a different philosophical tradition, on Kerala Hindus, for the reply came back, loud and clear.

Yes, they are escaping from the problems of family life (which include bereavement and poverty). In fact, they are most fortunate to have realised so early in life, that human attachment brings nothing but pain and misery. One *saṃnyāsini* even told me that she was fortunate never to have remembered her own mother. This way she was saved from 'that terrible attachment' that would have made it almost impossible for her to forsake a worldly life. This is necessary, for only without attachment can a person be free to 'think of God'. The aim of life is to be free from rebirth, and for this one must obtain *mokṣa,* liberation. First one must be able to discriminate between the Real and the seemingly real. The Real is Brahman, Pure Consciousness, but humans are dragged down into Maya, Illusion, that makes them believe that ephemeral matter and relationships are Real and enduring. It takes one or two good 'shocks' (by the grace of Sri Ramakrishna) to wake up from this dream. Therefore, those who forsake the world are on their way to breaking through Illusion, on their way to liberation. They are people with superior powers of discrimination. In due course, perhaps after many births, all humans will have to come to the same realisation, then they also will be freed.

By way of contrast, in Trichur Sarada Mandiram, during my fieldwork there were eleven candidates undergoing training from Karnataka. Next to West Bengal (the state from which Ramakrishna came) Karnataka was providing the most candidates, followed by Kerala. There was a newly opened branch of Sarada Math in Karnataka, in Bangalore, but in 1980–1 it was being run in a cramped rented house. Cement shortages were delaying the completion of the new Math premises. In the meantime, Karnataka girls seeking admission to the Order were frequently asked to go first to Trichur, in the neighbouring state, rather than to go initially to Calcutta, where it is felt the sudden adjustment to communal life, strange food, language and climate will be too traumatic. Karnataka candidates, after completing their training in Calcutta agree that it is a good idea to have a three year 'breaking in' period in Trichur first.

Of the eleven candidates from Karnataka, nine were from the major cities, and two from the hills in or near Coorg. Nine regularly attended the local Ramakrishna Asrama, and both they and members of their families had received *mantra* initiation from a member of the Ramakrishna Order. Unlike the recent candidates from Kerala, eight of the Karnataka girls were graduates, and one was still completing her degree, by correspondence, from Trichur. The other two had post-school diplomas. Five were in paid professional employment before joining. However, many Karnataka candidates (including some who are now in Calcutta and elsewhere) were not 'on the regular list', that is, did not meet the usual qualifications when they applied. Five of those from Karnataka presently in Kerala, were in his category.

In cases of candidates who do not fit the guidelines for admission, if the Head of centre is sympathetic, they are allowed to stay 'for some years' (usually about four), without officially being allowed to apply for membership. During this time they will live and work with those 'on the regular list'. If at the end of the trial period they are found to have 'adjusted' well, they will be allowed to seek admission, and the period so far spent as an inmate will be counted towards monastic candidature for eventual *saṃnyāsa.* In Trichur, if a girl has insufficient educational qualifications (as is frequent among Kerala candidates), the President will usually send her to complete College or a diploma, while residing at Sarada Mandiram or the Trichur College Hostel. This is a relatively easy problem to overcome. However, overage or physical disability are the reasons for the five mentioned above to be ineligible.

In the former case, if the candidate proves adaptable, she will be allowed to join, especially if well qualified, and formerly having had a responsible job. The two cases of disability were still to be resolved, for health is a major consideration in allowing a candidate to be formally admitted into the Order.

The two 'disabled' candidates were both particularly talented, but one had a withered right arm and the other severely impaired hearing. The former was able to do every chore expertly, with her left arm, but the left hand is considered 'impure' by orthodox Hindus, and herein lies the problem. The left hand alone is used to touch the body 'below the navel', and the right hand for handling food, and in giving and receiving articles. The right hand alone is used in many acts of ritual: in Sarada Math great emphasis is placed on correct ritual behaviour. Whilst in Kerala the girl was even allowed to do work connected with the shrine, but the main problem would arise if and when she went to Calcutta for training where such laxity is not acceptable. So far, no decision had been taken regarding her candidature. In another context, a *saṃnyāsini* who had broken her arm told me that 'virgins may use their left hand if necessary for *japa*' (repetition of the *mantra*, with the aid of either fingers or rosary to keep count). Non virgins are permanently defiled, as the left hand is used during sexual contact.

The second girl seeking admission although 'disabled' came from the hills. During childhood she developed a chronic cough and congestion, which led to repeated ear infections for eighteen years. 'But', she explained, 'my family is economically backward despite being Brahmin and I did not go to a doctor'. The result was loss of hearing. Her father purchased a hearing aid for her (her first) before she came to Sarada Mandiram. She had left school without completing her final certificate, but seven years later sat privately, and went on to study pre degree by correspondence. She is now completing a Bachelor of Arts by correspondence, while staying at Sarada Mandiram. Her father provided batteries for her hearing aid, but as he is poor, she only used them for classes, causing a great deal of strain during the rest of the day. It is interesting to notice that the girl with the deformed arm received more acceptance than this girl, by the Kerala inmates. I believe this is because they are from rural backgrounds and have an 'awe' of electronic equipment, the hearing aid being noisy and cumbersome. Nevertheless, despite two ear infections since coming to Trichur, she had managed to stay: now under the care of an ear, nose and throat specialist. She was very afraid of being sent home, but 'it is all God's will'.

The Karnataka candidates were, with one exception, from solidly middle class urban families, unlike the Kerala candidates who were from struggling rural or small town backgrounds. At least six of the eleven Karnataka candidates were Brahmins, living within walking distance of the local Ramakrishna Asrama, in the cities of Mysore, Bangalore or Mangalore. The Ramakrishna Maths and Asramas take on many of the characteristics of the local 'dominant caste',[6] wherever they are situated, for usually it is the dominant caste which forms the main patronage of their centres. In other words, centres in Kerala have many Nayar characteristics in food, local custom and even the dress of inmates, while the Karnataka centres show more Brahmin influences, in keeping with a large number of Brahmin devotees. For example, the Bangalore Asrama is situated in the midst of a conservative but well-to-do Brahmin neighbourhood, and enjoys the regular patronage of many Brahmin families, some of whom visit each and every day. It is from such families that the majority of Karnataka candidates are drawn, families in which the main worship in the home is dedicated to Ramakrishna. These girls have grown up hearing the stories of Ramakrishna-Vivekananda and Holy Mother, and are at home in the etiquette and jargon of the Ramakrishna Movement. They are used to the annual round of Asrama celebrations, and have internalised the values preached by the local Swamis of the Order. They have accompanied their parents to the Asrama over many years, and like them have received *mantra* initiation, during their teenage years or early twenties.

However, perhaps these daughters of devotees have listened too carefully to the Asrama classes, for the main emphasis of them is on *vairāgya* (dispassion), an appeal for the youth to remain 'pure' and to dedicate their lives to the pursuit of *mokṣa* (liberation). This is powerful stuff indeed, and by the time they are in College, young devotees must struggle between two ideals: that of renunciation or that of marriage. Their connection with the Asrama leaves them in no doubt as to which is nobler, but the draw towards home and family causes a storm within their minds. College is a time of relative personal freedom for urban Karnataka girls, a time during which they can go out to the cinema or eating houses with a friend or friends, and experiment with fashionable clothes, hair styles and even make up. It is a time when some girls are 'lost' to the Asrama, for there is little place there for the frivolous. Those who resist their peers do so by emphasising their Asrama affiliation: they wear simple, usually white sarees even to College, and refuse to participate in group outings, preferring to spend their time at Asrama classes.

It is at this juncture that many parents, however staunch their devotion to the Ramakrishna Movement, become alarmed. Maybe their daughter is thinking of joining the Order! Parents suddenly realise this possibility and begin to make enquiries as to a suitable husband for them. If a young woman shows signs of a tendency towards renunciation, who will marry her? The marriage must be arranged before gossip harms her chances of finding a match. The girl sooner or later hears of the plans, and approaches the Swami in charge of her local Asrama in a panic. What should she do? The Swamis usually advise girls to decide which they want in life: realisation of God or marriage and, if they declare that they want the former, plans are put into action for them to run away from home. This pattern has been repeated in over twenty cases.

The Swami concerned writes usually to the President of Sarada Mandiram concerning urgent cases (of which there have been many). If the case is less pressing, the girl will take a 'holiday' at Sarada Mandiram for a few days, to see how she likes the life there, and only then she will decide on which course to take. A few girls manage also to make a pilgrimage to Calcutta, and stay at the Sarada Math for a short time, as well as visiting the places associated with the founders of the Ramakrishna Movement. Devotee parents do not object to these pilgrimages, seldom if ever realising that their daughter is sounding out her chances of becoming a monastic member of the Ramakrishna Order.

For those who run away, the plan is simple. The example I shall give is an authentic one. A particular candidate came from a devotee's family, in which all the members were initiated and attended the Asrama regularly on weekends. The candidate herself had been initiated also, and used to go to the Asrama with a friend from College. She was thinking of joining the Asrama and told the Swami in charge. He advised her to write to the President of Sarada Mandiram, so that she could join after graduating from College. She wrote, and the reply was sent to her friend's house, as requested. Somehow her parents found out what was going on, and made steps to find her a husband. But, someone warned her and, borrowing money from her friend, she ran away, after confirming with the Sarada Mandiram President that she could come to Trichur at once. So, one evening, she set out for the Asrama with only a *bhajan* (hymn) book in her hand. She went straight to the bus stand, and caught a bus to Trichur, after sending a telegram informing Sarada Mandiram of the time of her arrival. In the meantime, her parents were very worried when she did not return home and phoned the

Asrama.[7] The Swami told them what had happened. On reaching Sarada Mandiram, the girl wrote to her parents explaining what she had done, and in reply her sister wrote that her mother had taken to her bed in grief. Finally, after some days had passed her mother went to the Asrama, where the swami consoled her, saying that she had brought up her daughter in the ways of Holy Mother, and she was blessed that she had chosen the path of renunciation. Her mother wrote that she was not angry, just upset. She said, though, her father had not forgiven her for running away. The exact reason for her father's anger she does not know: in the one and a half years since she left home, he has not written to her.

The candidate's attitude towards her parents is this: in all the years that they have attended the Asrama, they have not absorbed even the fundamental teachings of Ramakrishna-Vivekananda. Otherwise, they would understand why she ran away. This demonstrates the power of Maya, which causes even devotees of Ramakrishna to come under its ensnaring spell. At least they did not do the same as another candidate's parents, who in anger removed the photos of Ramakrishna-Vivekananda, Holy Mother and their *guru* from their shrine room. Moreover, as the President told me, a person who takes to *saṃnyāsa,* liberates seven generations of ancestors.

The candidate returned secretly the following year to complete her College examinations, but she stayed in the home of a trusted devotee, and her parents were not informed of her visit. Once the original anger calms down though, the President encourages mothers to visit Sarada Mandiram, or if this is not possible, the candidate will visit her home at least before going to Calcutta for training.

Two highly educated Brahmin Karnataka candidates decided to join the Order following the death of their fathers, both of whom were pious Asrama devotees. One said she was born as the result of his prayers at the birthplace of Holy Mother during the Centenary celebrations. This candidate had thought of joining as long as she could remember, whilst the other candidate confessed that she was an atheist until her father's death. In fact, she said, she used to ridicule his devotions, and caused him much anguish. After his death, she could only find solace at the Asrama, even though this caused a sensation among her friends. She received initiation as soon as the President of Belur Math visited her home town, and sought permission to join afterwards. As she held a highly paid position, she took leave at first, as advised.

In these last two cases, both girls 'realised' the transitory nature of life through personal loss, much in the same way as the early Kerala candidates had done, but here the similarity ends, for the Karnataka candidates would not have been resigned to a life of poverty on this account.

For the Kerala candidates (except the original five), family circumstances caused the girls to reject family life as too painful and unhappy, and so they sought an alternative. Only those who knew of Sarada Mandiram find their way there, others have to submit to unsatisfactory marriage alliances. I believe that as the Institution becomes more widely known, more and more girls with poor education and life prospects will seek refuge there, while the better educated and well placed will not be attracted but will seek employment and 'a good match' as they do now. It is common for girls in the past ten years to arrive at Sarada Mandiram without even the most basic knowledge of the ideals and teachings of the Ramakrishna Movement, and to have had next to no religious background. Most have not been 'religious' at home, and almost none has received *mantra* initiation or even read religious works on a regular basis. After arrival, however, they gradually learn 'religious' behaviour, which becomes a matter of habit. While many of the Karnataka candidates have a thorough knowledge of the main Mission literature, they are not as capable at managing the heavy domestic work required of them. For them, Sarada Mandiram represents a drop in living standards, whilst for the Kerala candidates, a considerable improvement on conditions at home.

The main picture that emerges, then, is that the Karnataka candidates are strong-minded, well-educated, employed and (in the majority of cases) good looking middle-class girls, with good to excellent family background and hence marriage prospects. They have a long association with the Mission, and the decision to join the Order is based on a desire to seek 'realisation of God'. Only one Kerala candidate gave this as her actual reason for joining, the rest giving the negative reason of 'not wanting to lead a married life'.

Not wanting to marry, however, is not the same as actively renouncing marriage in order to join an Order of *saṃnyāsinis.* In Karnataka, a young educated woman can postpone marriage by securing reliable employment and living in a hostel away from home. Some do this for indefinite periods, but this is most uncommon in Kerala, where employment prospects for women are few, and such hostel living rare. The girl is expected in Kerala to complete her education and then marry as soon as possible.

After discussing the reasons for coming to Sarada Mandiram with the Kerala candidates, most seemed to have sought institutional life merely as an (or rather, *the*) alternative to marriage. It was a question of having ruled out marriage as a happy lifestyle, and sought the only other one available. All the Kerala candidates had attended schools with Christian classmates, some of whom openly discussed becoming 'a Sister' as the 'other option', almost as if marriage and monasticism were the two careers for Kerala women! Kerala parents of candidates certainly miss their daughters, but seem relieved and satisfied that their secure future is ensured. Karnataka parents, on the other hand, once they have settled down after the initial shock of their daughter running away, are proud of their choice, especially as they are introduced as parents of a 'member' in Math and Mission circles. I do not think that Karnataka parents, however, nor the girls themselves, see life within the Order as primarily providing security. Good family background, and education are in themselves sufficient to ensure that the Karntaka girls who choose monastic life would also have succeeded in finding a good husband, considered the greatest form of security, the only real security for a Hindu woman. The Karnataka candidates expect to give up the option of security on joining the Order.

A late Swami of the Ramakrishna Order used to advise prospective candidates that *saṃnyāsa* was 'only for those who had something to give up'.[8] By this he meant that only those candidates who 'had everything going for them', good family, health, education, employment and marriage prospects, and who were not lacking material wealth, nor touched by life's sorrows, could be said to have true dispassion. Others were like the poor man who saw that *saṃnyāsins* were ensured alms, and so decided to put on ochre robes and sit in a meditative pose, so that pious passers by would fill his begging bowl and make offerings without him even having to beg. But, as time went by, the mere act of emulating a *saṃnyāsin*'s way of life gradually turned the poor man into a holy man, as he had to live up to his 'devotees' expectations of a *saṃnyāsin* in order to keep up the disguise.

The Ramakrishna Order, unlike the religious Orders of the Roman Catholic church does not see the religious life in terms of a vocation in the original sense of the word (meaning a divine call). The Presidents of centres are not impressed by candidates who claim to have had a dream, vision or presence calling them to the religious life, nor do members of the Order advise young men or women that they think they 'have a vocation'. They are simply willing to allow any prospective candidate to stay, who meets the basic qualifications of age, education and health, and who is prepared to try to 'live the life'. All that is really required apart from this initially is a willingness and an ability to adjust to the expected behaviour and attitudes within the Institution, a gradual process which extends over ten years.

According to Hindu belief, every person is under the influence of Maya, to a greater or lesser extent. Each will eventually become disillusioned by the so-called pleasures of life, and in time realise that the goal of life is indeed to become one with God/Brahman. For most, many more births will be necessary before they even realise that they are chasing ephemeral dreams which cannot provide happiness. Therefore, any young woman who has even begun to comprehend the only means real to fulfilment is already on the right path. Kerala candidates are, on arrival, at the first step, disillusionment. The Karnataka candidates, on the other hand, represent the second step, a positive desire to spend this life in the pursuit of realisation, with an informed knowledge of what this entails.

But, however carefully the Karnataka candidates have considered their choice to become a monastic candidate of the Ramakrishna Order, this decision to date had been largely on their knowledge of and acquaintance with their local Ramakrishna Asrama or Math. As they find out in due course, their knowledge of monastic life within the Order is essentially a visitor's view: possibly a highly romanticised one in which the candidate believes that the most serious struggle facing her henceforth will be a heroic struggle, fought on the philosophical plane, against Maya. It is this common preconception which forces some of the most introspective and sensitive Karnataka candidates to return home after a short period of trial within the Order, while their more robust Kerala sisters, who have few preconceived ideas about the religious life, remain.

As candidates will find out in due course, the battle against Maya is in fact an actual one, and they, the newcomers, are placed right in the front lines. The problem is that the enemy is very hard to identify, and the strategy is to be learned only through long and painful experience.

Chapter 7

Adjusting

The entire process of changing one's orientation from that of a lay person to an 'inmate' (as monastic inmates refer to themselves) is associated with the English word 'adjusting'. 'Adjusting' is a word used throughout the Order to refer to a specific set of attitudes and behaviour that set members of the Ramakrishna Order apart from others: including lay devotees. Adjusting involves a process which commences with arrival at a branch of the Order, and is not completed before *saṃnyāsa* is granted. Indeed, those who 'cannot adjust' will not be given either the vows of *brahmacārya* or *saṃnyāsa* on schedule or perhaps at all. So important is this concept, that I shall proceed to describe it in great detail, tracing its course over the ten years of candidature which precede full admission into the Order.

Although certain formal milestones are provided by the Order, so that the candidate knows at which stage of development or adjusting she stands, the actual process (of adjusting) is so subtle that the candidates are not aware that it takes place according to time-honoured traditions practiced within the Order since its inception. I shall endeavour to highlight the methods used to ensure that by the end of her candidature, the lay person has been so successfully stripped of her personal characteristics, that in the way she thinks, speaks, walks and acts she is readily identifiable primarily as 'a member of the Sarada Math'.

Arrival

A new candidate is referred to as a 'newcomer' within the Order. Before leaving for Sarada Mandiram a potential candidate will correspond with the President, and notify her of the expected date and mode of arrival, so that she can be met at the station or bus stand, if coming alone. As soon as she reaches Sarada Mandiram, she will be taken to the temple, to 'do *pranāms*' (prostrate) before the images of Sri Ramakrishna, Holy Mother and Swami Vivekananda, and then to meet the President, referred to simply as 'Mataji'. After prostrating before the President, she will chat briefly about her journey, before being taken to bathe. This is necessary, as journeys are not only hot and uncomfortable, but ritually polluting. After bathing and changing her clothes, the newcomer will be taken to the dining room for appropriate refreshments, according to the time of day. There is no formal admission ceremony, no dramatic crossing of thresholds, changing of dress or even signing of forms. Newcomers are not even introduced to other inmates of the Institution. In fact, it may be a few days before the newcomer can sort out just who is a monastic inmate, as opposed to resident teachers and others who live at Sarada Mandiram as lay women.

Nothing is taken away from the newcomer. Indeed, attention is seldom paid to her at all. She is in no way welcomed, nor made to feel that the Institution is happy to have a new recruit. It is very difficult for her to find out what to do or how to behave at first, because she does not readily realise that it is for her to seek the juniormost monastic inmates, and to try to emulate their behaviour. When she does realise that she must seek other juniors as her role model, and finally asks for advice, her questions and attempts at friendship are, often as not, met with aloofness or annoyance.

The newcomer's immediate concern is to fit into the daily routine. She has more than likely brought with her approximately three extra sets of clothes, and her own bedding – a mattress, pillow and linen wrapped in a canvas cover, or rolled up inside a ground sheet. Bedding is considered a personal item in India, in the same way as clothing, and it is customary to carry one's own bedding whenever travelling. The prevalence of head lice and bed bugs makes this sound hygienic practice, as much as one based on intrinsic fear and revulsion of bedding in general, as we shall encounter within the Order. The newcomer will keep her belongings with those of other junior inmates: her 'box' (metal suitcase) raised on two bricks on the floor, or placed on a shelf in the storeroom, and her bedding placed on a pile of inmate's bedding in one of the bedrooms of the Math (monastery) building. There is no unpacking, for it is common for Indian households to store clothing permanently in 'boxes', except in the most modern families, in which cupboards have been introduced. Empty incense packets are usually placed inside the boxes, in order to deter insects and mildew odours.

The Math building is based on the design of the *nalekettu*, the *taravād* of well-to-do Nayar. It is rectangular, with an interior courtyard, onto which all rooms open, via an all-around verandah. The construction is of locally hewn laterite, plastered and whitewashed, with a red tiled roof. In one wing asbestos ceilings have been added, while in the other three, the inside of the peaked roof is finished with lining tiles. The windows are shuttered on the outside, and have iron bars instead of glass. Inexpensive cloth curtains are strung across windows above eye level to ensure privacy. The Math building has been slightly modified over the years, for it originally housed the Hostel in one wing, whilst the other two wings were occupied by the shrine and prayer hall on one side, and the kitchen and dining areas on the other. Now the Hostel has a separate building, and a new dining room and kitchen has been constructed to the north. A separate temple was completed in 1975. The temple was the first to be built by a branch of Sarada Math. The Math building is connected to both temple and Hostel by a short covered walkway: a necessity in the long rainy season from June to September. Though based on traditional design, the original kitchen was placed in an untraditional location, in order to make maximum use of an existing deep well. This was a vital consideration, in a locality which experiences severe water shortages in the summer months.

During my period of fieldwork, a new set of rooms, away from the noise of the Hostel was being constructed, on the site of the old cowshed.[1] These rooms were to be used by visiting seniors. Since its initial construction, the original Math had not been renovated, and utilisation of space was very poor. There are seven bedrooms in two of the wings, each accommodating two to three inmates, with the exception of the largest room, in which the seniormost inmate sleeps alone, by choice. Junior inmates sleep on the floor between the wooden bedsteads ('cots') of their seniors, unrolling their bedding at night, and re-rolling it on awakening. Newcomers bathe at the well or in makeshift bathrooms, situated some distance from the Math building, and also use outside latrines. Seniors have attached facilities.

By the time the newcomer has bathed, she will have familiarised herself with the layout of the Math, though probably would not have dared to enter any of the bedrooms, although the doors are always left open. After hanging up her clothes (which she will have washed) she will more than likely approach an inmate, and ask her what she should do next. Almost all long distance transport arrives in Trichur during the early morning, so that by now it is only about 8.30 a.m.

The newcomer will be asked to assist with the vegetable cutting, a task commenced by senior Hostel children at 5.30 a.m., before prayers. Those inmates who are not school teachers all join in, sitting in a circle in the serving room off the main 'rice' kitchen. Their seats are small wooden rectangular slabs, raised about 5 centimetres from the floor, by the use of crossbeams on the underside.

Whilst at work, the inmates talk among themselves, usually about an incident that has occurred, or about problems with seniors (since only juniors cut vegetables in the early morning, the others being too busy). Teachers and students leave for school just before 10 a.m. At about 11.30 a.m. the newcomers all finish their chores and attend an informal class, conducted by the seniormost *saṃnyāsini.* Whilst I was there, they were studying the major *Upanisads* in turn, learning each day's verses by heart. There is a brief period before lunch available for personal chores, such as folding, washing or mending of clothes, learning portions for study or writing hymns into an exercise book. Most inmates (except those serving food) eat when the gong sounds for lunch at 12.30 p.m., at trestle tables outside the dining room, beneath an awning. Hostel children, who return for lunch, sit back to back in rows on the floor inside. Each person brings to the dining area her own freshly-rinsed steel plate and tumbler and sets it before her place. Hostel children, rostered to serve for the month, dart up and down the rows with metal buckets of food, depositing a ladleful of each preparation on each plate, without touching ladle to plate. A metallic ring spells trouble in the form of an instant scolding from a supervising inmate for the careless server, for serving vessels must not be 'polluted' by those of individual diners. The whole mealtime is supervised by the storekeeper, a senior inmate who is rostered for two months to oversee all food preparations, with the aid of two junior inmates.

The newcomer feels all eyes are watching her during the serving, as at this time all present chant a chapter of the Bhagavad Gita, a scriptural text. The Hostel girls learn it by heart, a few verses each week, so that in about four years of Hostel living, they would know the entire work, as would monastic inmates. Newcomers usually bring a small copy of the book with them to meals, so that they can read the text, rather than sit there mute. It is small incidents such as these, that make newcomers eager not to stand out, and to appear to others to be as senior as possible.

By the time the last verse is recited, and grace chanted,[2] many Hostel girls already have a handful of food ready to pop into their mouths with the final syllable. As they eat, they are offered second helpings, and there is certainly no compulsion to eat everything or to refrain from loading plates with favoured items. Once the sound of eating has ceased, the storekeeper pronounces the thanksgiving,[3] and the children stampede to the taps, to rinse their plates, their right hand (with which they have eaten) and their mouths. Plates are then replaced in their racks, children's in their own dormitories ('halls') and inmate's on a rickety wooden stand in the old dining area. Children and teachers return to school.

The intense heat of the midday sun, coupled with a heavy lunch, will have made the newcomer very sleepy, especially if she has come from a cooler climate. She will therefore be relieved to find that inmates who do not have to teach usually have time to rest after lunch. Newcomers lie on the bare cement floor in the old prayer hall to gain relief from the intense humidity, reading drowsily or chatting, before dropping off to sleep, often with an open book still in hand.

Sleep is fitful until mid afternoon, when the newcomer will be called to get up and return once more to cut vegetables for the night meal, which is substantial, but lighter than lunch. On many days, afternoon tea has to be prepared, especially seasonal fruit cut, or picked from the garden. At 3.30 p.m. a team of newcomers sweeps the Math verandahs and the prayer hall, in time for the reopening of the shrine at 4.00 p.m.

At 4.00 p.m. the meal gong sounds once more, for the children are back from school. Coffee or tea and a tasty snack is served, after which there is again work: either more vegetables to cut, or garden work, such as the 'plucking' of vegetables or, in the dry season, watering of the flower garden near the temple with the use of buckets dipped in the open cesspool near the bathrooms and well. Evening work will cease only at 5.30 p.m. when all the inmates bathe and change their clothes, so as to be ready for the *ārati*[4] (evening worship) which takes place after the conch is sounded at sunset. All is silent, and the temple ablaze with light when the bell rings for the children to assemble in the prayer hall, and they arrive in orderly lines, class by class, with folded hands as they (almost) silently take their places on the canvas carpets spread on the floor, towards the middle and back of the hall. The monastic inmates (with the exception of the President of the Institution) arrive less ceremoniously. Usually running late, they enter breathlessly at the last moment, from the side door, connected to the Math building, since inmates sit towards the front, on separate carpets from the children. Most 'get used' to a particular place, and look annoyed if someone else takes it. Newcomers do not know where they are supposed to sit. Some choose to take their place right at the back of the prayer hall, with resident teachers, visitors and other non-monastic personnel, whilst some are bold enough to sit with the monastic inmates. Those who opt for the latter course of action, probably wish they had not, as they soon find they have taken somebody else's place, or that inmates, suspecting their personal purity, take rather obvious precautions not to allow the newcomer's clothes to touch their own.

Inmates play musical instruments[5] during the *ārati*, and lead the singing of hymns.[6] After the singing is over (about half an hour on ordinary days), the children and the 'hall teachers' who supervise their homework depart, and the inmates spread out their personal oblong prayer mats, each wherever she wishes, in the dimmed hall. They are supposed to meditate until 8.00 p.m., but those involved in kitchen work or the supervision of children do not have time to meditate at all. In this respect, the information allegedly given by the President of Sarada Mandiram to a researcher into lifestyles in Indian religious Institutions would represent the ideal, rather than the norm. She states that, 'From 5.00–7.00 a.m., and again for two hours in the evening, the permanent members of the Ashram[7] meet in the oratory for *bhajans*, silent meditations and readings from Ramakrishna Paramahamsa and Swami Vivekananda, his most famous disciple. Visitors are not as a rule invited to the community meetings which precede these prayers, although they are, of course, welcome to attend the prayers themselves' (Vandana 1978:89).

The author is somewhat confused, maybe due to the brevity of her visit to Sarada Mandiram. Actually, no 'community meeting' precedes the evening prayers at all. She is obviously referring to the night 'reading', the last act of the day at Sarada Mandiram, restricted to monastic inmates. Between 8.00 p.m. and the supper gong at 8.30 p.m., those inmates without particular duties quietly read sacred texts, or articles from the Order's journals, or study, sitting on the floor of the old prayer hall or other thoroughfare (where a naked light bulb hangs from the high rafters on a long cord) springing to their feet if a senior approaches. Those with duties, eat hastily after the children have finished their meal. It is only after supper, at 9.40 p.m. that all the inmates assemble in the old prayer hall, the shrine workers, storekeepers and hall supervisors arriving (hopefully) just before the President enters, taking her place at a small wicker stool at a wicker table. She gives any notices, scoldings or information at this time but (unlike in other centres of the Order) it is not a time for sharing humorous anecdotes, or reading letters from inmates of other branches of the Order, or from local inmates on transfer elsewhere. The *Gospel of Ramakrishna* or *Great Master* is handed to the President, and she reads for ten minutes or so, before departing. Then, each inmate retires to her sleeping place, unrolling her bedding, and sitting on it for a few minutes to silently meditate or repeat her *mantra*[9] before lying down to sleep. A few inmates sleep in halls with their class, and after they have departed to the Hostel, the bolts are secured on the Hostel doors, echoed by those of the Math. The lights on the paths are extinguished, and by 10.00 p.m. all is still. This would mark the end of the first day at Sarada Mandiram for the newcomer.

At 5.00 a.m. there is a deafening clatter as the gong is struck, and one hundred and fifty or so children, each with a plastic or iron bucket and mug, towel, soap, toothbrush and paste (or burnt rice husks), stampede towards the wells to bathe. In summer, there is even more urgency, because the first out are able to grab the mangoes that have fallen during the night. The inmates fold their bedding with less urgency, and sleepily make their way to wash. Some have arisen earlier: those involved in shrine work, who have already bathed and changed, and the more austere, generally dedicated to early bathing. Hot water is only available to those who are ill, and for the seniormost inmates.

Rural girls from Kerala would be used to cold water bathing, but not those from the urban centres of neighbouring Karnataka, who also have to accustom themselves to the daily Kerala 'headbath'.[10] However, whether bathed and changed or simply washed, all inmates are assembled in the prayer hall by 5.30 a.m., when the shrine first opens for the day, with *mangalārati*,[11] followed by the chanting of two hymns, according to the day of the week, each being dedicated to a specific deity. Meditation follows until 6.30 a.m., when the children enter the prayer hall for their morning prayers and Gita chanting. The inmates are required to sit in front of the President during meditation, as many habitually drop off to sleep. At least, if they know that they will be seen, they will try to control this. The seniormost inmate, however, sits right at the back of the prayer hall, behind the President, often sound asleep. She is *senior* to the President! I shall follow the workings of hierarchy in a following chapter, as adjusting is closely related to seniority.

At 6.30 a.m. the juniormost inmates (and those seniors who are menstruating, and unable to carry out their rostered kitchen or shrine duties) pick up their brooms, consisting of coconut leaf ribs tied with a strip of red saree border, and proceed to sweep the prayer hall,[12] and Math building. Buckets of water and torn pieces of sarees are left in the corner meanwhile, and then the whole area wiped over. If the effect is too streaky (as occurs during the rainy season, or the dry dusty months of December and January) a scolding by seniors will follow. As 8.00 a.m. approaches, those who have not already done so, go and bathe and change their clothes. The daily cycle is now complete, and a newcomer may be forgiven for believing that she has finally 'made it'. She is now a 'member'.

Pre Probation

A member of what? Few candidates know on arrival (or even months afterwards) the main milestones to be crossed before *saṃnyāsa* is granted. Newcomers will hear the words 'member' and '*brahmacārini*' used loosely within the Order to refer to any candidate for *saṃnyāsa*, whether formal membership has been granted or not, or vows taken. The term *brahmacārini* is used to refer collectively to all the 'white sarees' as opposed to the *saṃnyāsinis*, who wear ochre. But, in reality, full membership is not granted until after *saṃnyāsa*, and a candidate is not strictly entitled to the title '*brahmacārini*' until after she has taken the relevant vows, after a minimum of five years' candidature.

A newcomer is officially a Pre Probationer, for about one year. At any time the newcomer is free to leave, as indeed she is later. In the first year of candidature, about two newcomers leave for each who stays. The dropout rate after this is much less, decreasing with each extra year until after *brahmacārya* when it is rare for anyone to leave. Those who leave shortly after arrival at Sarada Mandiram are still able to return home and to marry, virtually the only other opinion for a Hindu woman in Kerala. With the passing of time, it becomes increasingly difficult to resume lay life, as marriage chances lessen with the passing of years. It is hard to find a marriage partner for a woman who is known to want to lead a celibate life.

Those candidates whose health breaks down any time before the vows of *saṃnyāsa* will be sent home to recuperate, and if their health remains poor, they will be asked not to return. Great anxiety if felt for candidates who fall seriously ill, and Headquarters will be informed immediately, usually by telephone. For minor illnesses, the candidate will be placed under the care of a doctor. Traditional (Ayurvedic) remedies are mainly used as 'tonics' or to relieve aches and pains.

The candidate will embark on a ten-year training period, which commences with Pre Probation. The training is akin to an apprenticeship, during which the attitudes, skills and behaviour of seniors have to be thoroughly absorbed. At the same time, all those attitudes which testify to the candidate's former 'lay' status must be gradually given up. The method is subtle: the newcomer, lowest on the rungs of the hierarchical ladder, tries to climb up by emulating the behaviour of immediate seniors. At the same time, as other newcomers arrive, she asserts authority over them, as *their* 'senior', gaining prestige thereby. This is because she finds being a senior has distinct advantages, the main being that her juniors must obey her instructions, and speak to her with respect. In an environment in which she constantly has to defer to seniors, it feels good to command deference from juniors. Even just being a monastic inmate rather than a lay devotee gives prestige, and a feeling of delicious exclusiveness, especially on festivals, when visiting devotees of higher communal status than their own families, treat them with respect.

It does not take long, therefore, for the newcomer to feel self-conscious about her 'outside' clothes, which probably are (by lay standards), very conservative. She will have brought with her simple sarees or if poor whatever she possessed, probably cheap, printed cottons in gaudy colours. Suddenly, her blouses seem indecent. They are too tight and skimpy, when compared to the loose 'jackets' of the inmates. She notices what other newcomers have done about this, and requests a senior for a scrap of cloth from the 'machine' room, to be added to the lower edge of her blouses, to cover her midriff. If going outside the premises, she wears her lightest coloured saree to look like more senior inmates, and covers both shoulders, in imitation of the shawl worn by Probationers. Without even being asked, she will, within a week or so, remove any ornaments she is wearing (such as earrings, bangles and gold chain). As these are an indicator of 'householder' status, she no longer wants to wear them, because she wants to be identified as a *brahmacārini*. Ornaments will be given to the President for safekeeping. If she leaves, they will be returned to her, otherwise after some years, the ornaments will be given to a free boarder, or sold.

Essentially, absorption into the Order is a reaching out by the candidate for acceptance, in the face of seeming indifference, on the part of seniors. In the first few days or weeks at Sarada Mandiram, she has very little idea of what is expected of her, for she does not know if she is classified as a lay person or an 'inmate'. She does not know what she may touch, and whether (as is the right of inmates) she may enter the kitchen. Most feel lonely and unwanted during their first days at Sarada Mandiram. Why then, it may be asked, are not junior inmates compassionate towards newcomers who arrive after them, and share similar experiences?

The President of the Institution sums up the official attitude towards aggrieved candidates with one of her favourite sentences: 'Nobody invited you here'. In other words, candidates come of their own free will and, if they do not like the life, are free to leave. However, let them not complain, for this is not tolerated, nor is a sulky expression. Ramakrishna is the Avatar, the Incarnation of God in the present Kali Yuga or Iron Age. Thousands hear his message, but most are too involved in 'women and gold' to consider devoting their lives to the realisation of God. Those who do come, are blessed. They come through his grace but of their own freewill. Given this opportunity, candidates should try their utmost to conquer their worldly instincts, and the assertion of ego, two major obstacles to adjusting. Just as Ramakrishna brings candidates, for his own purpose, so he lets them leave also. He has his own reasons, for he can see into the hearts of all. Only those who struggle to be fit to remain in the Order can stay. Others will be sent away. After a candidate leaves she will hardly be mentioned again, except in a context of condemnation. A candidate who leaves must have had a fault in her character which did not enable her to adjust. If she returns for a visit, she will meet with a frosty reception, especially if she has married: a testimony to her 'worldliness'.

Gradually the newcomer settles down to the routine of life at Sarada Mandiram. The days are so busy that there is little time or energy to think of anything except work. Newcomers are assigned the work of cleaning the shrine vessels at night, and with the cleaning of rooms in the early morning, and afternoon. Between these duties, there are always other chores to be completed. At first the newcomer is happy to receive work connected with the shrine, that is, until she realises that there is a hierarchy connected with work, as with relationships between people, at Sarada Mandiram. Despite the official doctrine that 'everything is the Lord's work' certain work has more prestige attached to it, as a certain amount of seniority is required before a candidate is entrusted with it. Whilst at work the newcomer is carefully but unobtrusively watched by seniors, who soon form an opinion of her, which is based on two main criteria: willingness to do whatever she is told without answering back even in defence, and *śraddha*, in the local language context meaning 'care and attention'.[13] One *saṃnyāsini* told me of a monk of the Order who admonished a candidate newly arrived at the Headquarters thus: 'Daily Ramakrishna goes for a walk here, and you have not swept the place clean!' On another occasion she confided, 'You can tell the character of a candidate by the way she peels potatoes. If you cannot pay attention to such small matters, how will you purify your mind?' Yet, there seemed to me to be a world of difference between expectations of chores carefully executed, and the nagging, obsessive behaviour of certain seniors, who delight in finding fault, no matter how hard a candidate has tried.[14]

Scolding is the main tool for reshaping the newcomer into the required image of a *brahmacārini* of the Ramakrishna Order, and commences soon after the initial period of indifference, that is, as soon as the newcomer becomes established in a regular routine of work. There is a simple rule regarding scolding, which a newcomer must sooner or later learn: when scolded by a senior you must bite your tongue, even if the senior is in the wrong, or accuses you unfairly. Seniors are not open to suggestions or opinions from their juniors. Seniors by virtue of their seniority know better, and in any case must not be contradicted. One disadvantage in this (or advantage, depending on your seniority) is that the more senior you become, the fewer people there are who can censure your behaviour. This gives seniors ample opportunity to abuse their position, whilst juniors seldom think ill of them, let alone express this sentiment.

The most senior members regard the question of obedience in a different light to those who have sought admission in the last twenty years or so. The older inmates grew up under the shadow of the *taravād* system, in which similar values operated. Obedience and respect was due to seniors by their juniors, and the *kāraṇavan*, the eldest male of the *taravād* had absolute authority over all *taravād* members. In Sarada Mandiram, the President also has absolute authority over inmates, and I believe she sees herself as a *kāraṇavan* figure. I shall expand this theme in a future chapter. However, younger inmates have grown up not in *taravāds*, but in smaller units based on the nuclear family. In the modern Hindu family in Kerala, children are the centre of attention and concern, rather than elders. They are used to expressing opinions in front of seniors, and thus find the submission required of them in Sarada Mandiram very difficult to accept.

During the year of Pre Probation (and indeed throughout the years prior to *saṃnyāsa*) the candidate can expect numerous 'scoldings' from the President, not necessarily over major issues. It is not so much the subject of the scolding that matters, but the way the individual reacts to it. Or rather, *if* she reacts, it *becomes* major. It is

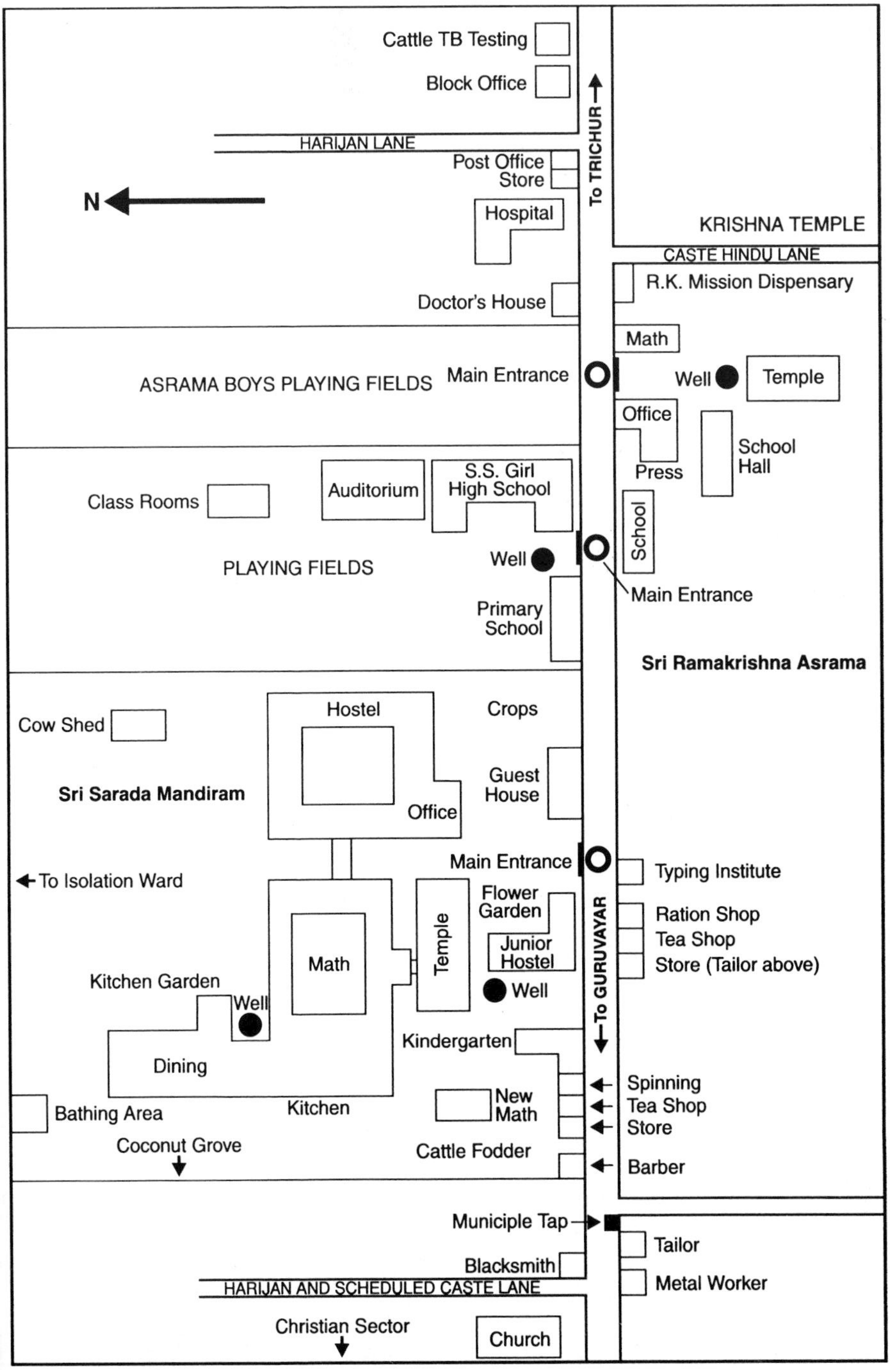

Rough sketch of village

Plate 1 Typewriting Institute

Plate 2 Guest House where author stayed

Plate 3 Sarada Mandiram Temple

Plate 4 Inner courtyard of monastic building

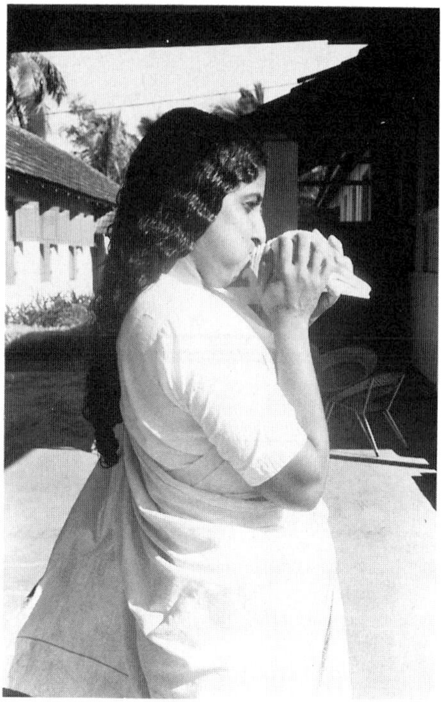

Plate 5 Brahmacārini blowing conch at sunset

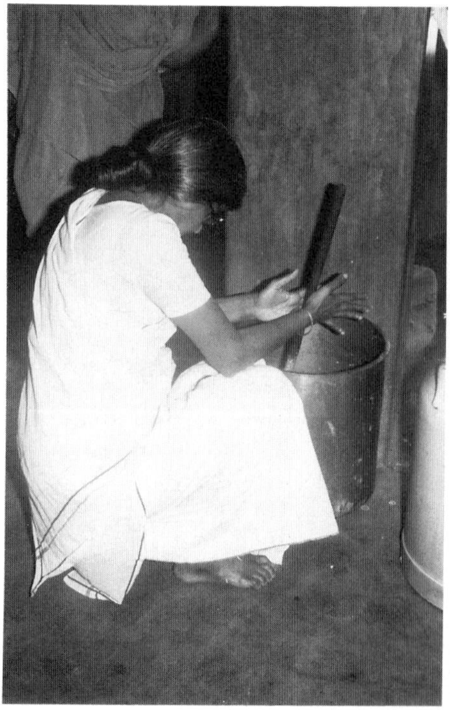

Plate 6 Resident teacher churns butter

Plate 7 Saṃnyāsini with food cooked for morning offering

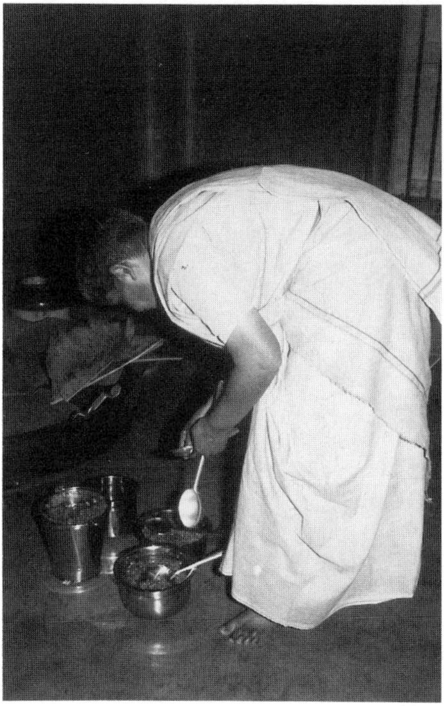

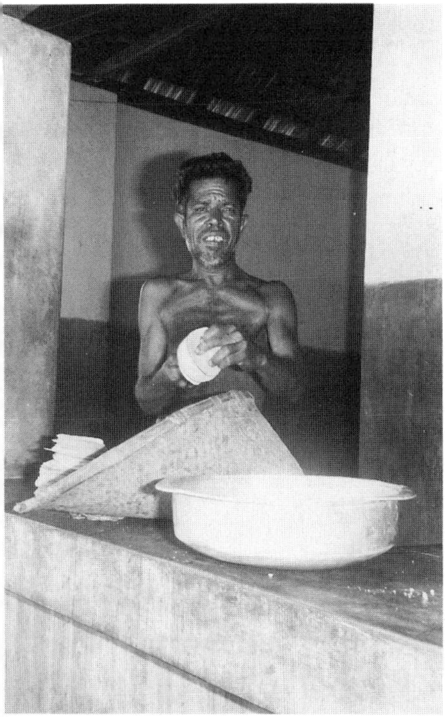

Plate 8 Professional cook prepares food in School grounds for festival

Plate 9 Brahmacārini helps hostel girls water garden

Plate 10 Food for feast being cooked outdoors

Plate 11 Hostel girls study in their 'hall'

Plate 12 School girls served a festive meal

Plate 13 Village girl at roadside tap

Plate 14 Christian village store

crucial to stress this difference, and so I shall illustrate this statement with an example. It involved Radha,[15] a Pre Probationer of nine months' standing.

Radha received a letter from a friend. There is nothing very terrible about that, except that the friend wrote in their mother tongue, Kannada, though both parties had received their education in the English medium. The President, who reads all inmates' incoming and outgoing mail[16] was displeased, as she could not understand the contents of the letter. She could of course have requested Radha (or, if she did not trust her skills as a translator, another Karnataka-speaking inmate) to give an indication of the letter's contents. But for some reason, her suspicion and annoyance was aroused. At 'Reading' that night she asked Radha, 'Why are you still writing to friends? And, why do they reply in Kannada?' Radha replied with indignation: 'I am not writing to them. Even when they send stamped covers[17] I do not reply'. She looked upset. Mataji read a paragraph of the book before her. Then, suddenly, she slammed down the book, and said, 'Why the long face? *We* have heard so many scoldings. You should *take* them. If you don't like this place, say so. SAY SO! This Sarada Mandiram is famous. You can do what you like here: no rules. If you don't like this communal living, that *means you are not fit for spiritual life.* Why are you looking angry with me? If this is how you start, how will you finish? I am reading the holy words of Swami Turiyananda,[18] and you show that angry face'. Mataji was now furious. 'I will not see that face. Go and sit in a corner somewhere. Why are you angry with me?' Radha replied, 'Mataji, you said that Bangalore people . . .' With that, Mataji threw down the book in a rage, and marched to her room. Radha, in a flood of tears, followed. The inmates looked stunned for a few minutes. One whispered, 'This is the first time you are seeing this, isn't it?' Another, with a broad smirk on her face, whispered, 'What did she do?' The exchange had been in English, so some of the Kerala candidates could not follow what was happening. 'She wrote to a friend', was the reply. Then, from Mataji's room came an urgent plea, 'May I talk to you?' 'GET OUT! I don't want to talk to you'. The inmates, still sitting in the old prayer hall, realised that there would be no more reading that night, and to the accompaniment of Radha's hysterical sobbing, silently got up, to retire for the night, eyeing each other nervously.[19]

Mataji had thrown down the gauntlet: you are not fit for spiritual life. An initiated candidate, such as Radha, far from walking out on that statement, overcome with grief at being publically humiliated (the worst feature of Mataji's scoldings), does exactly the opposite.

She feels a desperate need to prove to herself that she is worthy of the grace which Ramakrishna bestowed on her by enabling her to come to Sarada Mandiram. The ideal of renunciation is clearly for her the *highest* ideal, and the thought of failure has suddenly loomed before her. The next morning, a sorrowful Radha sat as usual in the prayer hall during meditation, and went about her duties (which included serving food to seniors) with swollen red eyes. No more was said. She had passed the test, for the time being, anyway. Mataji had demonstrated her absolute authority over Radha. She had the potential of adjusting. That night, Radha was sitting with her friend, another Brahmin newcomer from Karnataka, who was silently reading an article about Holy Mother in a Mission Journal. The latter said to me, 'Look at this article about Holy Mother. Whoever you were, she loved you. No "you love me and I will love you",' Radha said sorrowfully. 'That is divine love. Here it is all too human.' The article was entitled, 'Compassion and Holiness'. Radha clearly felt rejected and was comparing Holy Mother's forgiving nature with the President's fury.

The matter of Radha's scolding was not raised again, and after the passing of a few days, she cheered up. But, incidents such as this are never *forgotten,* because they are so painful, and so public. Even if the offender receives a scolding in Mataji's own room, the shouting is so loud that it can be heard by all and sundry. Sometimes the Hostel girls also hear the scoldings of inmates, some of whom are their teachers. The usual tactic during scoldings is for inmates to gather in the nearby machine room (the bedroom in which sewing was done), and listen as the whole drama unfolds, each eager to find out who is 'getting it' and what for. The 'kitchen people' (cooks and helpers), servants and even some of the more sophisticated Hostel girls also become knowledgable about scoldings, missing information being shared impartially. Gossip at Sarada Mandiram is the one valuable resource that crosses the otherwise rigid hierarchical boundaries. This is in line with the role of gossip in the traditional *taravād,* each so much isolated from its neighbours. Managers, labourers and members leaving the premises served to keep the *taravād* informed about important happenings outside. As I shall illustrate in due course, Sarada Mandiram is very much modelled on the *taravād* pattern, not only architecturally, but organisationally also, relying to a large extent on traditional roles, networks and sources of prestige.

As the months roll by, the Pre Probationer becomes accustomed to the various daily tasks which have to be performed at Sarada Mandiram. Each two months the 'routine' is changed. The President discusses the possible choices for each chore with other seniors, and then a list is drawn up, which is then given to a junior inmate to circulate, and finally pinned up on a wall. Within minutes it is the main topic of conversation. Who got storekeeper? Who got shrine? Who got *pūjā*, the performance of the ritual worship? The newcomer graduates to helping make the *pāyasam* and *luchis*,[20] the evening offerings, which are prepared after the evening *ārati*. She thereby misses meditation. In the morning, cleaning will continue for at least two full months. Then comes triumph. The next routine is likely to be *mālā*, the 'plucking' of flowers in the early morning and the threading of them into beautiful, colourful flower garlands, to be placed on the photos on the shrine. This duty, accompanied by minor duties connected with the shrine, is the most popular, involving two juniors and one senior daily. The senior cuts fruit for the morning offering, and enters the actual shrine to bring the garlands and food offerings. Newcomers are not permitted to enter the shrine until shortly before leaving for training in Calcutta, that is, after three years. The senior must also ensure that no error is made by juniors during their months of 'shrine work'. During this routine, those chosen will not have to perform any menial work, such as cleaning or vegetable cutting, or watering the garden. In the evening, they have to 'pluck' flowers, and so must keep their clothes both clean and ritually pure. They are, after all, *shrine workers*.

After a happy two months (despite inevitable scoldings) making garlands, the next routine will bring the incumbents back to earth. They will either be rostered for cleaning again, or store. While cleaning is unwelcome because it is 'menial', the announcement of two months as storekeeper sends the victims into an instant state of misery. Two juniors will assist the storekeeper, who is either a senior *brahmacārini*, or a junior *saṃnyāsini*. The work is heavy and exhausting, and by the end of the two months, at least two sets of clothes will be badly stained and torn. The storekeeper is in charge of all food supplies, and the preparation of meals. Provisions are kept under lock and key in the store, and given in measures to the cooks, before each meal. Supplies have to be ordered and put away, grains cleaned, spices pounded and ground, vegetables cut and menus planned, using home grown products as much as possible. Also, food has to be prepared on time, and without catastrophe, and the cooks kept in good humour. The lunch, which is prepared to strict ritual specifications, has to be made ready for offering and, perhaps most difficult of all, served later to the four seniors who, along with special guests (which included me) sit on chairs at a large table in the old dining hall, and receive individual attention and special food preparations.

At 12.30 p.m. when Ramakrishna has partaken of the offered food, the seniors sit for their meal: at the same time as the 'rank and file' in the main dining room. One storekeeper supervises the main dining room, filling food buckets as they are emptied by the children-servers, and leading in the chanting which precedes the meal. She also stands within earshot during the meal, to scold anyone who breaks the rule, 'Strictest silence to be observed in the dining hall', which is chalked in Malayalam on the wall near the entrance. In practice, strictest silence means that seniors should not be able to hear the noise, for if they do, the storekeeper will be on the receiving end of a scolding herself. Quiet conversation is not usually censured.

Children are served a pile of soft white rice, in which they make a 'well' with their right hand fingers. Into this a ladle of semi-liquid lentils cooked with vegetables and spices is poured. On the other side of the plate a blob of a 'dry' vegetable dish (often fried in oil) is given, along with homemade pickles. On Wednesday (the day on which Ramakrishna was born) and Sundays (when there is no school), *ghee* is given (rich homemade clarified butter) and fried *papadum* (lentil wafers) which are a delicacy. At the end of the meal, very diluted buttermilk seasoned with salt, fresh chilli, fragrant curry leaves and ginger root is drunk from the right cupped hand, then mashed into a little of the remaining rice, kept specially for this purpose. The buttermilk is both delicious and cooling, and a favourite with bland rice for those who are ill. Boiled water, served warm and flavoured with cummin, coriander or cinnamon, or cummin and dried ginger root, accompanies the meal as an aid to digestion. Fresh fruit, cut into pieces may follow. On special occasions, *pāyasam,* a sweet desert is served, much to the delight of the younger children, who express this with squeals of approval. By Kerala standards, the food is excellent in quality, except the rice, which is unfortunate, as it is the staple food.

Food in Kerala *is* rice, and the favoured type of rice is 'boiled', that is, the paddy is boiled and sun dried before husking. 'Raw' rice is not so treated. Good rice is fragrant. The rice which is offered to Ramakrishna is 'boiled', even though 'raw' rice is considered purer, and so offered in temples throughout both Kerala and Bengal. But, 'boiled' rice is considered much better for the digestion, and since Ramakrishna (who had a delicate stomach) is given typical Kerala Hindu food similar to that eaten by well-to-do Nayar, he is given the rice which they consider the best to eat themselves, rather than that which is ritually purer. While the children and others in the main dining hall eat ration rice, the seniors eat the small portion of offered rice, which is of the finest quality, often being grown in the paddy fields of a devotee. Ration rice comes complete with dirt, hair, worms, stones and other unattractive attributes. It has to be cleaned grain by grain by a team of children before being washed and cooked, the result depending on the zeal of the particular group. When cooked, it . . . there is no other word . . . stinks. It is very inferior grain, stored in often dangerously damp conditions, and open to contamination by rats and other vermin. Even the poor try to avoid it. Rice was freely available on the open market in 1980–1, and I could not understand why an Institution which has expensive boarding fees should economise on the main item of food. The President said that if you did not utilise your full ration quota when there was no shortage, it would be difficult to obtain rations if rice became in short supply. I feel persuaded, however, that the use of ration rice (and other grains) was a cost cutting measure, as ration rice cost less than half the retail price of rice in the open market.

As the children eat their lunch, the storekeeper or one of her assistants has to stand guard awaiting the President, in the old dining room. This is particularly difficult, as at the same time 150 people are being served in the new dining room. The food for the President and other seniors is kept covered, on a small serving table, always at the correct time, at 12.30 p.m. However, often the President chooses to be late, in which case the food has to be watched carefully, since crows and cats could contaminate it in a trice. As the President arrives, the storekeeper springs to her feet, as the other seniors follow in close pursuit. Covers are busily removed, with food ready to serve as soon as the seniors are seated. The President has special dishes prepared for her, instead of those prepared for the children and others. These include both her favourite foods, and those considered beneficial to her ailments, (diabetes, rheumatism and hypertension). If prepared in time, they will be offered to Ramakrishna, otherwise not. After she is served, others at the table are served, soft food only being given to the seniormost *saṃnyāsini*, who has neither teeth nor dentures. As the meal progresses, the President is offered 'curds' (yoghurt), and if she declines, thick buttermilk instead. There is a great art developed by seasoned servers of watching each person and anticipating what she will require next. This is only perfected after many months of carefully learning each person's idiosyncrasies.

The first few minutes after the seniors' meal has been served are very stressful for the server. The food can have too much salt or not enough, it can be poorly cooked, not to the President's taste, or rejected on numerous other grounds. The President uses mealtimes to let out anger that she may be feeling in general. And, the store personnel are the targets for this. Others sitting at the dining table do not join in the criticism, as this would be disrespectful to the President's authority. Only, on occasion, when a stone is found in the rice, a particular *saṃnyāsini* picks it up and drops it, with a resounding note, onto her metal plate. This is a cue for the President to scold the storekeepers for not properly cleaning the grain, a serious fault, since it has already been offered to Ramakrishna.

There were long periods during my fieldwork during which not one meal passed without scoldings for the servers, especially for the two months during which a particular *saṃnyāsini* had been appointed storekeeper. At one stage, every day for a week, the President left every meal in a fit of anger, and the storekeeper retreated into the kitchen in a flood of tears. On one occasion the coffee was not cooled sufficiently before being poured into the President's tumbler, making it too hot to drink immediately. On another, a special breakfast proudly prepared just to please her was sourly rejected as 'horrible', after the President had enquired who had made it. When she was offered coffee, she wanted buttermilk, when offered buttermilk, she wanted milk and water. The same went on at lunchtime, and again at night. Before every meal the storekeeper would say to me, 'Oh! I am so afraid. I just cannot please her, no matter how hard I try'. She and her assistants were scolded for wearing soiled sarees, though it is wellnigh impossible for a storekeeper to manage to remain clean, and one afternoon, she added for good measure, 'And, I told you *not* to give me fruits in the afternoon. And, you kept it, one vessel on top of another: like an exhibition!'[21] The vivid description, plus the sight of a woman of forty weeping over having done her duty and received nothing but criticism, was just too much. Especially as this scolding terminated in the President giving a series of loud belches, before she left the dining hall, in a huff.

An incident such as the one above (which was by no means an isolated one) causes profound shock to the newcomer. The official explanation of outbursts of anger, is by way of the oft-quoted saying, 'A *saṃnyāsin*'s anger is like a line drawn on water. It is only an appearance'. The meaning of this is that the *saṃnyāsin* (and by extension, the *saṃnyāsini*) uses a facade of anger as a teaching device. However, on one occasion the President confided in me that she was developing an angry temperament, which caused a physical reaction on her. I suspect that her poorly controlled diabetes has much to do with her moods. The behaviour of the President causes other doubts in the minds of some junior inmates, doubts that they felt they should not have, but on occasion expressed to me. Firstly, they worried about the fact that she has such an exclusive diet, and modern dining arrangements. She also had very fine quarters, with relatively luxurious furnishings and fixtures, and accepted a good deal of personal service. This did not seem to be in keeping with the ideal of *saṃnyāsa*, the ideal of total renunciation of worldly goods.

The President explained her attitude to some *saṃnyāsin's* seemingly opulent lifestyle in the following terms. I remarked that a *saṃnyāsin* of another Order who had visited Australia that year had stayed at the Hilton Hotel, and was surrounded by a retinue which would do a Head of State proud. She reacted with annoyance: 'We live on what the devotees give us. If the devotees arranged his stay there, it was not for him to be ungrateful. Nor to be angry if they arranged for him to stay in a hut. The secret is not what you have, but not to be attached'.[22]

Perhaps the most disturbing discovery for the newcomer, though, is to witness the conversations which take place at the senior dining table, during meals. The conversations are noteworthy in themselves, as mealtimes in Kerala are not traditionally regarded as social occasions. Moreover, in a monastic Institution newcomers could reasonably expect any conversation during meals to have some bearing on religious themes and aspirations, or at least address itself to practical matters. Instead, at meals, prominent people were often discussed, especially those involved in scandals. Or, local village or Trichur scandal, just broken, was the order of the day. If visitors had called that day, all the '*visesam*' (news) would be the topic, even if the conversation had been in confidence. Condemnation of local people who were not supporters of Sarada Mandiram was also a common mealtime theme. An example involved a very wealthy Izhava family which had never given a donation, even when approached. A month beforehand I had written down a lunchtime conversation in which the President had declared that one should not even talk to members of that family, because they had made their money from trading in liquor. Alcoholism among the middle class is a grave, but seldom aired problem in Kerala, and one which has affected the families of many Kerala inmates regardless of community. Now, the President had been invited to the house of one of the sons, and had accepted. She had just returned. At supper she said, 'Have you seen "Grand" Madhavan's house?'[23] And, she proceeded to describe it. 'All matching sofa-sets, and a *laminated* dining table with ten matching chairs! I asked how much it cost, and she (the wife) said, "How should I know, because we had no bill".' How else to get rid of undeclared money than to put it into a house? Toddy money.[24] And, their house was raided: two lakhs of gold biscuits.[25] So, he paid the Customs man. I mean, Government servants don't earn much. That is why they all take money . . .' She went on to discuss a blackmarketeer in Quilon, to the South, and money he rid himself of by painting the facade of the local temple with gold leaf. 'Kurians are different, though. Theirs is old *money*. They have *aesthetic* taste. But, Madhavan sits with his shirt open, and his legs apart on his expensive sofa set . . .'

Very often the conversation concerned marriage. 'Govindan in Hyderabad's son married a *madamu*.[26] I thought she was a Parsee, but no, she is an American. But dear me, the son is *black*, even though she is *fair*. He is like his father. His features – nose, teeth – are good, but he is black!' Mataji often confided that she was sorry that she was herself so black and 'not at all pretty'. Those who are serving when such conversations take place, must listen to all this without blinking, even if the conversation concerns someone they know well, and does not appear to represent the person accurately (such as criticism of a fellow inmate). Even an innocent reaction can bring a swift rebuke. One day Mataji mentioned that she had received a letter from the General Secretary of the Order, who had shortly before cancelled a visit due to ill health. 'How is she?' blurted out Lakshmi, a newcomer who was serving at the time. She received a furious look, for joining in the conversation of seniors, and retreated, hot faced, to the corner. On another occasion, a server smiled at an anecdote, to be quickly rebuked, 'How *dare* you enjoy our conversation?' Tears at once welled up in the server's eyes, but she turned her face away, lest she be scolded on this account also. All in all, serving can be the worst part of being storekeeper, because it is the one job in which you come to Mataji's attention constantly, day after day. As one storekeeper used to say to me daily, 'I am terribly afraid . . .'

By the end of the year the Pre Probationer will have sampled all the major types of work, except that involving shrine entry. Karnataka candidates will not be asked to supervise children or to act as temporary teachers (if qualified) until they learn sufficient Malayalam. Recent candidates from Kerala have not had teaching qualifications, except two with nursery training. One new candidate was sent at once to assist in the nursery while I was there, as inmates are preferred to lay women in the various departments of work undertaken at Sarada Mandiram. Not only is there more control over monastic workers, but their salary is used for the benefit of the Institution.

A 'year' within the Sarada Math and its branches is counted as beginning on Holy Mother's birthday, according to the Bengali calendar. This occurs in December-January and is the day on which vows are taken. A year thus extends from one birthday to the next. If a candidate arrives in June, for example, she will only be considered as having completed a year of candidature on her *second* Holy Mother's birthday, that is, after eighteen months. Within the Ramakrishna Math, a year begins on the birthday of Ramakrishna, that is, in February-March. According to the Bengali lunar calendar, a birthday is calculated by the number of days from the beginning of either the bright or dark fortnight of the moon, on the day of birth. This is known at *tithi*. In Kerala, *nakśetram* or the ascendant star for the month on the day of birth is the means of calculating birthdays. Only in observing local festivals is the Kerala calendar used at Sarada Mandiram.

The newcomer will receive her first 'cloth' from the President within her first few months. 'Cloth' refers either to a saree, the common garment of Hindu women, or *mundu* set, a Kerala garment consisting of two separate pieces of cloth, draped to give a similar effect to a saree. Cloth is usually given at Onam (September) and Vishu (April), two Kerala festivals. The President purchases and presents cloth to all monastic inmates just before these festivals occur, and newcomers will receive cloth along with the others. Cloth giving was the traditional presentation of the *kāraṇavan*, to all members of the *taravād*, tenants and servants on these occasions. The act of giving and receiving reinforced his control over all three categories of those who depended on him, in various ways. The gift was dropped lightly into the extended open palms of the recipient, so that there is no direct bodily contact. Junior members of the *taravād*, however, saluted him by prostrating and touching his feet, to receive his blessing, in high ranking families. Others saluted him without touching. Formerly, tenants and servants had to give gifts of produce to their *kāraṇavan*, as a token of their loyalty.

The President gives cloth in the same spirit as the *kāraṇavan* of yore. The recipients line up at different times when sent for, according to category: monastic inmates, domestic servants, outside servants and labourers, and lay residents. The last category receives cloth individually, as subtle status differences among the lay women residing at Sarada Mandiram makes it difficult to rank them, without causing offence to at least one of them. Each category will be given a different quality and style of cloth, depending on what is routinely worn. For example, female labourers usually receive a single *mundu* and blouse piece, while resident women receive a set of *mundu*, comprising two pieces of cloth, of finer quality, but not a blouse. Labourers do not wear a second cloth draped over their breasts, as do caste Hindu women when wearing the *mundu*. A blouse piece is given, so that the presentation represents a more or less equal 'set of clothes'.

Newcomers receive a saree with a 30–50 mm border in a colour other than red. Like other cloth, it is handloomed and unbleached.[27] The official 'uniform' for Probationers and *brahmacārinis* is a red bordered cloth, but this is not usually given to newcomers until after a year, unless the President has a surplus in stock. Sarees and *mundu* are not made especially for the Order, but purchased from local cloth shops or, occasionally, donated by devotees. There is therefore a great deal of variety in the 'uniform'. After the first year, the President will alternate red borders with other colours, and only by the completion of the third year (before leaving for training in Calcutta) will the candidate expect to have all red bordered cloth.

After the first red bordered cloth is presented, the newcomer will keep it carefully in her 'box', only wearing it on special occasions, or when going out. Each year, before Vishu, monastic inmates receive coarse 'long cloth' which is cut into five 'jackets' (blouses), and two petticoats, reaching from waist to ankles, to wear under the saree or *mundu*. A finer, soft cloth is cut into four 'bodices', a simple garment covering the breasts, tied in a knot at the diaphragm. No 'underwear' (underpants) is permitted in Bengali centres, but in Sarada Mandiram, though the older inmates wear a large, tight *onera* (the loin cloth of conservative Nayar women), younger inmates are now permitted to sew 'drawers', which are simple underpants with a drawstring at the waist. Sewn garments should last until next Vishu, and those who do not know how to use the sewing machines soon learn, though their first efforts may look and feel less than satisfactory. Expert cutters from among the inmates usually oblige and cut cloth for inmates who ask. Those who are able, spend the summer school vacation sewing clothes for the free boarders, under the professional eye of a *saṃnyāsini* sewing teacher. The seniormost *saṃnyāsini* and the President are the only two inmates who have their clothes stitched for them. This is interesting, because it is a tradition that *saṃnyāsins* do no stitching (nor wear stitched garments) though the latter seldom applies among 'middle class' *saṃnyāsins* today.[28]

As a newcomer gains confidence, she asks to try her hand at the musical instruments used during the evening worship: harmonium, cymbals, drums and gong and (if anyone has the ability to tune it) the tampura, a stringed instrument. There is no formal tuition for music, but new inmates ask those who usually play, to show them how. Experiments are made in the prayer hall by nervous but eager newcomers on days when the President (and if they are lucky, other seniors too) are absent. The standard of music and singing at Sarada Mandiram is very, very low indeed. In Kerala, it is only girls of high ranking families who are traditionally encouraged to learn classical vocal music and to play an accompanying instrument. It was these same families who were connected through *sambandham* with Sanskrit-knowing royal and Nambudiri men: traditional patrons of the arts in Kerala. The candidates from Kerala are not from these families, and have no 'ear' for music at all. On the other hand, Karnataka candidates, especially those of Brahmin families, even with little or no formal training, fare much better. But, the *bhajans* (hymns) at Sarada Mandiram are frequently off-key, sometimes so badly that inmates giggle helplessly. During the evening *bhajans* attended by the children, the smaller girls fall asleep from the monotony of the tunes, while others fidget or stare blankly ahead. A small number of girls actually sings, the children at the back often lagging behind the beat of the gong (which keeps the 'time') at the front of the prayer hall. The standard of *bhajans* at Sarada Mandiram has long been the subject of lament by the office bearers of the Order, for they are Bengali. As a people, Bengalis are exceptionally talented at both vocal and instrumental music. But, as Sarada Mandiram has so many other, pleasing features (such as the ability of the children to repeat the *Bhagavad Gita* in an expert manner) this lapse is forgiven.

One day, probably near Holy Mother's birthday, the Pre Probationer will be called to the President's room. She will answer the summons immediately, wondering what she has done wrong. The President will hand her a printed form and ask her to 'fill it up'. It is an application for Probation, the first step towards formal acceptance into the Order. On it the candidate fills in her name, home address, age, date of birth, education, qualifications, employment history, salary or wages, father's occupation and income, and caste. She is asked to state whether she is the sole or main financial support of the family and whether she has any outstanding debts. Finally, she is asked if she has her mother's permission to join the Order, and to undertake to make no claim for remuneration if she leaves.[29]

Within a few days, the Pre Probationer is sent into the town to a doctor for a medical examination, which includes a chest X-ray, pathology tests, and examinations of eyes, ears, teeth and general health. If anything is found to be wrong, she will have to undergo treatment before her application is forwarded to Calcutta. A full written statement is also required not only of all illnesses the candidate has had previously, but for all members of her immediate family, their ages and (if appropriate) age, and cause of death. The Trustees of the Order do not want to admit candidates who may prove a potential burden. If all goes well, however, the medical report and application are posted, along with a letter or recommendation from the President and, in due course, she will be called again to the President's room. This time she will be told that at the last Trustee meeting in Calcutta, her application was accepted. She is now a Probationer of the Ramakrishna Order of *saṃnyāsinis.*

No announcement of acceptance is made to the other inmates. The new Probationer will feel elated, but probably will only tell one or two other inmates, or maybe nobody at all.

After all the insecurity of the first year, all the new skills and behavioural patterns to be learned, all the adjustments to communal living, the acceptance is a *personal* triumph for the candidate. It is she who has struggled and won. She feels no need for congratulations. She has received with the news a boost to her badly bruised ego and (perhaps) faith. The crossing of the first milestone or threshold has finally been safely negotiated, and that is all that counts. She now looks forward to the next perilous two years, which will decide if and when she is deemed fit to embark on the long journey to Calcutta.

Chapter 8

Being and Becoming

The first year at Sarada Mandiram is really a trial period, during which the candidate gradually finds out whether or not she is suited to monastic life. At the same time, she is very carefully observed by her seniors, to see if she has the necessary qualities of docility and obedience to succeed. Bright girls who always have the urge to express or offer opinions are likely to be crushed early in the piece. Candidates are expected to passively accept what is told to them during classes, and heaven help the candidate who actually contradicts a statement by one of the 'leading lights' of the Order, such as she may feel tempted to do while reading an article in a journal of the Order. This is particularly so for candidates from Karnataka, many of whom had been actively encouraged to enter into religious debate by the Head of their local Ramakrishna Math or Mission, before deciding to come to Sarada Mandiram.

For the next two years, the candidate will have to prove her worthiness to be recommended for the long journey to Calcutta, where she will undergo two years of training at the Headquarters. By now her seniors will have a fairly good idea of her personality. They know the material: now they will set about remoulding it.

Religion is, according to Mataji (quoting Vivekananda) 'Being and Becoming'. That is, it is transformation by practice. 'Being' consists of living the Ideal, or following the path as shown by seniors. If you meditate and study regularly, and perform work in the spirit of service, then the required transformation will take place. This is the 'Becoming'. Inmates are, by their relative isolation from outside influences, protected from the grosser manifestations of worldliness, such as radio and cinema, magazines and (ideally) idle talk. As Ramakrishna said, 'the further you go east, the farther you leave the west behind.' The two main obstacles to spiritual life, however, come not from the external environment, but from within. These are in the form of manifestations of ego, and of the past impressions of the mind.

In order to merge in Brahman, or with the personal God, the spiritual aspirant must surrender his or her ego, to lose all concept of 'I-ness' or 'my-ness', me or mine. This works remarkably well in a rigidly hierarchical Institution such as Sarada Mandiram, in which total obedience to seniors is required. Any rising indignation at seemingly unfair treatment, and any opinion offered, is construed as ego exerting itself. From time to time, I would hear a candidate exclaim 'I must get rid of this ego', rather than 'I wish so-and-so would stop picking on me'. The war against ego is waged by the serious candidate in much the same way as the war against the 'devil's work' in old-style Catholic Institutions. The problems of an untamed ego stem from an even more untamed mind, the ultimate obstacle to spiritual progress.

Monastic candidates (and indeed lay devotees also) lament from time to time that during meditation their mind seems to bring up not pure thoughts, but dirt. This appears to be a common problem for meditators, as it is widely dealt with in articles on meditation, and in classes. The advice usually given is to pray for purity, and to repeat the *mantra* constantly. At the same time, consolation is given by likening the mind to an ink bottle. As clean water (the *mantra*) is poured into the bottle, it becomes blue and cloudy, until finally the residue of ink is flushed out, leaving the bottle clean and clear. The dirt in the mind has accumulated over many years, so the aspirant should ignore it, knowing that it will become diluted and eventually vanish, with constant spiritual practice. What this advice entirely overlooks is that a constant new supply of 'ink' is available to retarnish the bottle, even in a monastic environment.

Within Sarada Mandiram, indeed within the whole Order, there is no mechanism to help inmates with their inevitable mental crises, and 'spiritual' struggles. There is no priest who can listen and absolve you of guilt and doubt, no wise 'novice mistress' to encourage and counsel you. You are told to rely on Ramakrishna and Holy Mother, as can be witnessed after a scolding or even on the death of a relative, when a solitary monastic inmate can be found silently shedding tears before the shrine.

The first Pre Probation year is spent learning the 'routine': the daily way of life at Sarada Mandiram, and the seasonal round of festivals. There is now a welcome familiarity surrounding allotted tasks, and even the changes of seasons, with alternating wet, humid, and dry dusty season (January) following an expected course. Now, even candidates from urban homes have mastered the various arts connected with the seasonal harvest of crops: how to prepare tamarind for storage, coconuts for copra, acidic *nellikay* and green mangoes for pickles. Kapok must be cleaned in season, ready to be made into mattress and cushion filling. Probationers have become experts at churning curds in the early morning, until the pale butter can be collected on the surface with a jackfruit leaf, leaving thick, sour buttermilk behind. On many an afternoon, coconut palm leaves are brought by the labourers, and all newcomers sit in a circle, stripping each one with a swift movement, until only the ribs are left. Bundles of these are tied with a strip of cloth, to make soft, flexible brooms. The stress of constantly having to learn new skills, of having to change a lifetime of personal habits has lessened by the second year of candidature, but in its place new stresses emerge, those caused by constantly falling short of 'the ideal', of having to prove oneself worthy of being permitted to stay at Sarada Mandiram.

There is, however, a pleasant surprise in store for the Probationer, who finds that those who arrive after her are deferential towards her, as she has become towards her own seniors. She will begin to show as much annoyance at their worried enquiries, whenever faced with a new task or situation, as her seniors showed to her. It appears that within a year, the Probationer has forgotten her own first uncertain days at Sarada Mandiram. What she conveys to her own juniors is not understanding but a brisk assuredness. She wishes to distance herself from *newness*, and appear as senior (and hence, self assured) as possible.

Though the end of the Pre Probationary year has been marked by formal acceptance for candidates who were able to meet the Order's requirements, during 1981 there were five candidates (all from Karnataka) who 'were not on the regular list', that is, could not apply in the routine manner. These candidates feel it very acutely when their juniors apply for admission as a Probationer, and are accepted after only a year. Those lacking one of the necessary qualifications, or good health, or who are over age are often permitted to stay at Sarada Mandiram without obligation on either side. If they can prove their ability to adjust, they will be permitted to apply for admission after three to four years, all of which will be counted as years of monastic candidature. Of all branches of the Order, the Sarada Mandiram President has by far the most understanding attitude towards 'irregular' candidates, and no distinction is made between them and 'regular' candidates. She is prepared to give anyone a chance. Indeed, it is not considered etiquette to enquire of a senior whether she is actually a 'member' or not.

Probationers (including 'irregular' candidates of more than a year's standing) will spend their next two years in Kerala, unless another branch of the Order is short of workers, and the President agrees to send a candidate recruited through her own centre to fill the gap. Shortage of monastic workers is a problem in all branches, as the Order is still trying to establish new centres in the key cities of India. Unlike the Ramakrishna Order which often establishes centres with one or two monastic inmates, Sarada Math requires a minimum of four monastic inmates to open a new branch. This is not only because it is considered inadvisable for one or two women to live alone, but also because shrine work requires sufficient personnel. There always must be enough monastic inmates to ensure that at least one is available to perform shrine duties, quite a difficult consideration in an Order in which almost all members were still pre-menopausal. During menstrual periods, no inmate may touch any article connected with the shrine nor enter any area in which shrine objects or offerings are kept or prepared. Trichur is often regarded with envy by the Heads of other centres, as next to Headquarters, by far the most number of candidates is recruited through Sarada Mandiram, and there is always a supply of new candidates each year to make up for the two or three who depart for training in Calcutta.

Some time during the next two years, each candidate will spend a few months at least in the Mission centre in Trivandrum, the capital of Kerala. Usually, all transfers between branches of the Order must be referred to the Headquarters for approval, but in the case of Trichur and Trivandrum, it is informally arranged between the two centres, for their mutual convenience. The Trivandrum centre is quite different from Trichur. It is urban, and on its small plot, which once housed a modest bungalow, now stand randomly-built extensions, which house the Hostel for College girls. Twenty five girls were crammed into the tiny rooms in 1981, some of which had no outside ventilation. Ceiling fans had either been removed or disconnected, and the Hostel smelt dank and stale. Nevertheless, there was always a waiting list for admission, mainly by highly conservative families from rural areas who were worried that their daughters would be 'spoilt' whilst studying in Trivandrum. Hostel girls at the Ramakrishna Sarada Mission are extremely closely supervised.

Whilst monastic candidates seldom have reason to venture past the gates of Sarada Mandiram, in Trivandrum, they have plenty of opportunity to leave the premises: though always with a 'companion'. Junior inmates are sometimes sent to the market, or to the station to receive visitors. They also accompany the Head of Centre when she goes to give lectures or take part in meetings. The then Head of Centre was much sought after as a speaker, and had a considerable personal following, and on average sixty women attended her classes, held at the Mission on Saturday evenings. It is during their stay at Trivandrum that some Kerala candidates ride in private cars for the first time, and visit the drawing rooms of moderately westernised middle-class families. At all times, however, they must remain silent and in the background.

Trivandrum is the closest city to Kanya Kumari, a major place of pilgrimage on the southernmost tip of India. Just off-shore from the famous Devi temple, lies a small rock, on which Vivekananda is said to have meditated, pondering the future of India, and what he could do to bring about a national revival. A massive temple now covers the rock, and daily thousands of pilgrims and tourists wait patiently for the small ferries which ply the short but rough straits between Rock and shore. Each candidate will visit the Rock during her stay in Trivandrum, mostly making the round journey in one day. Likewise, candidates visit the temple of Guruvayur whilst at Sarada Mandiram. This temple is only about an hour's travelling time from Sarada Mandiram, and a regular bus service stops right outside the gates. It is one of Kerala's most famous temples and dedicated to Krishna. Usually a party of monastic inmates led by a senior is sent on these pilgrimages, when there is a member of the Order visiting from another centre. Visits to temples are virtually the only 'outings' for the junior inmates, and are much enjoyed.

Towards the end of the second year of Probation, candidates will begin to look forward, not without some trepidation, to being sent to Calcutta. All Probationers must complete two years training at the Headquarters, referred to simply as 'Sarada Math',[1] before being permitted to apply for *brahmacārya*. Actually, training does not have to take place in the *final* two years of Probation. Some candidates proceed to Headquarters, straight from their homes, or after one or two years at a branch centre. The latter part of their Probation (after training) is then spent at a branch centre once more. After completing the five years of Probation, they are again sent to Headquarters to receive their vows, since *brahmacārya* and *saṃnyāsa* are only given at the Headquarters. Those who travel to Calcutta for vows sometimes stay as briefly as a few days: especially those who are school teachers. But, in the case of Kerala, the journey is so long and expensive that it is considered better for a candidate to complete three years of candidature, then proceed to Sarada Math, only returning after *brahmacārya* has been granted. Each branch centre must meet the cost of sending its monastic inmates to Headquarters, but once there, the Headquarters pays the cost of maintaining the candidates. However, there is certain etiquette to be observed by Heads of Centres before sending their recruits to Calcutta.

Before being sent to Calcutta, candidates will be given cloth, from which to sew new blouses, bodices and petticoats, and at least two new sarees and a cotton shawl. They will also borrow warm clothing, such as sweaters and a woollen shawl, from others who have completed training, or who have come from the cooler areas of Karnataka, bringing these garments with them. It is not usual for clothes to be shared in other circumstances, as garments carry the 'vibrations' of their former wearers. However, winter clothing is not needed in Trichur's steamy climate, and it is far too expensive to buy new clothes for each candidate. Fortunately, both wool and silk are immune to the transfer of pollution (unlike cotton garments), so even the orthodox do not object to sharing them with others.[2] Similarly, mosquito nets travel back and forth between Trichur and Calcutta, until mended so repeatedly that they are forced into retirement. The cold, dampness, and incessant mosquitoes are just some of the rigours of life at Sarada Math, situated as it is on the edge of the murky Hooghly river, a branch of the sacred Ganges.

During the third year in Trichur, the candidate will receive only red-bordered sarees, instead of a mixture of red and other colours. For, only red borders will be worn in Calcutta. And, much to the candidate's satisfaction, the first outward sign of eventual acceptance into the Order is bestowed. She will receive the distinctive cotton shawl worn by members of the Order, both male and female. The shawl is a length of white cloth, approximately 2½ metres wide, with a 2 cm border of deep plum. It is the type of cloth favoured by Tamil Brahmins, who wear a matching lower cloth, from waist to ankles. This is also worn by *brahmacāris* and *saṃnyāsins* of the Ramakrishna Order, though the latter dye the cloth with ochre. Other types of border are, however, worn by members of the Order, according to availability, and gold bordered cloth (which is expensive) is also commonly worn as a shawl. While members of the Ramakrishna Order wear the shawl frequently as a 'dress' item, neatly folded over one shoulder, female inmates always drape it over their saree, to form a cape, which falls in soft folds from neck to below the waist, concealing the bodily contours very effectively. The shawl should be worn whenever monastic inmates leave the premises (including in their School compound), and on formal occasions when the public is invited, such as festivals. Strictly speaking, the shawl should also be worn whenever monastic inmates come in contact with the public, such as parents of Hostel girls, or devotees. Within the gates of Sarada Mandiram though, usually a saree drawn hastily over both shoulders is considered sufficient covering, when unexpected visitors arrive. Even the *brahmacārini* in the office sits without a shawl: Trichur is simply too hot for rules concerning the wearing of the shawl to be taken very literally. In cooler parts of India, a woman wearing a shawl would not receive a second glance, but in the intensely humid climate of Kerala, the shawl certainly marks out the wearer as an oddity. Nevertheless, the shawl is worn with pride, for it is becoming recognised locally as part of the '*brahmacārini*' dress of the Ramakrishna Order. Lay people assume that wearers of the shawl are all 'members'. However, this is not so, as senior 'irregular' candidates are also allowed to wear it, if there is every indication of their eventual acceptance into the Order.

The two years of training at Sarada Math Calcutta is closely supervised by some of the most senior members of the Order, many of whom reside there as its main administrators. Trainees stay in a separate building, in neat rooms, each accommodating two to three Probationers. Those who have already spent three years in a branch centre are grateful for this experience, for the slightest fault is unlikely to go unnoticed at Sarada Math. Since the daily routine differs only slightly from branch to branch of the Order, any skill already mastered, ensures one problem less for the trainee. The main hurdle to be crossed by non-Bengali candidates, is Calcutta orthodoxy. Kerala candidates are looked down on (by and large) by the predominating Bengalis for their humble communal status and rustic attitudes while the Karnataka candidates are generally highly regarded, as most are Brahmins, and of similar social status to themselves.

At Sarada Mandiram, communal differences between monastic inmates are a very sensitive topic. Except for the one Nambudiri Brahmin candidates, all monastic inmates from Kerala were either of Backward Communities or Sudras (Nayar). On the other hand, the majority of candidates from Karnataka was not only Brahmin, but middle class, and with tertiary qualifications. In these circumstances, any deference towards candidates of higher communal, economic or educational status would be at the expense of virtually all the local monastic inmates. But, at Sarada Math, apart from some caste-based feelings of superiority among inmates, there is also some frank snobbery, based on affluence including private school education, fluent English, as also high occupational status of parents.

The appreciation of South Indian Brahmins by their Bengali sisters is not without problems, since the two groups have conflicting notions of orthodoxy. There is no room for dispute, however, as the South Indian Brahmins simply have to follow Bengali custom, such as merely changing clothes in the early morning, instead of bathing first. The Bengali custom of bathing in mid morning and then replacing the same set of garments is quite repulsive to all candidates from Kerala and Karnataka, as is the Bengali Brahmins' attitude towards a pure diet.

With the exception of certain Konkani Brahmins, Karnataka Brahmins are usually strict vegetarians. Many Bengali Brahmins, though, eat fish, and it is cooked daily at Sarada Math. Although no monastic inmate is obliged to eat fish at Sarada Math, the smell of it cooking in pungent mustard oil is quite nauseating for vegetarians. One inmate (from a Vaisnava family) was so offended by the fish at Sarada Math that she told me that if she would have known, she 'would not have joined'. The vegetarian inmates sit together for meals at the end of the row, and consider themselves superior to eaters of flesh. But, they would never dare express such an opinion. After all, Ramakrishna, Holy Mother and Vivekananda were all non-vegetarians.

While some of the Karnataka candidates had visited Sarada Math before coming to Sarada Mandiram, and had undertaken tours and pilgrimages to various parts of India, almost without exception the Kerala candidates had barely ventured beyond the district of their birth. Karnataka candidates have the reputation at Sarada Math as earnest, dignified, well educated and 'cultural', while the Kerala candidates are regarded as villagers: very tough and capable of enormous amounts of physical work. Many of the Karnataka candidates' health breaks down while in Calcutta, and in this case they are sent home to recuperate. More often than not, a candidate leaves the Order not because of spiritual but physical unfitness. Great physical stamina is required during the Probation years.

Unlike Sarada Mandiram, where the day begins at 5.00 a.m., the bell for rising sounds at 3.45 a.m. at Sarada Math. Yet, as in Sarada Mandiram, inmates do not retire before 10.00 p.m. at night. Moreover, at Sarada Mandiram, monastic inmates can pile their plates with as much food as they wish, while at Sarada Math, portions are very small, and candidates are reluctant to ask for more. The food at Sarada Math is not to the taste of South Indian candidates, and is not well balanced. Added to this, is the constant threat of infectious diseases, mainly due to contaminated ingredients and an unreliable water supply, and many trainees complain of chronic digestive problems, made worse by fatigue. If the first years at Sarada Mandiram were a struggle to adjust, the two years at Sarada Math become a struggle for actual survival for many South Indians. Nevertheless, they treasure the memory of their stay there.

Though the two years spent in Sarada Math require the candidate to adjust once more to a new set of customs, all agree that the 'spiritual atmosphere' of the Math is a great aid to their inner development. Though Sarada Mandiram is situated in a large, tranquil village compound, inside there is always a great deal of activity, centred on the needs of the School and Hostel. Religious classes and meditation are to be 'snatched' between the frantic rush to complete chores, respond to bells, and answer the calls of seniors.

In contrast to this, trainees at Sarada Math are constantly reminded of the sacredness of their environment. The Math is situated in Dakshineswar, where Ramakrishna spent his adult life. The Kali temple, where he lived and taught, and where Holy Mother served him, secluded from the eyes of visitors, is less than five minutes away. Twice a week, offerings are sent there, and the inmates chosen to carry them offer their salutations to the shrines, before returning to the Math. Members of Sarada Math like to believe that Ramakrishna actually visited the Math premises during his lifetime, as he is known to have visited the garden houses of many of the local gentry during his days at Dakshineswar. Dakshineswar aside, the whole of Calcutta is sacred to members of the Ramakrishna Order, for so many of its localities are associated with the leading personalities recorded in both the *Gospel* and *Great Master.* Each trainee will have the opportunity to visit the key places of pilgrimage: the Belur Math, Holy Mother's Calcutta House, the Sister Nivedita School, and (if they are fortunate) the villages in which Ramakrishna and Holy Mother were born. The *Gospel*, read at night in sight of the Ganges, and in the tongue of Ramakrishna himself, adds extra meaning for those who had first read it in their mother tongue, in far off Kerala or Karnataka.

Religious life at Sarada Math is emphasised far more than in any of the branch centres. Not only is the ritual worship elaborate, but trainees find that their prestige is enhanced if they gain the reputation for practising extra meditation, whenever they are not engaged in work. There is almost no 'outside' talk among trainees, and since they come from many different parts of India, they have no common gossip to share except that concerning fellow inmates. There is no 'escaping' from religious duties at Sarada Math. There the day consists of prayer, meditation and classes, punctuated by work, and at night after meditation all trainees gather in the room of the President to listen to an article or some advice. The proximity of the Ganges, plus the knowledge that the place of Ramakrishna's earthy *leela* (play) is just nearby, makes days at Sarada Math very special for those who have come to join the Order from the farthest corners of India. And, for those who started their monastic life in Kerala, there is the added pleasure of being able to learn Bengali, so that the *Gospel* can be appreciated in its original language, and the opportunity to learn many of the songs that Ramakrishna and Vivekananda used to sing. Also, whilst in Calcutta, trainees meet the senior *saṃnyāsins* and *saṃnyāsinis* of the Order, about whom they had heard so much. Being and Becoming should be certainly much easier at Sarada Math, and those who return from there appear far more fervent, far more tranquil than their sisters, who are caught up in the whirl of duties in branch centres.

During the Trustee Meeting held annually before Holy Mother's birthday, it will be decided who will be given the vows of *brahmacārya* and *saṃnyāsa* for that year, and about a month beforehand, candidates will be informed. Vows are sometimes delayed for reasons of poor health or doubts about the candidate's long term ability to adjust. The Kerala candidates for *brahmacārya* will already be at Sarada Math, and others from various branch centres arrive in ones and twos as the day draws near. Before *brahmacārya* is granted, a second medical certificate is required and if this is in order, the candidate prepares herself for the ceremony.

Brahmacārya

A complete set of new clothes is required for the *brahmacārya* ceremony, and candidates residing at Sarada Math will be issued with cloth, for making into a blouse and undergarments. A new saree and shawl will be given beforehand, since all new clothes must be dipped in water and dried before wearing, to ensure their purity.[3] A week or so before the birthday, all candidates will be moved to a set of rooms a little secluded from other inmates, and given the vows to copy down, being warned not to leave their notebooks lying around. The vows and invocations, all in Sanskrit, are to be learned by heart. 'Are there eight vows?' asked Lakshmi at Sarada Mandiram, to a *saṃnyāsini* who had just arrived from Sarada Math. 'No, twelve', was the reply. 'Is it the same *homa*[4] as for *saṃnyāsa*?' 'No'. Then the *saṃnyāsini* changed the subject. Non inmates are not expected to be inquisitive as to the format of the ceremonies.

In accordance with the Bengali calendar, the day at Sarada Math begins at dawn. Vows are administered before sunrise on Holy Mother's birthday, which is the following morning by Western notions of time, a culmination of the celebrations rather than an inauguration. By this time, after a full day of *pūjā*, feasting, devotional songs and lectures the Math is charged with spiritual fervour, heightened by artistic decorations throughout the 'public' areas which are thronged by women devotees, freshly bathed and smartly dressed for the occasion. The copious use of shimmering silks and satins in the shrine, which is heavily decorated with fragrant garlands, flickering lamps, and sweet-smelling incense adds to the special atmosphere. The celebrations are ushered in before drawn, with plaintive *shenai* music, followed by special *pūjā* and chanting. Inmates wear new sarees, which by the end of the afternoon will be soiled from the day's duties, which include serving lunch to all present. The candidates for vows attend the religious ceremonies, but otherwise remain apart from the other inmates. All are anxious, and say that the day passes very slowly. At night they eat a light supper of fruit and retire soon after, for they will have to arise very early for their bath.

Pollution of tributaries of the Ganges such as the Hooghly is very apparent: all types of rotting refuse floats by the Math continuously, and the open drains of the neighbourhood (including those of the Sarada Math) empty straight into the river. Yet, the river is considered the ultimate purifier of both impurity and sin. Its waters are believed by orthodox Hindus to be bacteria free. It must be quite an ordeal to bathe in the river before dawn on the day of vows though, as it is mid winter, and the water very cold indeed. The surrounding atmosphere at this time is encased in thick, murky smog. Shivering and dripping with their soaking wet bathing sarees flapping about their legs (for one should not bathe naked) they walk awkwardly towards the bathrooms to change into their new, dry clothes, which have been placed there beforehand. At 4.00 a.m. the heavy double doors of the prayer hall are swung open from inside, and they are requested to enter.

The ceremony of *saṃnyāsa* has just finished, and inside the prayer hall all the *saṃnyāsinis* of the Math are already assembled, as well as senior representatives from other Calcutta centres. Only *saṃnyāsinis* may witness the ceremony, just as only those who have already been initiated into *brahmacārya* may witness the ceremony which is about to begin. *Brahmacārinis* residing at the Math now also enter, and take their places around the area marked out with chalk for the sacrificial fire. The newly initiated *saṃnyāsinis* are also present, but the candidates are too nervous to notice them. What transpires during the ceremony can only be pieced together from conversations with *brahmacārinis,* who were reluctant to give even the most general information regarding *brahmacārya,* and through an account by an American Swami of the Ramakrishna Order. Yale received his vows in Calcutta, and describes the event in his book *A Yankee and the Swamis* (1961). Since this book was written with the full co-operation of senior monks of the Order, it can be taken as a reliable source of information for both *brahamacārya* and *saṃnyāsa* ceremonies. In addition, other descriptions of ceremonies (particularly those connected with *saṃnyāsa*) are available in various Sanskrit texts, but these are not specific for the Ramakrishna Order, which follows its own format. However, lack of certain important details in the description of rites followed by the Ramakrishna Order, make detailed analysis foolhardy to attempt.

The description of the *brahmacārya* ceremony given by Yale applies to the Belur Math, and I shall make use of a substantial part of this, pointing out where possible when there is a variation in custom followed by Sarada Math. This is in particular during rites which occur before the candidate presents himself to the officiating *guru.*

At Belur Math prior to the day on which *brahmacārya* is given, candidates have their heads shaved, leaving only a long tuft at the crown. This style is traditionally worn by Brahmin *brahmācaris,* but all candidates receive this form of tonsure, which they will retain until *saṃnyāsa.* At Sarada Math, no tonsure is performed, candidates retaining their neatly tied long hair, until *saṃnyāsa.* In both Belur Math and Sarada Math, candidates enter the prayer hall after bathing in the Ganges (which flows alongside both Maths) and wearing new clothes.

> The candidates sit before a sacramental fire. The guru and other seniors take their places behind. First comes a prologue in which is declared the purpose of the ceremony and the step the initiate is about to take: 'The purpose of my life is to cultivate dispassion, to attain union with God, and to be immersed in the bliss of divine love. To attain these objectives, I will do my utmost to live according to the ideals of *brahmacārya*'.

These ideals are then enumerated, and constitute the vows proper:

To meditate every day with regularity.

To pray for devotion to God and feel the purity of one's own true nature.

To do work as service to God.

To be calm, sweet-tempered, enthusiastic, and fair in one's dealings.

To be moderate, constructive-minded, and self-effacing.

To ever remember that the consuming passion of a *brahmacārī*'s life must be to find God, who is dearer than any enjoyment, any personal relationship, and worldly responsibility.

To be practical in a practical world: 'When I have known the Truth that these vows lead to – but only then – I will try to help others reach the Truth'.

Finally comes the actual vow of *brahmacārya*, of continence in word, thought and deed, the practice of which is a necessary instrument for realisation of the other ideals . . .

Last of all, all present repeat the ancient prayer addressed to that Presence in the fire which, even as it consolidates one's good intentions, equally consumes one's ignorance:

> 'I who am an embodied being, endowed with intellect, life-breath, and their functions, now offer up all my actions and their fruits to the fire of Brahman. No matter what I may have done, said, thought, in waking, in dreaming, or in dreamless sleep, with my mind, my tongue, my hands, and my other members: may all this be an offering to Brahman. We offer ourselves and all we have at the feet of Sri Ramakrishna' (Yale 1961:202–3).

On completion of the *brahmacārya* ceremony, initiates are counted as Members of the Order, although full membership is not officially given until after *saṃnyāsa*. Apart from being counted in the annual statistics published by Headquarters, membership confers no special favours. More important to the initiate at Belur Math, is the reception of an insignia of Brahmin status, by those born of non-Brahmin parents. Though Yale passes over this lightly, it is of the profoundest significance, both for the individual and the Ramakrishna Order.

> . . . the Head of the Order now gives sacred threads to those who do not have them, for everyone becomes a Brahmin on becoming a *brahmacārī* if he is not a Brahmin already . . .' (1961:203).

Normally a male child becomes a 'twice-born' Brahmin during his *upanāyana* initiation, which occurs some time before puberty. During this ceremony he receives the sacred thread, a length of threads joined together at the ends, and worn over the left shoulder and across the right hip. From this time the orthodox boy has his head shaved, leaving only a small *śikhā* or tuft at the crown. The initiate has now entered the *bramacāri* phase of life, that of the celibate student, the first of four *āśrama* (phases) which Brahmin men should ideally undergo. But, only male children born of Brahmin parents have the right to this initiation, which marks the beginning of Vedic study. The initiate is taught the *mantra* known commonly as *gāyatrī*, which is to be recited daily, along with *saṃdhya* worship.

Though *brahmacārinis* of the Ramakrishna Order receive the *gāyatrī mantra*, and are henceforth considered as Brahmins, they do not receive the sacred thread, nor is their new status as externally obvious as is the case with *bramacāris*. It should be pointed out that no female candidate for *brahmacārya* would have previously undergone Brahmin initiation, even those of Brahmin parentage, and so for all of them the initiation bestows a ritual status otherwise unattainable.

But, while the *bramacāri* of the Ramakrishna Order can be transferred to a branch centre far from his home town or village, and perhaps be assumed to have been born of Brahmin parents, as his thread proclaims him, for a *bramacārini* the transformation is far more ambiguous and open to controversy. A Brahmin man may have the right to study the Vedic scriptures, to perform ritual worship, including the preparation of rice for offering, but not a Brahmin *woman*. The daily religious duties to be performed by a Brahmin cannot be undertaken by a woman, due to the ritual impurity incurred during menstruation and, if applicable, childbirth.

Thus, while in branches of the Belur Math, *bramacāris* undertake the performance of *pūjā* and associated tasks in the confidence that they are all indeed Brahmins and thus entitled to do so, in branches of Sarada Math there is uneasiness among some of the more orthodox candidates as to their right to perform duties expressedly forbidden them by tradition. However, seniors present the performance of religious duties not as Vedic rituals but as the service of the beloved Master, Ramakrishna, and during periods of impurity they abstain from performing them. Just as a mother serves her children, or a wife her husband, looking on these duties as a high ideal, so do devotees (whether lay or monastic) look on service as an important part of the relationship between God and the devotee. Indeed, the performance of service is one of the most important manifestations of hierarchy in Hindu society. The junior or inferior party is always bound to serve the senior by acts of obedience, abasement in both speech and gestures and general submission to demands or commands, without demur. I will discuss this at length in a later chapter.

The founder of the Ramakrishna Order, Swami Vivekananda, was a Sudra by birth, that is, as a member of the lowest caste, forbidden the right (along with all women) to even hear the Vedic scriptures, let alone to study them. Even after his triumphant return from the West, protests were raised in certain orthodox quarters of his native Bengal as to his right to wear the ochre robes of a *saṃnyāsin.* And, disparaging comments as to the authenticity of the Order, and the validity of its lifestyle are heard even today, especially from mainline orthodox *saṃnyāsins* of the Sankara tradition, including the present four Sankaracaryas, inheritors of the four Maths said to have been established by Adi (the first) Sankaracarya himself.[5] However, the Ramakrishna Order is now well-established enough in its own right to command its own following, and to largely disregard outside criticism. After all, as they believe that they are followers of the most recent and fullest incarnation of God, then the comments of detractors need only be acknowledged as manifestations of Maya, to which individuals in this Kali Yuga are particularly prone. However, in recent years, even the most orthodox of exclusively Brahmin organisations have come to realise that if they wish to prosper, then it is advantageous if not essential to cultivate goodwill and patronage among the powerful and wealthy. For the most part these are non-Brahmins: industrial magnates, overseas Hindus and especially, 'foreigners'. The old system of bestowing gifts on Brahmins as an act of merit has fallen into disrepute in many parts of India, and indeed Brahmins are viewed with unmasked hostility by fellow Hindus in some regions, notably Tamil Nad and Karnataka.

The vows taken by *bramacārin(i)s* of the Ramakrishna Order do not prepare the initiate for the traditional *brahmacārya* period of study and worship, far from the cares of the mundane world, but rather plunge them deeper than ever into secular work and responsibilities, certainly not as contemplated by Ramakrishna. The lifestyle of members of the Ramakrishna Order was designed by Vivekananda, who believed that life should be a harmonious blending of four *yogas* (paths to Union) namely, *karma, bhakti, rāja* and *jnāna.* He enshrined this in the seal which he devised for the Order, which Yale describes thus:

> The seal shows a choppy lake with a pink lotus in the water, lighted by a rising sun and encircled by a snake. On the waves rides a white swan. Below is a band of Sanskrit lettering . . .[6]
>
> The rough water stands for karma yoga, for spiritual progress through unselfish work; the lotus for bhakti yoga, for development through love of God; and the rising sun for jnana yoga, for the practice of discrimination and knowledge. All are held together by raja yoga, concentration and meditation, which arouse the 'serpent' of spirituality. The swan in the centre symbolizes the Supreme Soul (1961:205).

The notion of monastic members indulging in work as a form of service to God through man, though known in Christian Orders, was new to Hinduism. For, the Hindu quest for realisation is essentially as I have already stated, a lonely one, as the spiritual seeker struggles to withdraw from and lessen outside influences and duties, in order to make the mind 'one-pointed'. *Karma yoga,* a path expounded in the *Bhagavad Gita* is recommended not for *saṃnyāsins,* but for householders, as a means of learning to perform their inescapable duties with dispassion. It does not recommend that those who have renounced society, and hence social duties, immediately assume new duties as a form of spiritual discipline, as Vivekananda advocates. Ramakrishna condemned such action when counselling members of the Brahmo Samaj who (it should be remembered) were householders not *saṃnyāsins.* Commenting on Sambhu Mallick, who wanted to establish 'hospitals, dispensaries and schools' as a form of service, he cautioned them:

> Don't go out of your way to look for such works. Undertake only those works that present themselves to you and are of pressing necessity. . . . It is not good to become involved in many activities. That makes one forget God. Coming to Kalighat temple, some, perhaps, spend their whole time in giving alms to the poor. They have no time to see the Mother in the inner shrine! (*Abridged Gospel*: 201.)

He also added that in the Kali Yuga, *karma yoga* was a very difficult path (*Abridged Gospel*:202), and recommended instead that devotees lessen their duties lest they forget God among too many activities. And, he said, 'I may think I am doing unselfish work, but it turns out to be selfish' (*Abridged Gospel*:201). So, he advised devotees to 'First realize God, see Him by means of spiritual discipline. If he imparts power, then you can do good to others, *otherwise not*[7] (*Abridged Gospel*:200).

However, Vivekananda's avowed aim in founding the Order was to create a band of *saṃnyāsin*-missionaries who would seek, along with their own salvation, to uplift Indian society through educational and philanthropic programmes. The means to realisation in the Ramakrishna Order is through work, performed in the spirit of *jiver seva Siver puja* (service to man is the worship of Siva) as Ramakrishna is reputed to have said. Despite the uneasiness of Vivekananda's brother disciples concerning this policy of working *saṃnyāsins*, inaugurated at the turn of the century, it later neatly fitted in with the aspirations of the emerging Nationalist Movement. *Saṃnyāsins* of the Order, having no caste affiliation to lose, readily undertook to work among the poor and diseased, gaining as much support from Gandhians[8] as condemnation from ultra conservative caste Hindus, who viewed the weakening of caste observance as a threat to their prestige and security. Today, the Mission's policy of assisting the 'weaker sections' of society, is once more being undermined through a subtle but complex change in prevailing middle class attitudes towards Vivekananda's doctrine of social uplift.

In post-Independent India, Government help given to the so-called Backward Communities has frequently been regarded by caste Hindus as at their expense. This, combined with the rise of militant unions among manual workers has generated hostility rather than compassion among many of the educated youth who, a generation ago, would have applauded any plan for the 'social uplift' of Backward Communities. In answer to my enquiry among monastic inmates of both Sarada Mandiram and the Trivandrum Mission branch of the Order, only one gave 'service' as among her motivations for seeking admission. Others regarded 'service' as synonymous with their daily duties, none of which they consciously viewed as linked with a master plan for the regeneration of India. Indeed, one of the original five *saṃnyāsinis*, formerly an avowed Gandhian, said to me in scathing tones, 'What is this *social work*, compared to a higher spiritual ideal?' It is probable that Ramakrishna would have agreed with her.

* * *

The new *brahmacārinis* usually stay two weeks or so at Sarada Math, before being transferred elsewhere. There is a reason for this. Each new 'batch' of trainees arrives just before Holy Mother's birthday, along with candidates for vows. This means that branch centres are short of workers for this important festival, while Sarada Math is overcrowded. Vivekananda's birthday follows three weeks after Holy Mother's, and most centres require initiates to have returned in time for this. Initiates bound for Kerala face two nights on the train before stopping briefly at Madras, from which it is a further overnight journey to Trichur. Depending on which train they catch, they may have time to visit Sarada Math Madras, but if not then an inmate will come to the station with a packet of cooked rice for their supper. When possible, monastic inmates avoid restaurant food, and carry their own supplies, which include drinking water, when travelling.

A *saṃnyāsini* will be waiting in Trichur station for the newly initiated *brahmacārinis* and, perhaps, *saṃnyāsinis*. Soon their taxi is sweeping up the driveway of Sarada Mandiram, stopping just before the temple. Those junior to the travellers run to pick up their dusty bedding and boxes, plus assorted baskets or cartons, which may contain either books for sale, cloth or other articles, as requested. The new arrivals, tired but triumphant, kick off their sandals, and enter the prayer hall to prostrate before the shrine. Even though their clothes are soiled and polluted by the long journey, still they must 'tell Ramakrishna and Holy Mother' that they have arrived safely, just as they do whenever leaving or arriving back at any Math or Mission premises. Then, they proceed to the President's room to prostrate before her also. After a few polite words about the journey, they will emerge in the Math courtyard, to be met by their juniors, eager to offer their *pranāms*, and their seniors, who stand with folded hands in return for the travellers' *pranāms*. All are eager for news from Sarada Math. In fact, the return from Headquarters was the only time I witnessed unmistakable excitement among the inmates of Sarada Mandiram.

The usual plan for arriving inmates is to bathe and change as soon as the initial greetings are over. Their belongings wait in the corridor, as they are too dirty to bring inside. Bedding will be unpacked and linen placed in a pile for washing. The cotton mattresses will be placed in the sun to air, along with pillows, groundsheets and blankets. Woollen garments will also be spread in the open, before storing with pieces of camphor. Any clothes for washing will be added to the pile of linen and, if hot water is available, they will be placed in a sturdy iron bucket of hot water, soap shavings and washing soda. This is all part of a well-rehearsed routine of managing polluting substances, for clothes are highly contaminated from the journey, and must be dealt with before bathing. Otherwise, the freshly-bathed person will become polluted once more, if garments or washing water come into contact with her clean clothes. As the traveller removes her soiled clothes before her bath, she thrusts them with a stick straight into the soapy bucket. She will have already placed clean clothes over the bathroom door. The laundry will not be further dealt with until evening, just before she changes for the evening prayers.

Bathing completed, the traveller now goes straight to the prayer hall, pausing on the way to take a pinch of sacred '*bhasmam*' (ashes) which she applies in a horizontal line to her forehead. Even though she has been away from Sarada Mandiram this becomes once more a reflex action.[9]

Later, after the morning worship is over, a round dot of mixed red and white sandalpaste, offered in the shrine, will be added. The first bath back in Kerala does not pass without comment, for despite the dank bathrooms with rickety taps and frequent need to draw water directly from the well, the water is clean and soft. In Calcutta the water from the tube wells is so hard that soap is next to useless, and the hair remains itchy and sticky.

After visiting the prayer hall, *pranāms* must now be hastily made to those seniors who were not available on arrival, for once the school bell sounds, there will be no chance to perform this most necessary act of obedience. If it is not yet time for breakfast, other *brahmacārinis* and junior *saṃnyāsinis* will come to see the new initiates in their room, and newcomers will hang back shyly, waiting to be introduced. Their room! When the Probationers left Trichur for training they would have been simply occupying space at night on whatever floor was available. Now a room has been made ready for the new *brahmacārinis*' use. At night a newcomer will sleep on the floor between their cots, but the cots are theirs, and the shelves recessed into the wall have some room for their few personal books, photos and *mālās* (rosaries). Newly arrived inmates from Calcutta will have also adopted the custom of carrying a small bottle of Ganges water with them, so that they can smear a drop or two on their right hand before touching their *mālā* in the prayer hall during meditation time. After some days the water will be exhausted, and the custom abandoned.

It was interesting to hear the conversation between Calcutta 'veterans'. The first question concerned the seniors of the Math: how were they? Then, about Trichur candidates who had completed a year of their training. What work were they doing? How was their health? How were the newly-arrived trainees when they saw them last? Then ensued a detailed conversation about which inmates were occupying which rooms, who had been transferred and where, and why so-and-so had not received vows that year. News of operations and illnesses followed, along with questions as to the progress of the new temple. When would it be finished? All this time, newcomers stood in the doorway, not able to participate in the conversation whilst seniors were talking. Later they would get a chance to ask about the Trichur trainees. Perhaps they had sent a scribbled note, on a page of notebook paper, via the *brahmacārinis.* Junior inmates do not usually write or post letters to anyone, except parents. At least, correspondence is frowned upon. But, notes do circulate between centres, by hand. From what I have seen the contents are all general and harmless, for they may pass via more than one hand, and no envelopes are available. Anyway, I doubt whether any inmate would be foolish enough to express anything controversial on paper. By the time breakfast is over, the excitement has died down, and the new *brahmacārinis* take their place in the small room off the rice kitchen, where vegetables are being cut. They select a knife, and join in . . .

Gradually Calcutta is pushed into the background. Only on special occasions, those who have been there valiantly try to sing Bengali *bhajans* or to make a Bengali food preparation. Those who can produce a Bengali book and *read* it are met with awe by newcomers. It does not take long though for the Calcutta-returned to wish they had a set of Kerala *mundu*, which is so much lighter, (both to wash and to wear) than a saree. But, some retain their Bengali hairstyle, just to remind others that they have *been to Calcutta.*

There are five more years to be spent within the Order before the possibility of *saṃnyāsa* being bestowed. As the training period is officially completed before the granting of *brahmacārya*, why are a further five years necessary? After returning from Calcutta, *brahmacārinis* perform much the same duties as before, except that they will seldom if ever be rostered for cleaning duty. They will however be expected to help with cleaning during menstrual periods, when shrine and kitchen work is not permitted, and work must be rearranged to find a replacement. Occasionally, when there is need to go to the station or bus stand in town, or to take a child to the village Dispensary, a *brahmacārini* may be entrusted with the task, after first having rehearsed the procedure, by going along with a senior on a few occasions previously. Though responsibility increases marginally with seniority, it is only permitted to the extent of the careful carrying out of simple and explicit instructions. Still, nothing is to be done on one's own initiative, and no opinions given. Being and Becoming involves the suppression of initiative, if indeed it was ever evident. Some of the Kerala inmates in particular had never been required to exercise initiative, had never handled money, nor ventured out alone.

Brahmacārinis do not attend the classes for newcomers. Whilst newcomers are at classes, *brahmacārinis* must be available for duties: someone must sit in the office at all times, in case of visitors arriving or the phone ringing. One monastic inmate must also remain in the kitchen-store area, in case the cooks require an ingredient, as all provisions are kept under lock and key. In addition, another inmate must be within call of the President, in case she needs someone to bring refreshments, take a message or to call someone.

During training at Sarada Math, all candidates for *brahmacārya* are taught the ritual *pūjā*, the worship of Ramakrishna. Those who have come from Mission centres may have already performed the simple offering of fruit, or evening *ārati*. However, in Math centres, where rice offerings are made, only those who have received *brahmacārya* are permitted to perform *pūjā*. In Mission centres, offerings approximate those made in the shrines of private homes, which today are made by virtually anybody who so desires, except those in a state of ritual impurity, such as occurs during mourning, menstruation or following childbirth. The *pūjā* performed in Math centres is more akin to that of temples, so that only those who have received Brahmin status may perform it. In the Ramakrishna Maths, any candidate who has received initiation as a Brahmin in youth can perform *pūjā*, even before *brahmacārya*. Although *brahmacārinis* perform *pūjā* at the Mission branch in Kerala, at Sarada Mandiram only junior *saṃnyāsinis* performed *pūjā* whilst I was there. I was told, however, by more than one monastic inmate that authorities at Sarada Math wished the Nambudiri *brahmacārini* to perform *pūjā* at Sarada Mandiram, but as she was in charge of the office, including accounts, she had not been given the responsibility of *pūjā*.

The reason for a further five years of candidature for *brahmacārinis* before *saṃnyāsa* can be granted is not then for more formal training, or the need to acquire new skills. It is rather the period of time deemed necessary for the candidate to distance herself from her previous environment, and to have truly become part of the Order. The chance of wanting to return home after ten years is remote: what family would welcome as a daughter-in-law one who has taken the vows of *brahmacārya*? As the years go by, despite perhaps internal conflict, *brahmacārinis* try harder than ever to endure whatever difficulties come their way, as the threat of failure is always before them. Even if a *brahmacārini* is unhappy in a particular centre, or with the duties allotted to her, she is constantly reminded that she is there to be *an instrument*, to have no will of her own, no opinions, to ask no questions. The easiest way, perhaps the only way, to be happy within the Order is to become as Ramakrishna said, like a leaf plate, blown by the wind, with no resistance. This takes time to learn.

During the years leading to *saṃnyāsa*, the Trustees will be informed of each candidate's progress. When any office bearers from Headquarters visit Trichur, they will observe each inmate carefully: how she performs her duties, whether she appears cheerful or sullen, and whether she is docile and obedient. Each will be called for 'a few words', and each will be discussed at length with the Head of the Centre.

As the fifth anniversary of her *brahmacārya* draws near, if everything is satisfactory, the Head of Centre will submit the candidate's name to the Trustees for *saṃnyāsa* during the coming birthday of Holy Mother. Once again, ill health or problems of personality or behaviour may postpone the candidature even further, much to the candidate's shame. Now, along with candidates for Probation, another medical examination is arranged. If this is satisfactory, the *brahmacārini* is called by the Head of the Centre, to start making preparations for Calcutta.

Saṃnyāsa

As soon as the train reservations are made, the candidate for *saṃnyāsa* begins her preparations. Once again, new clothes are stitched for the ceremony, and the local President will give her at least one new saree, this time with a very narrow border, and shawl. She will once again borrow warm clothes and the usual mosquito net. Early in December, she will depart for Calcutta, along with two or three new trainees, carrying the customary gifts of homemade produce from the Trichur President to be presented at Headquarters. Shortly before departure it is customary to visit parents to receive their blessings, for after *saṃnyāsa*, the tie between parents and daughter will no longer officially exist. On the day of departure, she will be permitted to visit the Asrama opposite to seek the blessings of the President, after prostrating before the image of Ramakrishna in the shrine. That evening, the taxi pulls up before the Sarada Mandiram temple, and the travellers make their final *pranāms* to their seniors, and receive those of their juniors. The boot is piled with boxes and bedding and, with the escort of the *saṃnyāsini* from the town Hostel, they depart, to the cry of '*Jai Sri Guru Maharajji ki jai, jai Mahamayi ki jai, jai Swamiji Maharajji ki jai! Durga, Durga!*'[10]

used throughout the Order. This is echoed by the other monastic inmates, who have gathered in the courtyard for the departure.

At Sarada Math, arrangements are similar to those before *brahmacārya*. There are *mantras* to be copied and learned, and candidates are kept in semi-seclusion in a block of rooms. Once again, I have to rely largely on Yale's account of the actual ceremonies connected with *saṃnyāsa*, as *saṃnyāsinis* were most reluctant to discuss any part of the proceedings, or even peripheral events which led up to the day of the ceremony. As is the case with all forms of initiation within the Ramakrishna Order, details are not disclosed to non-initiates. Yale's book was published outside the Order, before he became a *saṃnyāsin*.

Three days before the ceremony, candidates are helped to dye their clothes with the sacred *gerua* (ochre) powder, used by many ascetics in India. The Trichur candidates will already be experts at this, as they will have helped to dye the clothes of seniors on many occasions. Clothes are soaked in boiling soapy water, and redyed after every menstrual period during which they were worn. The soft *gerua* clay is powdered on a grinding stone with a little water and the resulting paste added gradually to a bucket with water, until the right colour is obtained. The dye is then left to settle, and then strained before use.[11] White clothes are then dipped in the dye, making sure no streaks or dark patches occur. For this reason, new clothes are washed once before dyeing, to make them more absorbent. The clothes are then spread on lines to dry, and carefully pulled into shape and folded. After *saṃnyāsa*, any sarees with wide borders possessed by candidates are given to juniors, as well as the clothes worn during the pre-*saṃnyāsa* ceremonies. *Brahmacārinis* consider it a great honour to receive clothes from those about to embrace *saṃnyāsa*.

Three days before Holy Mother's birthday, a barber visits Sarada Math and shaves the head of candidates for *saṃnyāsa*. The number of candidates in recent years is between three and five. The candidates now appear at meals with their heads covered with their shawls, to hide their tufts, which will be removed during *saṃnyāsa*. On the day prior to Holy Mother's birthday, a secular priest comes to the Math to help the candidates perform *śrāddha* or funeral offerings, for seven generations of ancestors, their parents, and themselves. If their parents are still alive they pray that the offerings be kept and handed over at the proper time in their name. After their own *śrāddha*, they have relinquished their present birth, and remain as ghosts, until their rebirth as a *saṃnyāsini*. The candidates now appear only for meals and meditation, subdued and aloof. On the eve of *saṃnyāsa,* they are supposed to fast, but any candidate who is less than robust will be pressed by seniors to take a little of the fruit offerings.

Holy Mother's birthday commences at dawn, but it is not until the next morning before dawn that the vows of *saṃnyāsa* are administered. The candidates bathe in the Ganges at 2.30 a.m., before changing into their new *gerua* clothes. This is a concession to female 'modesty'. At Belur Math the candidates approach their *guru* naked. They then enter the prayer hall, where senior *saṃnyāsinis* are assembled before the area marked out for the *homa* fire. The *homa* for *saṃnyāsa* is known as *viraja,* and with preliminary purificatory rites, this is now kindled.

Of the actual ceremony of *saṃnyāsa,* Yale says:

> It is a ritual, essentially, of disowning forever matter's false illusions, and espousing Spirit as the one true ingredient of man and nature. For example, here is a typical affirmation:
>
> Om. Oblations to the Supreme Self.
> May my skin, flesh, blood, bones, fat, marrow,
> and nerves be purified.
> Free from ignorance, the root of all evil,
> may I realize myself as the Light
> of Pure Consciousness,
> the self-luminous Brahman.
>
> Thus the body, mind and senses are purified, one's ego is surrendered, one's mind relieved of all impressions of past deeds, thoughts, and limiting memories, by the enunciation again and again of: 'I am the Atman, the non-dual Brahman, pure and free'.
>
> Now the candidate proceeds to the *sannyasa* guru, prostrating himself before him.
>
> The guru cuts the tuft of hair. This, along with his sacred thread, the man consigns to the flames, signifying his severance from caste, sex and society. The guru then hands the candidate the ochre cloth. He gives him his name and teaches him the secret mantras known only to monks, by which any *sannyasin* of any order can identify any other as ordained and genuine. The man dresses himself in the clothes of renunciation. Last of all he burns in the fire, with all that is holy as his witness, his desire for enjoyment of life here and hereafter – all cravings for wealth, for progeny, and for name and fame. . . . The man utters the sacred

> promises attesting that no living being need ever in future have anything to fear from him, avowing all living creatures to be extensions of himself. Thus the ceremony, which really turns a mortal into a God, ends. Through utter renunciation of humanness one has gained immortality (1961:204–5).

Candidates for *saṃnyāsa* at Sarada Math undergo a similar ceremony, including the severing of the tuft, leaving the head clean shaven.[12] However, I do not know whether candidates are supplied with sacred threads before the ceremony, in order to be able to cast them into the sacred fire.

Yale's opinion that the burning of the tuft and thread signify 'severance from caste, sex and society' is, in my opinion, open to dispute. I believe this is ensured before the *saṃnyāsa* ceremony when, during the *śrāddha* the candidate surrenders his or her present birth, and becomes a ghost, awaiting rebirth. The ghost brings with it all the impressions of its previous birth, including the desire to be reborn as a *saṃnyāsin(i)* but *not* its former caste, sex or social status. Moreover, I do not agree that *saṃnyāsa* 'turns a mortal into a God', and dismiss this as a flight of poetry on Yale's part: not the only example of hyperbole in his book, incidentally. For, the *mantras* accompanying the *saṃnyāsa* oblations express only: 'a longing on the part of the aspirant to become divine – by freeing himself from all blemishes of body and mind'[13] (*Mahanarayan-opanisad* Section 65:1–5). They clearly do not *transform* the candidate into a God at all.

The English verb 'renounce',[14] used in connection with *saṃnyāsa* I believe is misleading in a subtle way. No *saṃnyāsin* actually 'renounces' his family, in the sense that he or she formally denies or repudiates a former kinship connection. At no time in any part of the ceremonies does this occur. In particular, the suggestion that a pious Hindu would renounce a mother is highly questionable, so valued and sacred is the bond between mother and child, especially mother and son. In fact, what alters this relationship is *death*, which occurs during the candidate's *śrāddha* ceremony. In the new birth, as a *saṃnyāsin(i)* the candidate is reborn as the child of the officiating *guru*, taking on his or her spiritual lineage, rather than a biological one. When the guru dies, the *saṃnyāsin(i)* observes mourning, as I have myself witnessed at Sarada Math on the death of the first President. Moreover, as Yale remarks, legally as well as socially, a *saṃnyāsin* in India is not regarded as related to his (former) parents, wife or children (1961:204), and has no claim on them or their property, even if he should later return to the lay world. This further reinforces my conviction that *saṃnyāsa* should be understood as a new birth (in the Hindu understanding of rebirth) and not merely a change of social status.

I was interested to find that some members of the public who are acquainted with the *saṃnyāsinis* of Sarada Math believe that they are not completely women, even though they have female bodies. In particular, I found some who did not believe that they menstruated, even if they had not reached the apparent age of menopause. One *saṃnyāsini,* a well-known speaker, found it so difficult to have to refuse religious honours in devotees' homes or public venues, that she had her ovaries removed, during surgery for a totally unrelated condition! Sometimes, however, *saṃnyāsinis* choose simply not to disclose their unclean condition to the laity, especially when in another town for a visit, and devotees (without enquiring first) arrange to take them to visit the local temple. The rationale for this behaviour, is that it is *clothes* that are polluted by menstruation, by their contact with blood, as would be the case with any sore or wound. However, the sacred *gerua* cloth is immune from pollution, so the point does not apply. The wearer of *gerua* is always pure.[15]

There is another curious ambiguity surrounding the *saṃnyāsinis* of the Ramakrishna Order. Are they to be permitted, as are Hindu holy men, to move freely in society, being bound neither by family nor communal constraints? Or, as holy women, must they be even more protected and circumspect in their behaviour than female householders, lest their modesty and chastity be called to question?

Ohja has noted in her study of the few female ascetics residing in the holy city of Varanasi that they generally live in a community or are settled in a house (1981:266), unlike the traditional *saṃnyāsin,* who is free to wander from one place of pilgrimage to the next.[16] Moreover, the ascetics whom she met were not members of the Dasanami Order, and for the most part followed sects which allowed women to adopt an ascetic way of life. These women were, however, mainly either simply living a pious life (as do many orthodox Brahmin widows), or had only taken the equivalent vows of *brahmacārya,* not *saṃnyāsa.* As Ohja discovered, these women were not at all happy to discuss the legitimacy of their choice of lifestyle, for even if they were not formally initiated into *saṃnyāsa,* they were still living away from male custody, a situation very much condemned by the orthodox.

Members of Sarada Math have no doubts as to the legitimacy of their lifestyle, since Vivekananda was chosen by Ramakrishna,

Incarnation of God, to found their Math. They believe that they have a particular mission to uplift Hindu women. As Vivekananda stated, 'They [women] must be put in a position to solve their own problems in their own way' (*CW* Vol.V:229). In this context, the opinions of other religious movements or of lay people, opposed to their existence, do not really count. They have a mandate from the Lord Himself to carry out his work.

In addition to the Rules, which apply to the whole Order, members of Sarada Math are very aware of the personality of Holy Mother, who stressed the 'feminine' virtues of modesty, docility, chastity and domesticity. The members of Sarada Math do not disguise the fact that they are female. Rather, they have found it to their advantage to stress their female attributes. Since the mid-1970s they have increasingly discarded the oral use of the title *Pravrajika* (ascetic) encouraging junior monastic inmates and devotees to call them 'Mataji' or Revered Mother instead. There is a profound reason for this, as I shall endeavour to explain.

Sādhana or intense spiritual practices are centred on *tapas* or austerities. *Tapa* literally means 'heat', and this heat is generated by the building up of energy within the body of the *sādhaka* (spiritual aspirant). *Brahmacārya,* or the observance of chastity is the key to *tapas.* It is based not merely on the abstention from sexual intercourse, but from the positive strength derived from the retention of semen. An ejaculation of semen (even if involuntary) depletes the bodily store of energy. A *sādhaka* become virile by *storing up* semen, which is then consumed in the internal fire of *tapas,* giving the *sādhaka* great psychic and other powers, a special bodily lustre, and great beauty. According to *yoga* practice, a *sādhaka* who can prevent semen from leaving its storehouse in the brain, and journeying downwards through the central canal (*suṣumṇa*), to be finally ejaculated, is a *yogi,* a person of high spiritual attainment. *Yoga* practice even prescribes ways in which ejaculated semen can be once more drawn up through the penis, and some are said to have mastered this art, by practising with water or milk.

The *yogi* has learned to arouse the *kuṇḍalinī,* the curled up snake, depicted as female, which resides in the genital area. This *kuṇḍalinī* is forced up through meditation, driving the seminal fluid upwards, in its path. When *kuṇḍalinī* reaches the brain, she embraces the deity residing there causing their union (for a fuller account, see Cantlie 1977). The ecstasy experienced by the *yogi* is 'the pleasure of psychic intercourse' (Cantlie 1977:254), during which *kuṇḍalinī* drinks the nectar (semen) of her Lord. The person who has experienced this ecstatic union is henceforth described as a 'realised soul', that is, one who has personally witnessed the union of the god and goddess, or the Cosmic Mind with the Cosmic Body. Such a person has attained the goal of life: he will not be reborn.

A senior *saṃnyāsin* told me that a man who practises unbroken *brahmacārya* for twelve years, develops a special nerve in the central canal, known as *medha.* It is this which gives the *saṃnyāsin* his power, for *medha* allows a man to have super knowledge and intelligence. The man is known as an *urdhvaretha,* or one who keeps his seed drawn up. It is thus curious that a *saṃnyāsini* of the Ramakrishna Order has Medha as the first part of her name, since it cannot be possible for *medha* (according to the *saṃnyāsin*'s definition) to be developed by a woman.

Here we come to the main problem associated with the *yoga* concept of realisation. It very obviously only applies to males. Women possess no store of semen, no penis through which it flows. Since asceticism through *yoga* was a male ideology, there is no provision for women to attain liberation through this means. Nor for that matter, can those of lowly birth, as they are considered lacking the self control to make this possible. Therefore, even if a woman manages through unorthodox means to become an ascetic, even a *saṃnyāsini,* what method of realisation is open to her?

For those denied the right to Vedic knowledge, various *bhakti* (devotional) sects of Hinduism offered an alternative path to realisation. Religious exercises designed to foster an intense love of a personal deity are considered sufficient for realisation, and many *bhakti* sects welcome devotees who are not twice born, and also women, as full participants in their activities. The *śakti* cult devoted to the Goddess Kali in her various manifestations can be approached from a *bhakti* point of view, as was demonstrated by Ramakrishna, during periods of intense devotion to Kali as the Divine Mother, manifest as Sakti. Kali is worshipped though, according to Tantrik rites.

Saṃnyāsinis of Sarada Math seldom speak in terms of *kuṇḍalinī,* but frequently stress in classes and lectures that women should realise that they are all no less than '*śakti swarupini*': Sakti herself. But, society tells you that you are weak and dependent. If you believe that, that is what you will be. Women forget that Sakti (including *kuṇḍalinī*) is female. The Cosmic Mind is male, but the power without which it cannot be activated, is female. Without Sakti, there is no creation, no universe.

Woman is Sakti, but Sakti is also Maya, the world bewitcher, which hides the Truth behind her veil of illusion. Women are ensnared by

Maya as are men, but if they can overcome her, and tear away the veil they will behold the Reality, and realise Sakti as their own true nature. A woman who has realised herself as Sakti is all powerful. The powers of a woman with this realisation are awesome, according to a senior *saṃnyāsin*, one thousand times that of a realised man. In the final analysis, though, members of Sarada Math believe that realization can be achieved *either* through devotion (to Ramakrishna – Sarada Devi) or through Advaitic discrimination. This follows the teachings of the *Bhagavad Gita* highlighted by Swami Vivekananda.

* * *

Thus, while Being and Becoming for the candidate for *saṃnyāsa* centres on the need to learn obedience, and a gradual modification of behaviour, the result of ten years of 'simply living the life' is that an individual is readily recognisable as a member of the Ramakrishna Order. Her dress, speech, attitudes, and the whole rhythm of her life may be in harmony with other monastic inmates. The process of rounding off any rough edges will by now be as complete as it will ever be. Though the monastic inmates of Sarada Math exhibit conformity to set patterns of behaviour, certain aspects of their personality are not stifled by their seniors. The very active individual will be appreciated for her enthusiasm in work, but may be cautioned not to neglect formal spiritual practices, while those of a meditative nature may be reminded that whilst this is commendable, somebody must do the work. Those with professional qualifications may be able to use them, though some may be transferred to a Math centre from time to time to 'charge their spiritual batteries'. Monastic inmates may remain basically introverted or extroverted, mainly neat or scruffy, mainly urban or rustic. But, each must have learned to obey all those senior to her, in order to survive.

Saṃnyāsa does not bestow on members of Sarada Math the freedom which is celebrated in Vivekananda's poem 'The Song of the Samnyasin': the ability to wander freely over the face of the land, unbound by any social conventions, sleeping anywhere, eating whatever chance may bring. After *saṃnyāsa*, members are even more careful than ever to preserve the good name of their Order by 'setting an example' by their behaviour. It is thus not permissible for a *saṃnyāsini* to travel alone, except in the direst of necessity, to mix with *saṃnyāsins* (including those of the Order), except those of great seniority, nor to be seen in the company of unaccompanied males. The President of Sarada Mandiram told me that if members fall short of public expectations then they should be prepared to hear criticism. They must set up a model of behaviour for other women to follow.

It should be remembered that Sarada Devi is the role model for *saṃnyāsinis* of Sarada Math, and she was at once celibate and the Mother figure for the *saṃnyāsins* of the Order. *Saṃnyāsinis* in the last decade are increasingly stressing this aspect of their life, discarding for all but official purposes the title of *Pravrajika* (Ascetic) for *Mataji* (Mother). They appear to devotees as maternal in their attitudes, plying devotees with food, comforting them in their sorrows, greeting them with affection. Their Maths are essentially homely: well decorated to the point of being frankly pretty, and from underneath many a *gerua* saree can be seen dainty sandals, not very durable, but definitely feminine. Though their shaven heads declare them to share the sad, celibate and often barren state of high caste Hindu widows, their title stresses that *saṃnyāsa* has bestowed on them spiritual motherhood of the devotees. They follow the example of their founder, Sarada Devi, incarnation of Sakti, and wife of the greatest incarnation of God, Ramakrishna.

The *saṃnyāsinis* of Sarada Math see themselves as combining the spiritual qualities of ascetics, with the power of Sakti and the compassion of Mother. Thus they are much sought after, especially in those regions of India, such as Bengal and Kerala in which Sakti worship is particularly prevalent.

Ohja has pointed out that the majority of female ascetics in Varanasi are Bengali, and associates this partly to the great veneration of Sakti in that state (1981:267–8). While it may be true that women more readily identify themselves with Sakti in Bengali, Ohja also mentions 'favourable' circumstances there which eased the way for females to take up asceticism as a way of life. I believe that it is more likely that the *unfavourable* circumstances experienced by caste Hindu women in many a Bengali joint family are possibly a high contributing factor in the flight of women to Varanasi. Though Sakti worship is widespread in Kerala, until the recent abolition of the *taravād*, women there enjoyed a high degree of security. Apart from the specific example of the Ramakrishna Order in Kerala, very few women have taken to an ascetic lifestyle, even today. The very existence of Sarada Mandiram and the Mission branch of the Order in Trivandrum, I suggest, is a direct response to the rapidly changing social structure in Kerala, with an adverse effect on certain well defined categories of Hindu women.

But, while Kerala Christian families, long plagued by the problem of dowry, have frequently offered one or more daughters to become brides of Christ, so that they are ensured an escape from a life of poverty, for Nayar families in particular, the threat of a daughter entering a Math is regarded as shameful. The Nayar or Izhava father of this generation is responsible for the education and marriage of his daughters, and his prestige largely depends on his ability to secure 'good' husbands. But, if a girl approaching marriageable age realises that she is unlikely to secure a satisfactory match, or that this was the case with her parents, she may well panic and try to find a way out. If she knows of Sarada Mandiram she may end up there. Perhaps only one in five or less candidates in Kerala succeeds in remaining within the Order and is granted *saṃnyāsa*, but those who do, *can* expect lifelong security. As the years go by, and young *saṃnyāsinis* hear news of former relatives and friends, of separation and divorce, alcoholism, unemployment and ill health, few would have cause for regret. And, moreover, even those parents who were most hostile initially to their daughter's vocation, sooner or later admit that she has chosen the one path in which her needs will be met, even in old age.

Chapter 9

Hierarchy and Rank

In this and the following chapter I would like to examine the principles of hierarchy and purity within Sarada Mandiram. This is a particularly interesting topic, as generally *saṃnyāsa* is understood as a state in which the usual constraints of hierarchy and purity (applicable to Hindu householders) do not apply.

Dumont (1970) regards caste as the basic organising principle of Hindu society, a statement unlikely to cause disagreement, but he also stresses that caste is based on the pure/impure dichotomy, which seals of caste groups at their various levels. The 'renouncer' as Dumont calls ascetics, cannot be placed within the caste/hierarchy system, and so becomes a paradox: an 'individual-outside-the-world' (1970:46). Renouncers exist 'outside the caste system' (1970:231) in contradiction to it (1970:230). Renouncers do not participate in *saṃsāra,* the social world.

Although the monastic inmates of Sarada Mandiram should then after *saṃnyāsa* rightly be classed as individuals outside the caste/ hierarchy system, in fact as well shall see, the Institution operates on rigid lines of hierarchy, which encompass not only the monastic inmates, but their relations with non inmates. The Sarada Mandiram rules of hierarchy (though unwritten) place the Institution squarely at an identifiable level within Kerala Hindu society. By examining the workings of hierarchy and hierarchical notions of purity within Sarada Mandiram I shall aim at a deeper grasp of the principles of communal ranking in Kerala. I shall also suggest an alternative to Dumont's understanding of pure/impure as a series of dichotomies, when applied to hierarchy.

The first point to bear in mind when discussing hierarchy within Sarada Mandiram is that not all monastic inmates are devoid of communal affiliation. Only those who have taken *saṃnyāsa* are officially 'casteless', and it may be said that the Ramakrishna Order has a highly ambivalent attitude towards caste observance. Whilst on one hand, candidates for monasticism are accepted regardless of their communal background, on the other, the training which candidates receive culminates after five years in their becoming Brahmins. In other words, all candidates must become Brahmins before they are admitted to the ranks of *saṃnyāsa.*

Moreover, as I have already stated, whilst some Mission centres allow all senior Probationers to perform the daily offerings, in Math centres only *brahmacārinis* (i.e. those who have been made Brahmins) may do so. And, as far as I can ascertain, those who are chosen to perform worship at Sarada Math are actually of Brahmin parentage. In Sarada Math, all the cooks in the main kitchen are lay Brahmin women, although breakfast and afternoon tea, prepared in the 'tiffin' kitchen, are prepared by monastic trainees. No offerings are prepared in the tiffin kitchen, so while Ramakrishna's meals are fully prepared by Brahmins, all monastic inmates, no matter how orthodox their backgrounds, have to eat food prepared by their non Brahmin fellow inmates. I was told by a monastic inmate that in 1972, during a visit to Sarada Mandiram by the first President of Sarada Math, after meeting the kitchen staff, she enquired, 'the cooks are all Brahmins, aren't they?' The question caught all the seniors off guard, and they replied that they were all initiated devotees of Ramakrishna. In fact, at the time one cook was a Harijan and one an Izhava. It would not be possible to find a Brahmin woman who would be prepared to cook in the kitchen of an Institution entirely run by non Brahmins. Indeed, on special occasions, such as the opening of the temple, a team of Brahmin cooks is hired, but they bring with them all their own equipment, and cook in the open, in the school compound.

There is no doubt that the prestige of Sarada Mandiram would be enhanced (even in the eyes of devotees) if Brahmins regularly prepared the food and performed the ritual worship. Twice since the temple was constructed, South Indian *saṃnyāsinis* of Brahmin origin trained by the order in the performance of ritual worship were sent to Sarada Mandiram to take over the responsibility of the daily *pūjā.* Whilst the seniors of Sarada Math would prefer a Brahmin to take charge of the temple (since only they have the proper '*saṃskāras*' or tendencies carried over from the previous birth), for the seniors of Sarada Mandiram, the reason is different.

The illustrious royal and aristocratic *taravāds* of Kerala, were distinguished from those of lesser stature by their ability to secure the service of Brahmins, both to enter into *sambandham* with their women, and to act as cooks and priests in their kitchens and temples. Even today, there are elderly aristocratic women who declare that they only eat food prepared by Brahmins, and thus refuse to eat in the modern homes of their own children. Some devotees would prefer the food at Sarada Mandiram to be prepared by Brahmins, but since the main meal of the day is offered to Ramakrishna, even the orthodox accept it, as *prasād*. Orthodox Brahmins and other high ranking individuals who are not devotees of Ramakrishna would not be offered a meal at Sarada Mandiram, and so far there has been no problem of the rejection of food on these grounds.

Among monastic inmates at Sarada Mandiram, community is rarely mentioned, although those from Kerala are well aware of the communal affiliations of their fellows. They have very little idea as to which communities the Karnataka candidates belong. In response to my enquiries, not one Kerala candidate correctly identified the Brahmins among the Karnataka candidates, and the Karnataka candidates assumed that the Kerala candidates were Nayars. While lowliness of birth is a sensitive topic at Sarada Mandiram, appreciative mention is made of those who are of 'good families' on appropriate occasions. Any monastic inmate who has a well connected relative enjoys extra prestige, both with seniors and devotees, and gossip of well known Kerala families is a favourite pastime.

Every *taravād* in Kerala held a well-defined rank vis-a-vis other *taravāds* in the region, and Sarada Mandiram, established during the time when the power of *taravāds* was still intact, early on established its own place among the local hierarchy. The local Asrama President who built Sarada Mandiram, constructed it in the style used in *taravāds* of wealth and renown. The monastic inmates 'at home' wear the *mundu* and *vesti* favoured by women of good families, and the food served at meals is that enjoyed in families of high rank. For example, certain preparations using buttermilk suggest families in which the cooks were traditionally Brahmin. *Taravāds* which formed *sambandham* with Nambudiris were strictly vegetarian, as is Sarada Mandiram, whilst lesser ranking *taravāds* were not. The major Kerala festivals are celebrated even today as far as possible as they were in the heyday of the *taravād*. Feasts are lavish, and ritual articles, long condemned to attics and storerooms in disused *taravāds*, are still in use, polished bright by a team of monastic inmates, instead of by the customary servants. Throughout Kerala, members of the 'old' *taravāds* have lost their land-based wealth, and have scattered. The older generation has no alternative but to watch the family homes crumble and decay, as without the income from their former lands, maintenance is impossible. It is the older women in particular, from these once proud families, who look on Sarada Mandiram as the last vestige of Kerala culture and tradition.[1] It is its adherence to 'our' values that enabled Sarada Mandiram to enjoy the confidence of women of the 'old' families, and made it a popular choice when they were seeking a boarding school for their daughters or grand daughters, or a cause to support. The situation is changing, however, with the gradual demise of the last of the *taravād*-born. The mothers of today's boarders at Sarada Mandiram have most likely been raised in a small family unit, and are far more interested in tomorrow's trends than yesterday's lifestyle.

It is its adherence to 'good family' Nayar values which makes it difficult for those of lowlier birth to identify with or feel at ease at Sarada Mandiram. And, there are some of the so-called 'good families' who actually resent the Institution as a hotchpotch of undistinguished women who are trying to create the illusion that they themselves are of good families, making themselves ridiculous in the process. Despite the view of this minority, those who know Sarada Mandiram identify it with an adherence to conservative 'old' Nayar values, even though the Institution is far from Nayar dominated at the present time.

Ranking within Sarada Mandiram

Dumont stresses that caste is firmly based on the belief of the superiority of the pure over the impure. Hierarchy occurs because 'the pure and the impure must be kept separate' (1970:81). This view of hierarchy, as based on a graded series of dichotomies, I find gives a false view of the nature of caste interaction, in a subtle but important manner. I would like to approach the subject of hierarchy not as a series of oppositions, but from the point of view of the individual in his or her interactions with other individuals.

Hierarchy is the most important organising principle within the Ramakrishna Order, but it is based on monastic seniority, rather than communal status. In this respect it fits well with the traditional Nayar notions of internal *taravād* ranking, wherein respect should be given to all elders, and received from all juniors. The main *taravād* house, which in the case of 'old' families was likely to be a massive *nalekettu*, was entirely occupied by women and their children, the men sharing a barrack-like building to one side. The oldest female member of the *taravād* was accorded great respect, and it was she who communicated and negotiated the women's needs with the *kāraṇavan*. However, for all the women, the *kāraṇavan* remained a distant figure, held in great awe.

Until 1968, the President of the local Ramakrishna Asrama opposite, was also in charge of Sarada Mandiram, and it was the seniormost *saṃnyāsini* who had to approach him for advice, supplies and assistance. As was the case in the *taravād*, the women ran their own day to day routine, and a *kāristhan*, or manager (a male who has not a *taravād* member) who served as an accountant and advisor, kept the *kāraṇavan* informed as to what was happening among the women, the servants, tenants and other personnel connected with the *taravād*. In a similar manner, a *kāristhan*-like figure, a male in employment of the Asrama used to visit Sarada Mandiram, to keep the account books, check orders for supplies, inspect projects and generally keep an eye on the Institution, so that he could report back to the President. In true *kāristhan* style, he also conveyed gossip between the two Institutions, adding any information he had gleaned from other sources, including from the labourers as they went about their work.

The President of the Asrama at that time was the son of a Prince and a Nayar mother, and was every bit the *kāraṇavan* figure. Tall and austere, of fair complexion and distinguished in bearing, he dominated the entire village. On festivals he presented cloth to all the inmates of the two Institutions and their workers, all of whom lined up to prostrate before him. On government election days, he 'opened' the ballot box by casting the first vote, even though the majority of villagers voted for a Marxist candidate.[2] Like the *kāraṇavan* of old, his signature held the corporate property, on behalf of all the members. Though none could claim a share, each member was entitled to maintenance for life. In this case, the *taravād* 'members' were the monastic inmates of the two Institutions. Discipline was also meted out by the *kāraṇavan*, and it was in this capacity that often he was the most feared person in the hamlet or village. The President of the Asrama likewise kept a close watch on the inmates of Sarada Mandiram, and was a severe disciplinarian.

After Sarada Mandiram became independent of the Asrama in 1968, ties with it gradually lessened. The Asrama ceded 6 hectares to Sarada Mandiram, and a senior *saṃnyāsini* became a President in her own right. This process was similar to the dividing of a *taravād* which had grown unwieldly, into *tāvazhi*. This could occur by mutual agreement, when a senior woman and her descendants were provided with their 'share' of the property, and permitted to build a separate *taravād*. Sometimes a ceremony of severance took place, when the new *tāvazhi* no longer wanted to be bound by observance of all the ritual obligations required of members of the parent *taravād*, in addition to their own. The completion of the Sarada Mandiram temple, with the performance of elaborate daily *pūjā*, and the separate observance of festivals, marks the effective watershed in Sarada Mandiram-Asrama relations. Nevertheless, a close bond remained between the two Institutions until 1975, the year in which the venerable President of the Asrama passed away. The new President was roughly the same age as the President of Sarada Mandiram, and the relationship between them was more one of equals, who confer on matters of mutual interest, rather than the former situation of Sarada Mandiram's total dependence on the advice, support and counsel of the previous incumbent. The President of Sarada Mandiram is now very much a *kāraṇavan* figure, probably more so than the President of the Asrama. The appointment of a female to the position of *kāraṇavan* was not unknown, in *taravāds* with no surviving male member. And, according to an informant from such a *taravād*, a female in this position exercised a great deal of power.

In keeping with the *taravād* model, monastic members of Sarada Mandiram all rank downwards from the President, the criterion of ranking being relative age. However, age at Sarada Mandiram derives not from date of birth, but from the date of arrival as a monastic candidate. Relative rank is expressed at Sarada Mandiram through a system which ensures that there is no concept of peers: only seniors and juniors. Each monastic inmate must call all those who arrived before her '*chechi*' (elder sister) if they still wear white garments, and 'Mataji' (revered Mother) if they wear the ochre of those who have taken *saṃnyāsa*. This is similar to the *taravād* in which all elders of one's own generation were called 'elder brother/sister', and all those of one's mother's generation by titles incorporating the word '*amma*' (mother). All one's juniors within the *taravād* were called simply by name, as were all those of inferior communal status[3] regardless of their age. Individuals of higher communal status were called in turn by respectful titles, regardless of their age. In order to establish a workable system of nomenclature, the original monastic inmates had to assign to themselves (or be assigned) a position in the communal hierarchy, so that consistency was used in dealing with each other and outsiders.

It was the President of the Asrama at the time who set the pattern of address terms, when he first opened the Hostel for Harijan girls. From the beginning, inmates called their elders '*chechi*', and eventually the Warden also was known to all by this title. Later, as caste Hindu girls began to seek admission, they too accepted this form of address. In its relations with outside Hindus (such as devotees) the monastic inmates adopted an interesting course. They called Nayars only by title if they were older, and by name if they were younger. All people of below Nayar rank were called by name, regardless of age, if they were in manual occupations. All those of higher than Nayar rank (including the aristocracy) were called by title. And, gradually as Hindus of Backward Communities (Izhavas in particular) gained middle class status, the monastic inmates began to follow the pattern adopted in most educated or middle class circles. Those who were elder were called 'Mr' or 'Mrs' plus the husband's name, or in the rare cases of an older single woman, 'Miss' plus her own name. Those who were not quite middle class were generally called '*chechi*' or its male equivalent, '*chetan*'. This was especially the case for parents of Backward Community monastic members, and quite a step forward for those (generally Nayars) who would never before have called a person of inferior communal status by a kinship term.

The point I am trying to make by giving illustrations of nomenclature, is that Sarada Mandiram established by this means a rank among Nayar *taravāds* of repute. This was further emphasised by the habit of senior inmates calling elderly Nayar men and women of 'old' families closely associated with the Institution, by the titles 'aunt' or 'uncle', thereby further implying that they could be related to members of such proud lineages. Those of aristocratic background, royal houses or clearly superior communities (such as Nambudiris) monastic inmates proudly call by their titles, demonstrating thereby that they do indeed interact with such illustrious persons. This behaviour is very striking, as in the days of *sambandham*, much of a *taravād*'s glory was in how many relationships and connections it had with those of high rank.

Though manual labourers are all called by name by monastic inmates of Sarada Mandiram, the President does not permit the curt form of verb to be used in addressing them. Though this habit is still prevalent in the wider society, workers at Sarada Mandiram soon become used to the extra courtesy accorded them. I witnessed on one occasion when a visiting *saṃnyāsini* attempted to call one of the Nayar cooks from the kitchen, by saying '*va*', which means 'come here'. In her own language (Tamil) this is acceptable, but in Malayalam, the language of Kerala, this is a verb form reserved for inferiors. The more polite *varu* is used in Sarada Mandiram. It so happened that the *saṃnyāsini* was of Brahmin origin, as the cook knew, and so she was highly offended. She reacted by henceforth being most unco-operative towards the *saṃnyāsini*. The *saṃnyāsini* did not realize the question of insult had arisen.

Monastic inmates from Kerala are very quick to pick up the customs of nomenclature at Sarada Mandiram, just as they would have been required to do if they had entered the outside workforce. However, Karnataka candidates are unfamiliar with the subtleties of rank in Kerala, sometimes with embarrassing results. A reasonably new Karnataka candidate had recently been appointed to the position of assistant storekeeper, when a *saṃnyāsini's* sister (whose two daughters are monastic inmates) came to stay for a few days. I noticed that other inmates referred to her obliquely as 'Leela's mother', and in addressing her directly, as '*chechi*', though she was of advanced age. This was entirely lost on the new storekeeper who up to the present, had heard all visitors invited to sit at the senior dining table addressed by the title *amma*. So, in serving the relative during her first meal at Sarada Mandiram she continuously addressed her in this way. The woman was obviously highly embarrassed by the newcomer's behaviour, since she was in fact an Izhava, and the title *amma*, though meaning mother, reserved for Nayar women. Nobody corrected the newcomer at the time, but I noticed that at the next meal she refrained from her use of the term *amma*. I presume that one of the other monastic inmates must have had a 'quiet word' with her in the meantime.

As I have mentioned, *taravāds* gained great prestige by association with people of illustrious families. Sarada Mandiram has from the outset been able to attract patrons and devotees from some of the most prominent families of both Trichur and even outlying districts. However, few of such families have become monastic candidates, even though numerous daughters have received *mantra* initiation. This is not surprising, though, as daughters of good family usually have the best marriage prospects: they have the necessary fairness of complexion, family name, education and 'culture' to attract a doctor, engineer or other professional spouse, often with overseas qualifications and prospects. To these young women, monastic life holds little appeal.

The importance of 'good family' was illustrated by some comments passed by a very senior monk of the Order of royal background himself. He complained that, 'those who come here these days have so little. I ask them, "What have you to renounce?" They have neither beauty, nor family, nor education, nor wealth. The real renunciation is one who has all these, and who says, "no, I have had enough. None of this will bring me contentment". Such a one was the Buddha'. He then remarked that his attendant, who was in the room, was of a famous family of scholars. I asked him whether he should give such information in front of the boy, who had come to renounce his background. The Swami replied candidly, 'I *like* such people. I like *white* people.'[4] The boy flushed visibly, and left the room.

It should be pointed out that no other Womens branch of the Order is organised in quite the same way as Sarada Mandiram, and that the *taravād* model cannot be applied even to the smaller Mission centre in Trivandrum. No other branch is based on extensive agriculture, or with the participation of local villagers as income-producing labour. Moreover, the senior *saṃnyāsinis* (and women who joined more recently) have actually grown up at Sarada Mandiram, and maintain extensive family ties. In this respect, the monastic members of Sarada Mandiram certainly do not fit Dumont's description of 'renouncers' as 'individuals-outside-the-world'.

The term 'individual' applies even less to monastic inmates of Sarada Mandiram than does the phrase 'outside-the-world'. The President certainly does not tolerate individuals, any more than did the *kāraṇavan* of old. For, individuals threaten the united front of the Institution/*taravād*. *Taravād* members knew that the secret of communal living was *not* to be an individual, but to blend in with others, accepting what was given, and never demanding special treatment. Only the *kāraṇavan* had access to special privileges, including an expense account and the right to entertain visitors at will. That is, he alone had some right to individuality. But, the *kāraṇavan* was aware that he represented the whole *taravād*, and in this capacity built up his own following of allies and flatterers, and also enemies. The President of Sarada Mandiram knows that she should not be sought after as an individual, but only as a representative of the Order. However, although in theory any incumbent should receive the same support and respect, it is inevitable that each will attract her own following, and almost inevitably, her own enemies and detractors. The President, like the *kāraṇavan*, is the only member then, with the opportunity of becoming an individual. Only in Headquarters can curb her individuality, if it goes too far.

Maintaining Rank Within Sarada Mandiram

As is well known to readers of Kerala ethnography, members of the various communities were formerly kept physically separate by a system of distance pollution, by which members of each community had to keep a specified distance from members of other communities. Not only was there no interdining between communities, but even among Nayar themselves, *taravād* members interdined with only very few other *taravāds*, of roughly similar status.[5] When having occasion to dine at higher ranking *taravāds*, the visitor would be seated in a separate 'line' from the other diners or even in a separate room, and served after *taravād* members. This was especially so in the case of the *sambandham* partner of the *kāraṇavan*, who in some cases resided at his *taravād*. Moreover, a woman had to take as her *sambandham* partner a man of higher ranking family. In other words, in relationships the emphasis was always on *receiving* from superiors. In the case of *sambandham*, the woman was seen as the recipient, and the man the donor. A similar principle operated in the reception of food, in which the donor should not be of lesser rank than the recipient. These rules applied only to 'prepared'[6] food, not to ingredients. To come into close contact with inferiors was considered polluting, the seriousness depending on the relative rank of the two parties. An example relevant for the purpose of this discussion was the *sambandham* male partner who could only touch his Nayar partner (or children born of the union) at night, after his ritual duties had been completed for the day. He would bathe very early in the morning in a tank, before resuming ritual duties, or entering his own home.

I aim to demonstrate that ranking within Sarada Mandiram is similarly based on the desire to receive from higher ranking individuals, and a corresponding desire *not* to receive from those of lesser rank. That is, a network of receiving from seniors and giving to juniors operates, and this network binds together all the monastic inmates, from highest to lowest. The same theory applies in relationships with non members, so that each individual stands in a particular ranked relationship with each other individual.

Expressions of Hierarchy

One of the earliest lessons to be learned at Sarada Mandiram is how to behave towards seniors. And, as was the case with work, the main way of learning is by making mistakes. From the rebuke, the newcomer learns what her behaviour *should* have been, in a particular instance. She may be fortunate, however, and learn on occasion by witnessing or hearing about a fellow inmate's error. She will make a mental note that when faced with the same situation, she must remember not to commit a similar mistake. A simple example will illustrate my point. After a short time at Sarada Mandiram, a newcomer will have observed that all inmates wash their clothes with hot water once a week, and on the fourth day of a menstrual period. So, she will do likewise. She will also have observed that clothes are not ironed, but pulled into shape and folded neatly in a specified manner. The correct way of doing so will be learned when folding clothes for senior *saṃnyāsinis.* Daily she will be called to help in this task. Sarees and shawls require two people to fold them properly. So, the newcomer will call an inmate who does not seem occupied (possibly someone she has already helped to fold cloth), to help her when she washes her own clothes. The inmate will react with annoyance, and maybe even tell her to ask someone else. Finally it dawns on her: she must only ask juniors to help her, not seniors. If she is the juniormost, she will ask one of the office helpers, or even a Hostel girl. As soon as another newcomer arrives at Sarada Mandiram, however, her problem is solved. In Sarada Math, where there are no non monastic inmates except the cooks (with whom junior inmates have no dealings) possibly newcomers who actually commence their monastic life at Headquarters spend many an hour valiantly trying to pull their own sarees into shape: alone.

The principle of respect for seniors is easily grasped for the Kerala inmates: for they know that superiors (based on the criteria of age or community/*taravād* status) were traditionally to be respected. In schools and Colleges, girls of senior classes (and within a class, senior in age) are still accorded respect. But it takes a while to realize that the basis of seniority for monastic inmates at Sarada Mandiram is neither age nor caste. I have even heard a Kerala-born anthropologist, well over the official retiring age, protest over an overseas appointment accepted by a well-known colleague, 'Why was I not asked? I am his *senior.*'[7]

The most powerful expression of hierarchy within Hindu society in Kerala was in forms of greeting and salutation. Throughout India it is common for Hindus to greet each other by placing the palms together at chest height, raising them to the level of the nose if the person being greeted deserves extra respect due to superior caste, age or individual achievement. In keeping with the extra emphasis on hierarchy in Kerala, individuals do not greet each other in this manner. Tenants and servants of the *taravād* stood before members of the household in a stooped posture, their mouth and nose covered by their cupped right hand when summoned, and spoke only when asked. Language to superiors was ultra respectful, whereas language to inferiors was in the form of curt commands, devoid of courteous verb endings and flattering pronouns and titles, used in speech to superiors. Nayars in turn would adopt a respectful even servile attitude before Nambudiris and royalty, and their greeting would be acknowledged in a haughty manner such as a nod of the head rather than reciprocated. Juniors of a *taravād* would salute the *kāaṇavan* by prostration on special occasions, such as festivals on which cloth was given, birthdays and before and after a journey. The individual would kneel down and touch his or her forehead to the floor in front of the *kāraṇavan*. A well-bred child would also do so before a mother and grandmother on similar occasions.

Within Sarada Mandiram, all inmates (whether monastic, Hostel girls, teachers or servants) are expected to prostrate before the President in the same manner as *taravād* members did before their *kāraṇavan*. Devotees learn to do the same whenever visiting the Institution. Parents may or may not adopt this form of salutation, but when a child is about to leave for a vacation, she will be asked, 'Have you done *namasker* to Mataji? Then go and do it'. The child will ask 'May I go *and come*?' 'Go and come!' the President will reply. To tell someone to 'go', means just that. It is tantamount to saying 'get out'. She will return the salutation by placing her hands together at chest height, a form of blessing in the case of *saṃnyāsinis*. On festivals, all the inmates of the Institution will line up to prostrate before the President, and on the two Kerala festivals she will present cloth to each, except paying boarders, (most of whom go on vacation for the Kerala festivals). Labourers will also receive cloth in return for their prostrations. Theirs will be single cloth of rough coarse weave, and they will look to see if there is either a blouse piece or shirt folded inside it, exchanging glances if there is not. The cooks will receive slightly better cloth, either a saree or *mundu*, depending on what the individual normally wears. Free boarders will receive stitched garments, usually of ugly printed Khadi (handspun cloth), and the blouse is often ill fitting and clashes with the skirt. So on festivals, normally happy days especially for children, the free boarders feel embarrassed rather than pleased with their new clothes. The *saṃnyāsinis* are well aware of this, for usually a few paying boarders will be in the Hostel: those whose parents are interstate or overseas. They will be dressed in finery, perhaps 'foreign' clothes, purchased in the Gulf States or Malaysia. They will be of synthetic material and fastened with buttons, hooks or even zips, not safety pins, as are the clothes of the free boarders. Monastic inmates will receive quite good quality cloth, either presented during the year by devotees or purchased by the President. She herself is presented with cloth periodically, and if it is fine and of correct size, she will keep it. I presented a set of Kerala *mundu* of fine quality. 'No *kasavu*?' was the comment. *Kasavu* is thread of real gold. 'I did not think it was appropriate for *saṃnyāsinis*'. 'If we are given it, we wear it.' *Kasavu* has long been far more prestigious than cloth with woven borders of dyed cotton. Only the wealthy could afford to wear it. It was the cloth of the aristocracy and of royalty.[8] As the '*kāraṇavan*', *kasavu* cloth *is* appropriate for the President, and she will not usually give it to a junior, except if it is her own used cloth. The admiration that *kasavu* inspires, is part of the Kerala enthusiasm for gold itself. Ask a selection of daily wage labourers what they would do with a windfall of money.[9] The answer is: buy ornaments for the women of the family. By ornaments 22 carat gold is meant. The sight of a *saṃnyāsini* wearing *kasavu*, therefore does not go unnoticed, nor without scathing comments from non devotees. The ample clothes of the monastic inmates (especially the seniors) is a source of resentment by the villagers. Even the President is aware of the extent of her clothes. 'How many sets have you?' she asked a newcomer whose clothes from home were becoming ragged. 'Four? You will have to wait till you are a *saṃnyāsini* before you have a lot of sets.'

However, the outside assessment of the *saṃnyāsinis* is not always just. One *saṃnyāsini* wore only Khadi cloth, which evokes Gandhian ideals of austerity. In fact, her 'austerity' amounts to an idiosyncratic indulgence. Fine Khadi is far more expensive than everyday handloom or mill cloth counterparts. And, unlike the *kasavu* cloth worn on occasion by the President, the Khadi is not usually presented to Sarada Mandiram, but has to be purchased. But, the President has other benefits denied the rank and file. Visitors, including Hostel girls' parents from overseas, lavish her with gifts ranging from coveted Parker pens to packets of biscuits. They also press money into her hand some of which is entered into a Sarada Mandiram account, and some of which is not. The money the President keeps in her own name is modest, but it gives a power denied her charges. She can also order taxis to take her on a shopping trip to the town, and keep it waiting until she has finished, the way an aristocratic or wealthy lady keeps her driver waiting, outside each shop in turn. Some years ago, she used to catch buses, but despite the high cost of taxis, did not do so now, even though the bus passes the Institution's door, and inexpensive 'autos' can be caught from the bus stand to the main shops.[10] Taxi catching began with the separation of the Institutions, marking the beginning of the President's *kāaṇavan*ship.

The President has other extensive powers. She can dismiss or expel anyone who deviates from her expectations. Nevertheless, she is often extremely patient with her erring subjects, giving them 'chance' after chance to mend their ways. Numerous times she has given shelter to women with nowhere to go. Once it was a Muslim woman of 'immoral' conduct with a small child, driven out of her village. She gave her work as an outside labourer. Some of the male labourers threatened to leave. She told them they could do so. They would find work elsewhere. The woman would not. Monastic inmates from other centres, suffering from various degrees of physical or mental affliction, are almost routinely sent to Sarada Mandiram for an opportunity to recover. However, there is a limit to her patience, and those who have been on the receiving end of her furious temper, will never forget it. On occasion she is capable of using physical force. I have questioned many informants concerning violence in the *taravād*, and it appears that it was widespread. The *kāraṇavan* chastised *taravād* members, and the *kāristhan* often chastised tenants, or had them beaten by his 'men'. To touch them himself would have polluted him. Hence, his 'men' would do the job. At times tenants were put to death, and I personally have known two Nayar families in which incidents of murder were related to me in a matter-of-fact manner. The *kāraṇavan* was the object of awe, fear and often, deep hatred. The President tolerates many wayward and difficult people because, as she says, Holy Mother had to put up with her 'mad' niece, Radhu, and a host of quarrelsome, scheming relatives. She also admitted regretfully that she cannot control her temper. 'It harms me, more than they.'

So much does the Institution revolve around the fear of the President, that when she is absent, a perceptible change in behaviour occurs among the monastic inmates, and to a lesser extent, among children and labourers. The night that the President went with 'delegates' to Calcutta for a Conference of the Ramakrishna Movement, I entered in my notebook 'Tonight we all were relaxed. After *ārati* (evening worship) Devi *chechi* (a *saṃnyāsini*) sat in the office listening to the radio'. After *ārati*, the children go to study and the monastic inmates should sit for meditation unless they have other specific duties. Except for the morning sacred songs and news (which is on the air just when morning chores begin) the radio is never turned on, unless by the President, for a rare special programme (such as her own 'radio talk'). The sight of four or five members chatting in the office, just outside the temple, during meditation time, a time of silence, was indeed unusual, and I put it down to the excitement of the day, in preparing the delegates for the journey.

However, the next night, four inmates, including the seniormost *saṃnyāsini* had a 'foot stamping competition' in the corridor between the Math and Hostel buildings. This occurred only two days after an incident during which a boarder was severely beaten by the President for talking during study time at night. The hullabaloo accompanying the rhythmic stamping, which became faster and faster until one of the competitors collapsed in a giggling heap, drew amazement from the children, who came out of their 'halls' to see what was going on. The following morning, after tea, when all had morning duties to perform, four inmates (one of them the same *saṃnyāsini* who had joined in the foot stamping) sat in the corridor with the newspapers (which usually go to the President's room, and stay there until she has read them), and mocked the lecture series that was being held in the town by the leader of a rival Hindu 'Mission'. The article describing the lectures was read out in the tone used by old-fashioned scholars giving a religious discourse. For the two weeks of the President's absence there was a general laxity in behaviour among inmates, especially after supper at night. The culmination was on the night of Sarada Jayanthi,[11] the most sacred festival of the year, when at night a newcomer and a teacher put on a 'programme'. All sat in expectation in a semi circle. The two entertainers performed a skit in which they imitated inmates sweeping and wiping the floors, avoiding many places, or angrily flicking back the end of their sarees. They then gave a bouquet of plastic flowers to the 'guest of honour', the seniormost *saṃnyāsini* present, who was staying overnight from the town College Hostel before embarking on the 'Address', in which one spoke in Kannada, and the other translated into Malayalam sentence by sentence. The humour was that the address was in Sanskritised Kannada, and the so-called translation was almost identical to the original. They then imitated a *bhajan* group that had come to Sarada Mandiram recently for the Inauguration of the auditorium. Although the inmates laughed, they were not sure that sacred subjects should be held to ridicule, and some felt it was insulting to give the plastic flowers to the *saṃnyāsini*. You should respect seniors, not play jokes at their expense.

Whilst the President was absent, the next senior was in charge, the usual '*kāristhan*' figure. But, instead of assuming an aloof '*kāraṇavan-*

like' image, she did the opposite. She fraternised with the other members, chatting at night with them until reading became later and later. The Karnataka inmates at no time were seen to join in the chatting, mainly because it concerned local people and events, which they could not follow. However, they did not set up an opposition gossip circle among themselves. For two weeks, the prayer hall at meditation time was theirs exclusively. This interested me particularly in the light of information available on Catholic girls from Kerala who had been sent to join a convent to Florence. Sonia Dougal noticed that when not under observation, they did not bother to attend Mass daily, nor to carry out other devotions expected of novices (1974:157–8). The difference was that in their case, *their superiors deliberately did this* to test their vocations, about which they had serious doubt. At Sarada Mandiram, the *saṃnyāsini* who took over the running of the Institution when the President was absent, was the Manager. She slept in the same room as the President and ate in the seniors' dining room, which isolates her from the other members. The President's absence was a good opportunity for her to enjoy companionship and a certain amount of levity, both denied her when the President is in residence. At the same time, she indulged in her opportunity to exercise extra authority over the labourers, whose daily supervision was her domain. Usually in true *kāristhan* style she encouraged gossip from the labourers, which was then relayed to the President. In the President's absence she behaved in an aloof manner with the labourers, imitating the behaviour of the President, when she came to inspect a piece of work, standing a little distance from the workers, shaded by an umbrella and only speaking to give a curt direction.

We can conclude from the above evidence that not only is hierarchy important at Sarada Mandiram, but the President is the key figure, around whom the Institution functions. Her actual physical presence is needed for the familiar routine to continue, for the simple reason that when she is in residence, the inmates are afraid of transgressing, lest they become objects of her wrath. She ultimately has the power to not only punish but to report to Headquarters on the conduct of an inmate. She has, in fact, power over their ability to remain in the Institution. Even though there is strict ranking which defines the relative position of each and every member, in the final analysis, the members are merely 'members' and the President is the *kāraṇavan*, the head of the family, the one true 'individual' who represents it.

Chapter 10

The Concept of Purity

I have established that within Sarada Mandiram, ranking follows the *taravād* model. Individuals are ranked according to 'generation' (*saṃnyāsinis, brahmacārinis,* Probationers and Pre Probationers), and within each rank, according to relative age. In its relations with the outside world, the *saṃnyāsinis* of Sarada Mandiram have ranked themselves on an aristocratic *taravād* level in food, dress and custom. Perhaps even more importantly, the monastic inmates assume this level when speaking in Malayalam, both within the Institution and in discourse with non inmates. Since Malayalam cannot be spoken without the relative rank of all parties being taken into consideration, my assertions regarding the self image of the monastic inmates can easily be demonstrated.

The relative ranking of Hindu communities and indeed of *taravāds* in Kerala is clearly connected with their relative levels of purity. However, internal ranking within the *taravād* does not obviously fit this pattern. Yet, I believe there is one overall scheme, whose underlying principles make sense of hierarchy in all its manifestations within the Hindu context. It is the same principle, based on notions of purity, which governs commensal and marital relationships, and which can be demonstrated to underpin the organisation of Sarada Mandiram.

Personal Purity

The concept of purity within Sarada Mandiram can be divided into three main categories, though these cannot always be easily separated from each other. These are: personal purity, hierarchical purity, and purity maintenance when associating with 'outsiders'. A newcomer to the Institution must try to grasp all three very speedily, a particularly difficult task for those who are not familiar with local etiquette and idiom.

The most basic rules regard the daily cycle of bathing and changing clothes. At the sound of the bell of 5.00 a.m., on arising the newcomer will clean her teeth, wash her face and go to the prayer hall, where at 5.30 a.m. the shrine room opens and the morning *ārati* and chanting takes place. She will sit for meditation until 6.30 a.m., when she must report for the morning sweeping and wiping of the floors of the monastic building and temple, along with four or so others. She will finish at about 7.30 a.m., pausing at 7.00 a.m. for a cup of milk coffee, which is served in the dining hall, for all the inmates except the most senior, who have theirs prepared specially. When the cleaning is over, the newcomer will then bathe, rinsing her clothes with cold water and rubbing any stains with soap. She will then put on a completely fresh set of clothes, which she has kept folded over the gap at the top of the bathroom or well enclosure door. While carrying her clothes she must take care not to touch them to the clothes she is wearing, for the latter are ritually impure. After bathing, she will hang her washed clothes on the line in a place shown to her, which she will use from that time on. Such places are made by wire stretched across the supporting pillars of the square of the inner courtyard, the pillars making convenient divisions. Two sides of the square are reserved for *saṃnyāsinis* and two for *brahmacārinis* and newcomers. Each person leaves a gap between her clothes and those of the people on either side, but nothing is said if the wind blows the clothes on top of each other, as there are no pegs, except for the President's clothes. Straight after hanging her clothes, the newcomer will go to the prayer hall and prostrate before the shrine, pausing on the way to take a pinch of *bhasman* (white ashes of burnt cowdung, offered to Siva) and smear it on her forehead in a horizontal line. During menstrual periods she will not use *bhasmam*. Vegetable cutting will take up the newcomer's time until 8.30 a.m., when the ringing of a bell in the shrine denotes the end of the morning *pūjā* and the commencement of *ārati*. All will go to the prayer hall to witness the *ārati* and to sip the *tīrtham*, the sacred bath water of Ramakrishna.[1] Two small stainless steel cup-shaped vessels are kept beside the *tīrtham* containing red and white sandalwood paste. White has been placed in a round dot on the forehead of Ramakrishna's photo, and red on Sarada Devi's and finally white on Vivekananda's.[2] Each inmate dips her right fourth finger in each container in turn and presses it lightly onto her own forehead, leaving a dot there. Some, following the Kerala custom, make a short horizontal bar of white sandalwood paste, and then place a red dot in the middle of it. Sandalpaste is used even during menstruation in Sarada Mandiram. When I asked why sandalwood is permitted but not *bhasmam*, I received the standard answer 'It is our custom', but I believe the reason is clear: *bhasmam* is smeared on the Siva *lingam* just as red powder or paste is smeared on images of goddesses. The devotee is united with Siva through receiving his *bhasmam* which represents his seed (O'Flaherty 1973:245–7). A woman who is menstruating is not permitted to receive seed, i.e., have sexual intercourse.

The newcomer may assume that she is 'clean' after her bath, but this depends on her timing in visiting the latrine. The importance of this is illustrated from the following conversation that I had with a *brahmacārini* from another centre:

> 'Here it is very difficult. The latrine is very far away. I have the habit of opening everything (taking off my clothes) to go to the latrine. But how can you here?'
>
> I said: 'Here all go to the latrine early and then take bath'.
>
> She replied: 'But I can only go to the latrine by 9 o'clock. I take bath at 8, so how can I go to the latrine in a clean cloth?'
>
> I said: 'There is an inside latrine. Use that. Do you know where it is?' She replied: 'I have seen it, but isn't it for seniors?'
>
> I told her: 'The President and Devaprana have their own latrines. Nirmalaprana only uses it when either Jayaprana or Tulsiprana are visiting. Otherwise only junior *saṃnyāsinis* use it'.
>
> She said: 'Shall I ask? Shall I explain?' (Fieldnotes: 3rd January 1981).

The point of the conversation was this: there is a clash between the custom followed at the Headquarters and that of Sarada Mandiram. In Calcutta, inmates must change their clothes of awakening, but do not bathe until much later, even up until just before lunch. It is usual to wait until it is necessary to go to the latrine, during which time all clothes should be removed. The latrine is attached to a bathroom, so it is convenient to bathe straight after a bowel movement. In any case, after a bowel movement the anal region and the feet must be washed well with water. Clothes need not be removed while urinating, but again washing is absolutely necessary. The use of toilet paper is regarded with absolute horror, and indeed is often one of the few facts known about the habits of foreigners. Because of this, all visiting foreigners are regarded as walking around covered in excreta.

Actually, at Headquarters the most purifying bath is taken in the Ganges which flows right beside the Math compound. It is considered especially good to bathe in the Ganges daily, but if not, at least on special occasions. It is not always convenient since the river is tidal, and in winter, extremely cold. Because of the murky nature of the water, a special old saree is kept for Ganges baths. With repeated use the cloth becomes a deep grey. This notwithstanding, the devout argue that Ganges baths are spiritually cleansing as they have the power to remove sin. The colour or muddiness of the water or clearly visible garbage does not lessen this.

At Headquarters, if an inmate needs to visit the latrine at a time other than before her bath, she must remove all her clothes first in the bathroom area, and only replace them after a thorough washing of the anus, hands and feet. The whole problem of defecation becomes complicated by the widespread constipation of inmates in winter and in the rainy season, of equally widespread 'loose motions'. The state of bowels is actively discussed, and appropriate laxatives and anti-diarrhoea treatment taken.

However, changing one's clothes on awakening is not sufficient to ensure personal purity by Kerala standards. Early bathing is absolutely necessary for the orthodox, and formerly this was in the family 'tank' or a river. Today tap water is sufficient for all but the most orthodox, but well water is slightly better. As in Bengal, the hair must be wetted daily, though washed with soap only once a week. Therefore, in Sarada Mandiram any monastic inmate who has shrine or kitchen duties will bathe before the shrine opens at 5.30 a.m., and change all her clothes. One or two orthodox inmates bathe early daily, regardless of their work, because they believe that it is not correct to even touch one's own small meditation mat or rosary without bathing, after sleep. Only the initiated have a rosary, but many of the Karnataka candidates arrive already initiated, and in possession of both rosary and mat. They will be told not to touch or use either without bathing or at least changing their night clothes, the latter being a concession to Kerala customs. As I have stated, they could neither do any shrine nor kitchen work at Sarada Mandiram after merely changing without bathing.

Why must these rules be followed? To begin with, inmates sleep on 'bedding', which is a mattress of cloth stuffed with kapok, covered by a removable cotton sheet. Bedding is permanently contaminated, because it is used during menstruation, and although the bedsheets are washed in hot water on the fourth day (along with all clothes worn during this time) the mattress absorbs pollution through the sheet, which is polluted by contact with the polluted clothes on the person's body. For a male monastic inmate bedding is polluted through nocturnal emissions of semen, and in the case of 'householders' through contact with sexual fluids. The bedding of householders is thus regarded with particular revulsion by members of the Ramakrishna Order. Even if bedding were not used, the clothes worn during the night are usually polluted by the ingestion of boiled rice, which is served for supper almost daily.

The question of boiled rice is a perplexing one. No other food causes the *consumer* to be polluted at Sarada Mandiram except boiled rice. And, the pollution can be removed by bathing and changing. A person who has eaten rice can pollute another (or even her own washed clothes) by their clothes touching. Bodily touch does not transfer this form of pollution. Similarly, with menstrual pollution: polluted clothing contaminates unpolluted clothing, but a menstruating inmate may, for example, hand a book to a person without causing contamination. She should, however, keep away from inmates who are involved in shrine or kitchen work, lest their clothes touch inadvertently. Also, during morning and evening *ārati* when all inmates sit together on a carpet, menstruating inmates should sit slightly apart, lest their clothes contaminate those of others who will shortly wish to use their rosary and mat. At Sarada Mandiram this rule is far less observed than in Headquarters, where there is obsessive concern over 'touching'.

After her bath in the morning an inmate at Sarada Mandiram remains in a state of ritual purity (unless menstruating) until lunch, when her meal of boiled rice causes her to become polluted. If she does her weekly washing, however, she becomes polluted, (since she will be splashed by polluted soapy water) or if she goes to the latrine without removing her clothes first. Also, going outside the compound, where she comes into contact with 'outsiders' causes her clothes to become polluted. For example, inmates must change after going to town or even to school if they want to do any work connected with kitchen or shrine, or touch their rosary or mat. Clothes also become polluted by touching any bedding, so that the first act on awakening is to fold the bedsheet and cover, and place them inside the rolled up bedding along with the pillow. The bedding is kept on one end of the 'cot' and only unrolled at night. You can sit on your wooden bedstead during the day, but your clothes must not touch any bedding.

There is one more means of becoming polluted followed in Calcutta, but which is all but ignored in Sarada Mandiram. In Headquarters, clothes must not be starched with rice water. Only the clothes of newcomers and *brahmacārinis* are starched. Their clothes are white, and are worn daily for a week, one set being worn in the morning and one in the evening. After wearing, clothes are merely dipped in water and hung up, so that the starch is not removed. Morning clothes are rinsed in the evening and worn again the next morning, and the same with evening clothes which are rinsed each morning. A third set may be needed during the rainy season. After a week, all clothes worn during the week are soaked for some hours in boiling water to which soap shavings and soda are added. They are then washed with a kneading motion (in Calcutta) or beaten on a washing stone (in Kerala) until clean. In Calcutta, on the day of washing, starch must be requested beforehand, as it is made of white flour boiled until clear. Only a small amount is permitted, as flour is expensive, and the individual must tell how many 'sets' she has to wash. The starch is diluted with water in which a blue bag is used. The clothes are hung up and folded, ready for use again. By the fifth day the clothes look decidedly grubby. If going out, at least a freshly washed and starched saree and shawl (if worn) will be used, underneath which can sometimes be seen very soiled blouses and petticoats.

In Calcutta the water is very hard, and it is a waste of time to try to keep clothes clean by washing them daily with soap. However, in Sarada Mandiram, the water is excellent and more soap is given per month than in Calcutta.[3] Inmates are thus expected to keep their clothes both clean and white. The Kerala inmates are usually used to beating clothes from childhood, and can dazzle you with their cleaner than clean brightness. The Karnataka inmates, usually used to servants, end up with their clothes becoming greyer and greyer, as blue accumulates, instead of being beaten out fully each wash. Clothes in Sarada Mandiram should look clean, not just 'washed'. But, according to Headquarters, the dazzling Trichur clothes are very impure.

Every day at Sarada Mandiram the rice is cooked in a large quantity of water and the rice water is drained away and used to starch clothes. Even shrine cloth is starched in rice water. The inmates know that this is not permitted in Headquarters, for the practice renders all the inmates permanently polluted, making their bathing and changing to no avail. But, there is no way that the President of Sarada Mandiram is going to allow the purchase of white flour, when rice water starch is available. The Calcutta rule is simply ignored and even the most orthodox use the offending starch, including *saṃnyāsinis*, who are not permitted to use starch at all at Headquarters, since it is considered too 'smart'. Incidentally, the starch is not contaminating because the rice taken from the water is offered to Ramakrishna, and thus *prasād*, because the rice water used is from the Hostel lunch which is not *prasād*.

I have wondered a lot about the problem of rice pollution. Rice is considered a 'special' food in much of India because it involves the use of a plough and thus '*himsa*' or violence, as small creatures such as worms are injured in the process. Rice is not eaten on certain fast days, such as the bi-monthly *ekādaśi*, though other grains may be eaten. Those who observe fasts strictly, either do not eat or drink, or eat only fruit and milk. But, boiled rice is the first food to be avoided during any fast. In Kerala 'rice' is almost synonymous with 'food' as it is the staple diet, but in other parts of India where it is not, the restriction still holds. What is so special about boiled rice that it contaminates without even being eaten, that is by merely using rice water starch?

There is strong evidence that rice is used in Indian ritual contexts as a symbol of male 'seed'. Indeed, marriage ritual includes rice in this role in parts of India, including the custom of sprinkling rice grains into the freshly-made part in the bride's hair, along the length of which a red powder has first been spread. Also, in South India, Jagadisa Ayyar reports that a woman emerging from menstrual seclusion before going to her husband must eat boiled rice and salt, as 'rice and salt stand for semen' (1925:166).

On fast days, when spiritual aspirants abstain from rice, they are also to abstain from sexual intercourse.[4] Rice water must thus not be used to starch clothes that come into contact with sacred objects as they are semen polluted. Boiled rice is moreover the least transferable food, and as a general rule, an individual will only eat rice cooked by a member of the same community as him/herself or members of select higher ranking communities. In Kerala, *taravāds* whose women had *sambandham* relationships exclusively with Brahmins, ate food cooked only by Brahmins. Among Nayars, although a menstruating woman may eat rice, she may not go near the granary where it is stored nor cook it. Menstrual seclusion was rigidly enforced within the *taravād*, as a menstruating woman is said to make seed or even paddy go bad.

Once the newcomer has mastered the principles of personal purity, she is gradually allowed to enter the kitchen, and later is given simple tasks involving the shrine. Entry into the actual shrine is not usually permitted until after the candidate has received *brahmacārya*, except in the case of a Brahmin. During training at Headquarters all are given the opportunity to enter the shrine, while rostered for shrine duty. In Calcutta, it is possible for worshippers to enter the shrine and to touch the image in many temples, while in Kerala only the appointed priest may do so.

So far I have discussed concepts and rules which concern the need to be in a state of ritual purity primarily at times when the individual has to perform some religious duty in Sarada Mandiram. This includes kitchen work in the main kitchen, where food is offered to Ramakrishna. Few rules are observed in the 'old' kitchen, where breakfast is prepared, a meal which is not offered. At times when this kitchen is used for offered food (such as at night when a light offering of fried wheat cakes and semolina boiled in milk is prepared there) the kitchen is first thoroughly cleansed and only those engaged in preparing the offering may enter.

Hierarchical Purity

There is another series of concepts discernible at Sarada Mandiram, that appear at first to be quite apart from those outlined above. These rules concern the individual's place in the Sarada Mandiram hierarchy, and join the newest of the newcomers to the seniormost *saṃnyāsinis* in a system of graded links.

The basic principle behind hierarchical purity is the principle that seniors must be respected. Each inmate has her own 'plate and glass', both of which are made of stainless steel, and are brought to each meal. Those who have been in Calcutta may have acquired their own tiffin plate, a smaller steel plate used for non rice meals: such as breakfast, afternoon tea, and supper on the occasions when *dosa* (lentil pancakes) are served. In Calcutta not only separate plates but a separate kitchen and dining room are used for non rice meals. No offerings are prepared in these areas, and very few precautions of ritual purity observed. Trainees prepare and serve these meals, and may do so even when menstruating. In Sarada Mandiram the old kitchen serves a similar function, though there is only a single dining room.

Clothes, bedding and bathroom bucket with a plastic dipper are the other major personal items of an inmate. It is unthinkable to take or use any personal belongings of a senior, just as it is to call her by name, or to ask her help in folding your clothes. For example, if a Trichur inmate is visiting Trivandrum overnight, she will need to borrow a bucket and mug. She will take these from a junior (though she does not like to borrow at all), most likely from the inmate closest to her in seniority. Sometimes an inmate is called to go out at short notice and may not have a freshly washed saree or shawl. She will borrow one from a junior inmate if she herself has to ask. But, if a senior offers to lend her one, she can accept it. The rule is: you can commandeer help or possessions from a junior, but can take them from a senior only if offered. In the case of borrowing, the rules sometimes differ from those generally observed.

A senior will give you her cloth, but will not lend one. Yet, when there is a gap of some years between two inmates, it is very flattering to be given something by a senior. For example, before *saṃnyāsa,* the candidates give to juniors their broad red bordered sarees. Also, holy pictures or small booklets are often given by a visiting *saṃnyāsini* to junior inmates. The most prized gifts are those given by the very seniormost *saṃnyāsinis,* especially the President and General Secretary of the Order. Sarees or shawls given by them will be kept carefully and used only on special occasions. Indeed, any attention shown by seniors is eagerly sought and the source of envy for others.

Serving Seniors

Senior *saṃnyāsinis* are (according to custom within the Order) permitted to exact 'service' for their juniors. A prime example is the custom of Heads of Centres and very senior *saṃnyāsinis* of choosing a Probationer or *brahmacārini* as a *sevika* (one who serves). The duties of a *sevika* include arranging the bed of the senior, hanging up her washing, dyeing her clothes, bringing light refreshments to the senior and visitors, and 'personal service'.

'Personal service' involves massage. All Heads of Centres and most other senior members of the Order, to my knowledge, accept this form of 'service'. After lunch, and again before retiring for the night, the *sevika* is called to the bedside of the senior, to give her a massage. Massage is a common practice in Hindu homes, and a girl may be called to massage her grandmother, and later her mother-in-law in many parts of the country. In Kerala, massage was widely practised in the *taravād,* and the rules of hierarchy surrounding this were once again similar to those in Sarada Mandiram. In the *taravād,* a woman of the 'grandmother' generation would be massaged by a girl of the 'grandchild' category. In Sarada Mandiram, a senior *saṃnyāsini* would be massaged by a *brahmacārini* or Probationer, a similar 'generation gap' applying.

I questioned the General Secretary of the Order about the practice of massage. She replied, 'I tried massage once, but the sensation was such, that I decided it was *not* for *saṃnyāsinis*'. But the practice is widespread in all centres, including Headquarters. There are well documented cases of an erotic attachment arising between the two parties, and of the Head of Centre being involved in a relationship with a junior.

Whilst I was at Sarada Mandiram, a *brahmacārini* arrived there from another centre, in an obviously agitated state of mind. On the second day, she burst into my room, and told me that she had been expelled from the Order, and was leaving for home the following day. She wanted to tell me the reason, so that somebody would know 'what was going on'. According to her, she became the personal attendant of the Head of her Centre, and used to be called on twice a day for massage and to 'smooth her wrinkles'. She said that at first she was flattered, and carried out her duties in all innocence. It therefore took her quite a while to realize that the relationship was becoming 'intimate', although she had seen a similar occurrence in another centre, between a Head of Centre and a *sevika*.[5] After a few months, a new candidate had replaced her as *sevika*, causing her much distress. She was so hurt and angry that she told a visiting *brahmacārini*, who promised not to repeat what she had heard. But, the *brahmacārini* was from Headquarters, and told the General Secretary on her return. The Head of Centre was informed to send her former *sevika* forthwith to Trichur. The Trichur President was to arrange for her immediate dismissal. The *brahmacārini* phoned her family to tell them she was coming home.

The next day, the *brahmacārini* left with the President for Cochin. A lay devotee took her to the airport, as the *brahmacārini* had wealthy parents who had agreed to pay for the air ticket. Before leaving, the *brahmacārini* told me of other instances of homosexuality within the Order, mostly involving naive girls like herself. She said that she had joined the Order to lead a 'pure life' and instead had lost her innocence and become corrupted. Moreover, she was being punished, and not the guilty party, who had simply embarked on a new relationship. She was very bewildered and emotionally shattered by the past few days. She guaranteed that her parents (who were initiated devotees of Ramakrishna) would pursue her story with the officials of the Order. After her return, she wrote to a lay devotee that she had arrived safely and that her parents were very happy to have her home. That was the last I heard of her. I did not hear her name mentioned again a Sarada Mandiram.

Apart from the relationship of seniors with their *sevikas*, there are more complex and more frankly homosexual relationships discernible within the Order. These occur between inmates with a lesser hierarchical gap between them, but still, as far as I could discover, not between inmates of similar standing. The extreme emphasis on hierarchy within the Order ensures that there is little or no concept of 'peers'. This in turn minimises the mutual sharing of affection and confidences among inmates 'in a similar boat', as is apparently common in Catholic religious communities, where such relationships are referred to as 'particular friendships' (Moorhouse 1969:188).

In Sarada Mandiram a homosexual relationship flourished between a particular junior *saṃnyāsini* and a Probationer, and was not the first one in which the *saṃnyāsini* had been involved. Their behaviour was obvious to not only the other monastic inmates, but to the students and domestic staff as well, and was widely discussed. However, a lay devotee who had been very much part of the Kerala education system, informed me that homosexual relationships among unmarried adolescents were not regarded as particularly 'deviant'. She explained that since girls were expected to remain virgins until marriage, and since marriage was no longer consummated by puberty, young girls in high school and College (especially those residing in hostels) readily formed 'crushes'[6] on their seniors. This, she said, was far preferable to the bold girls who had sexual relations before marriage, and ended up having abortions. 'The hospital in Trivandrum is crowded with them', she said. Crushes were just a phase, which was 'cured' by marriage. However, relationships of this nature among monastic inmates *were* regarded as deviant, by fellow inmates, students and domestic staff alike. *Brahmacārya*, referred to continence in 'word, thought and deed', was often preached at Sarada Mandiram. In one centre, a particular relationship was regarded as nothing short of scandalous, but when a visiting *saṃnyāsini* took up the matter with the Head of Centre, according to her she received a swift and stinging rebuke. The *saṃnyāsini* concerned had certain connections within the Order, so she could not be openly censured.

Cautious enquiries enabled me to ascertain that homosexual attraction was indeed of some concern within the Order, and during my fieldwork I heard that two candidates whose applications for vows were deferred for this reason. I heard also of at least three previous cases in which the junior party had been transferred elsewhere, and kept under careful observation, to see if she could mend her ways.

Campbell-Jones notes that transfers occurred in Catholic convents for similar reasons (1979:86).

In general, the level of sexuality among inmates was difficult to assess, except in the rare instances where I directly observed either sexual behaviour or conversations.[7]

Another form of 'service' is hair cutting. *Saṃnyāsinis* have their head shaved once a month. There is no set day for this, but many prefer the last day of menstrual pollution, as hair cutting is a polluting activity, after which a bath and change of clothes is necessary. It is thus best to start the monthly cycle freshly shaven and cleanly dressed. Juniors cut hair for *saṃnyāsinis*, though not all inmates master this skill, mostly because it is hard to find willing heads on which to practice. The clippers used can become caught in the hair, with painful results. Before commencing hair cutting, the 'barber' must touch the feet of the *saṃnyāsini* to apologise for being audacious enough to touch the head of a senior. Normally, the head is regarded as the seat of the *guru* in the form of Siva, and should not be touched by anyone except by a very senior *saṃnyāsini*, such as the President of the Order, by way of blessing. Inmates are told never to touch the feet of anyone with the head (except their own *guru*) while prostrating. Though the 'barber' becomes polluted by cutting hair, and has to bathe, she has to again touch the senior's feet at the end of her hair cutting, to once again apologise. The senior will murmur a blessing in reply.

There is a hierarchy in the receiving of food also. Normally once food is served on a plate, the individual either eats it all, or throws the remains onto the refuse heap. However, a very senior *saṃnyāsini* may give food from her plate to a junior, as *prasād*. The food may already be the *prasād* of Ramakrishna, if it was first offered in the shrine before being served, but in any case, the food from the plate of a senior such as the President of the Order is equally regarded as *prasād* and received with respect and gratitude, as it denotes a special favour. The President of Sarada Mandiram would not give anyone food from her plate once she has commenced eating, but does give a piece of fruit or a biscuit from her morning or afternoon snack to anyone who is present when she receives it. In this case, the plate has not been in direct contact with her saliva, for snack foods are broken into bite size pieces and popped into the mouth without touching fingers to lips, unlike a meal during which the hand returns repeatedly from lips to plate, thereby polluting the whole plate with saliva. The President of the Order does, however, give food from her plate after she has commenced eating. In this respect she is like

Ramakrishna, whose *prasād* leftovers are eaten daily, by inmates and devotees, for that special contact.

On the other hand, the clothes, bedding, plates and glasses of non monastic people, whatever their age or status are to be avoided by all inmates. I shall give some examples.

Firstly, all bedding, linen, buckets, plates and glasses used by non monastic visitors are stored separately from those of monastics and the linen is marked 'SG' (Sarada Guests) instead of 'SM' (Sarada Math). Moreover, monastic inmates sit on a separate carpet during prayer times. At Sarada Mandiram inmates sit on the floor or benches for meals, but in Sarada Math there are separate mats for monastic inmates and 'outsiders', the latter being distinguished by a tacked-on red saree border: a sure danger signal. These mats must never touch the monastic mats. On one occasion at Sarada Mandiram the mother of a monk arrived and sat down on the monastic carpet in the prayer hall just before evening prayers. She was told politely to sit behind on the common carpet, but replied 'I like to sit here with you people', with a broad smile. She refused to move. As the inmates entered the prayer hall they looked at her, but she took no notice. The two inmates who usually sit in the place where the visitor had seated herself, sat down nearby, one sitting half on the carpet and half on the bare floor, to make her point. As she sat down she drew her saree close around her crossed legs, so as not to touch the intruder's clothes, which would pollute her. The second inmate behaved in a similar manner. In Sarada Math, if a visitor even treads on the monastic carpet, an inmate will jump up and escort her away, as if she had just stepped onto a minefield. In Sarada Mandiram, this would not happen.

Another illustration happened when a newcomer served me milk at night instead of buttermilk. I did not want to get her into trouble, but milk is one of the few vegetarian foods that I just cannot tolerate. The President noticed the error and scolded her, asking her to change my milk for buttermilk. Immediately there was a problem. Milk is a valued and scarce commodity in Sarada Mandiram, and believed endowed (as the product of a cow) with multiple lifegiving qualities. It should not be thrown away. Yet, since it had touched my tumbler,[9] no inmate could now take it. Those children who pay for 'special milk' had already had theirs. The milk was transferred to a guest's cup and placed on a shelf. An hour later, after we had eaten, the cup and its contents had disappeared. I have no idea who drank it. One of the lay teachers? One of the cooks? Would they have taken it from my glass? I shall never know. During the day, if too much food or too many places are served, the extra portion is given to the sweeper, who always looks affronted when called to take it, even though she is never offered food from a plate once a person has commenced eating. If the food is from Mataji though, she would feel pleased. This sweeper informed on other workers when she brought Mataji hot water and cleaned her bathroom and latrine.

The most extreme case of aversion to food of inferiors within the Order came to my notice during a visit to Sarada Math Calcutta. A newcomer from Karnataka moved her numb foot during a meal and knocked over her glass of water. As it spread across the line of diners (who are seated on the floor in hierarchical order at Sarada Math) they jumped up, leaving their plates, and evacuated the dining room by the middle door, which was normally closed. It was as though some deadly slime was about to devour them one and all. The Karnataka girl looked bewildered. What had transpired was this. Bengalis sip their water (and all liquids) from their glass, which is held in the right hand, the same hand with which food is eaten. South Indians, on the other hand, pour liquids from their glass with their left hand, without touching the rim of glass to their lips. Therefore, a South Indian glass of water is not polluted by saliva and thus not contaminated. In their estimation there was no need for the evacuation. The Bengalis, however, had not realised this. They had not thought about the significance of the difference in custom and in any case, may not have accepted the South Indian reasoning.

I have suggested at the outset that there is an underlying principle that links notions of purity with hierarchy. The three types of purity behaviour in Sarada Mandiram are:

1 personal purity linked with religious duties;
2 hierarchical purity linked with seniority of inmates; and
3 purity linked with outsiders.

In the case of the first category, the individual must keep herself ritually pure to approach Ramakrishna-Sarada Devi. The inmate must be alert to keep herself as far from contamination as possible, lest it be transferred to her. Even when in a state of ritual purity, an inmate engaged in shrine work must wash her hands if she touches her own body or clothes, and Ganges water is liberally used to cleanse items of worship from any contamination.

In interaction between inmates, the same applies. Those senior should not be contaminated by their juniors. In this respect, Ramakrishna-Sarada Devi and Vivekananda can be regarded as the most senior inmates of Sarada Mandiram, with the President in reality coming a close second. While inmates should be careful not to contaminate seniors, they are eager to gain an intangible 'something' through receiving food, cloth or even a touch of their superiors. And, the more superior the superior, the more valuable the gift. This is especially so of food given by a senior (or *prasād* from a special temple, such as the Headquarters or Guruvayur) which the recipient will share with others, even if each receives only a minute crumb.

On the other hand, all non inmates are to be physically avoided. Their clothes, food and associated vessels are all regarded as polluted, and inmates feel a revulsion towards them. I believe this is exactly the same as the behaviour associated with hypergamy, in which the flow of prestations is always downwards for the giver.[10] That is, no matter what the object: marital partners, cooked food or cloth, the donor is always superior to the recipient. In those communities in which the two partners in marriage are of equal status, the man should be older than his wife, which introduces relative age when relative status is lacking in a relationship. This is the same principle as seniority within a family, and also within the Ramakrishna Order.

I believe there is a connection between the desire of women as the recipients in conjugal relationships (including *sambandham*) to secure spouses of higher status, and the practice of taking of *prasād*, or the desire to be near (have *darśan* of) or receive gifts from individuals believed to possess superior qualities, such as successful political leaders or *gurus*. In each case there is a desire to assimilate the qualities of the superior person into oneself.

Food after assimilation becomes part of the consumer. This is why Hindus are careful to eat only 'spiritually beneficial' foods if they wish to progress spiritually. *Prasād* is the most beneficial of all foods, and embued with the good qualities of the donor, it therefore increases these same qualities in the recipient. A devotee wishes to be like his or her *guru* or favourite deity and to be one with them and so consumes their *prasād*, which is saturated with their good qualities, by contact. By the same token, the food of inferior people is saturated with their inferior qualities, and to be shunned, lest these qualities also be transferred to and become part of the consumer. Hence, members of the Ramakrishna Order wish to partake of the superior qualities of their deities, their guru and their seniors, in order to assimilate part of these into their own bodies, but fear the food of non members who are all – according to them – worldly. Non monastic people are involved in *kāmini-kancana* (women and gold), the two activities against which Ramakrishna has warned. However, initiated householder devotees of Ramakrishna are somewhat safer than other householders, as presumably they are purified by his *mantra*, and through trying to live up to his ideals and being alert to the snares on the path. But still, anyone involved in 'women and gold' still threatens the purity of a monastic inmate, and his or her food and clothing is to be avoided. Members of the Order therefore try to eat only food cooked in their centres, and while travelling try to arrange to take food with them, or at least to eat in the homes of close devotees. Such devotees in cities where there is no centre, even keep special sheets and plates for visiting *saṃnyāsinis*, so familiar are they with their inclinations.

Hypergamy in Kerala centres on similar beliefs. The woman, the recipient of seed, should take that only of a man of superior status, so that any child born will enrich her lineage.

This brings me to a discussion of ritual pollution rules and bodily margins, as discussed by Mary Douglas (1966), and by Marglin (1977). Briefly, Douglas sees exclusive groups such as castes and even Jews as obsessed with sealing off their social margins so that assimilation (exogamy) does not take place. The body becomes a metaphor for this concern, and hence the need for purity rules, which centre on the crossing of bodily margins. Eating, excreting and sex are the main ways in which the bodily margins are crossed, and so many rules exist to regulate these activities. Marglin stresses how the separation of castes is about the separation of the powerful from the less powerful, by the closing off of social and bodily boundaries.

I suggest that purity rules concerning Hindus are not about the sealing of social boundaries, or group closure, *but of a carefully worked out system where there is interaction, but not assimilation.* This is the basis of caste. The Hindu believes in ranking the social 'evolution' of the individual over many births, until he/she is free from all the negative results of past actions, and free from desire for everything except liberation from life itself. The individual evolves by sealing himself off from bad influences and opening himself up to good influences. Hence, he does not take food cooked by those of lower castes, who are less highly evolved, but *does* take food from higher castes, who are further on the 'evolutionary' scale. Positive benefits can be had by taking the food of superiors, as I have already stated, *prasād* being the supreme example, as it is the food of the gods or of holy people. Since the prime ideological concern of members of a monastic Order is liberation, it follows that purity rules will be a prime concern also. In this respect they are similar to Brahmins, who also as a priestly caste are highest on the evolutionary scale and closely connected to religious duties. They follow the rules most closely as they have the most purity to lose. They, like gods and *saṃnyāsins* are the prime givers of food, as they have the most highly prized qualities to transmit.

Conclusion

From the above analysis it should be clear that hierarchy is essential to the fabric of Hindu society, including *saṃnyāsins.* Contrary to Dumont's assertion, though the *saṃnyāsin* belongs to no caste, he is at least as equally involved in hierarchy as are householders, and perhaps even more so. The example of the workings of hierarchy in Sarada Mandiram provides an explanation as to why this is so. Hierarchical thinking is embedded in the notion of pure/impure, which is not a series of graded dichotomies, but a system which operates not unlike a one way valve. The Hindu opens him/herself up to higher influences, and blocks off access to lower influences. The basis of this practice is based on the 'evolutionary' nature of Hindu philosophy. In each birth the individual should struggle to raise him/herself higher, to become more *sattvik* (pure) in mind and body. An individual is born into his present social position by virtue of the level of purity reached in the previous birth. The 'valve system' acts as a safeguard, allowing the assimilation of higher and purifying influences, while at the same time blocking out the low and the impure. The line drawn between the lowest caste and the three upper 'twice born' castes is based on the assumption that the former have not yet reached the level of purity at which they even concern themselves with higher thoughts.

Hierarchy in Hindu society thus begins with the *individual,* for each is born at the level which he/she has attained by self effort. Families consist of individuals of similar levels, and castes and their divisions, of larger groupings of families of similar levels. The individual must strive to achieve greater purity by assimilating purer influences into the body (such as *prasād* or other food cooked by pure categories of people) and by blocking out impure influences. At the same time the 'power' of the body must be maintained by celibacy. Thus, although the *saṃnyāsin* in theory should not be involved in caste and its underlying hierarchical base (as these belong to 'the world') he cannot avoid it. For, a low caste person denotes a low level of purity, and this person poses a threat to the *saṃnyāsin*'s own purity. This is why a *saṃnyāsin,* although in theory devoid of caste, usually eats food which is either *prasād* (offered to a deity, and so of a higher level of purity than the *saṃnyāsin* himself), cooked by a Brahmin, or a member of his own Order or sect. Indeed, some ascetics (including Ramakrishna himself) are so acutely aware of the danger to their person by impure influences, that they become fanatical in guarding against them. Deep concern over the source of their food, the proximity of low caste or 'worldly' people, and with their own bodily margins, especially the 'nine gates'[11] or points of entry and exit, renders the *saṃnyāsin* especially vulnerable to considerations of hierarchy. For, his person, more than that of even a lay Brahmin, has most to lose by purity-loss or contamination.

Rules of purity and impurity do not constitute a series of dichotomies in classifying Hindu society, but graded steps on a staircase which each individual is born to explore. Each Hindu (*saṃnyāsins* included) has a place on the staircase, and therefore is in a hierarchical position vis-a-vis fellow Hindus. A *saṃnyāsin's* whole lifestyle is aimed at an attempt to reach the top, to reach liberation, and until this is attained, maintaining and increasing his position is of the utmost importance to him. The social freedom promised by the formal absence of caste does not in fact exist, for purity/impurity and hierarchy, the underlying principles of caste, are very much part of his/her life, as part of the Hindu process of liberation.

Chapter 11

Sarada Mandiram and the Local Villagers

Religious communities are invariably studied as social isolates, as they are often assumed to be. It is convenient to draw an investigatory boundary corresponding to the Institution's walls, and to concentrate only on structures and relationships occurring within. However, in the case of Sarada Mandiram, it is vital to an understanding of the Institution to extend the enquiry further, to include the village in which it is situated, especially as it is ostensibly for the benefit of the local population.

Relations between Sarada Mandiram and the villagers were (without any qualification at all) bad. There was a constant undercurrent of tension and hostility on both sides during my period of fieldwork (which brought the underlying tensions sharply into focus). On the other hand, careful enquiries revealed that such a situation did not exist between the Asrama and the villagers, although the Asrama presumably operated on parallel lines to Sarada Mandiram.

The most frequent and basic accusation against Sarada Mandiram by the villagers was that the *saṃnyāsinis* lived in luxury and 'do no work', and the only interest expressed in the poor villagers was to exploit them to the fullest extent. I endeavoured therefore to investigate these claims.[1]

A typical village daily wage labourer lived literally from hand to mouth. The general labour pool in the village could expect Rs 12–15 per day for males and Rs 7–8 for females, working in nearby fields. By way of contrast, Asrama workers received Rs 12 and Rs 6 respectively, while Sarada Mandiram paid males only Rs 9 and females Rs 4. The working day at the two Institutions was from 8.00 a.m. until 6.00 p.m., with an hour's break for lunch, during which the workers could return to their homes. They worked seven days a week, and there was no holiday, or sick leave.

It was the seemingly harsh terms of employment at the two Institutions which in fact made them the most sought after employers by the villagers. Generally, labourers could expect no more than 200 to 250 days of work per annum, as during the height of the rain, and in mid summer, they were laid off. This was known as the lean season, when hunger was common. In summer, the schools were closed, and the bread rations[2] given to junior children ceased. Many families survived on edible leaves from their parched gardens and whatever green fruit that was on their trees. Rice, the main source of calories, was no longer taken for granted, and in this season, tempers flared easily.

Despite the lower rates of pay, the Asrama and Sarada Mandiram both offered its employees a degree of security. Daily, they lined up at the office window to receive their pay, and with this, the rice ration was purchased on the way home. Women in particular benefitted from this arrangement, as most of the village men drank, gambled and smoked *beedis* (tobacco). When women had daily work, the family had daily food, otherwise, this was by no means the case.

Not one of the labourers from Sarada Mandiram admitted that there was any benefit in working there, though those employed by the Asrama expressed a great deal of satisfaction with their employment. The latter received almost the outside rates of pay, as well as a guarantee of work, the optimum conditions, if other benefits (such as interest free loans) were also taken into consideration. On the other hand, the very low rates of pay offered by Sarada Mandiram were seen as a prime example of exploitation. The *saṃnyāsinis* knew that work was scarce and so, without conscience, paid half the going rate of pay to the women employed there. At the same time, the *saṃnyāsinis* claimed to be working for the uplift of poor women and families. They lived well using cheap labour to cultivate produce, which they then sold to their Girls Hostel at a profit. It generated a great deal of hostility when the women working at Sarada Mandiram, struggling to feed their children saw the fine food served to the monastic inmates, their plentiful clothes, and comfortable quarters. Village Communists were quick to point out the classic example of exploitation in the name of religion, as exemplified by the *saṃnyāsinis* of Sarada Mandiram.

In their resentment towards the Institution, not one villager volunteered to tell me that workers frequently obtain loans from Sarada Mandiram, which are paid back by small deductions from the daily wage. To receive a loan from the village Co-Op they would have to pawn their ornaments, and pay a high interest rate (16%). Sarada Mandiram gives loans for any request that is 'reasonable', and charges *no* interest at all. At the time of the two major Hindu-Kerala festivals nearly all workers take an advance of Rs 50, which helps them to purchase extra food, and clothes. I found out from the Sarada Mandiram office that indeed at any one time at least two labourers had substantial loans of Rs 200 or more. Surely this does not constitute exploitation.

Labourers' Grievances

When the labourers compare their standard of living with that of Sarada Mandiram they come to the conclusion that the *saṃnyāsinis* live in luxury. Three groups of buildings stand out in the village: the Asrama, the church complex and Sarada Mandiram. But, the villagers only level the charge of 'living in luxury' against Sarada Mandiram, though all three Institutions have similarly impressive buildings.

It is ironical that it is (in my opinion) the care that the Sarada Mandiram takes to keep 'Guru Maharaj's house'[3] as clean and attractive as possible, that creates the impression of opulence. In Kerala, it is the custom of every family to sweep and wipe every floor of the house after dawn and to sweep the immediate surrounds of the house, to clear away leaves. But, almost no care is taken above the floor level. In even the wealthy homes, dust and grime accumulates on furniture and woodwork, cobwebs adorn the beams (as ceilings are not common, except in very recent slab concrete constructions), and the window curtains hang limp and smelling of dust. Kitchens are blackened with soot, and bathrooms (if there is such a facility) slimy with the build up of oil used on the hair daily, and for a weekly 'oil bath'. Cockroaches thrive in the dankness of both bathroom and kitchen. After the rains each year, the *taravāds* used to be whitewashed for the Onam festival. Today, many homes cannot afford such maintenance, and even the daily 'sweeping' is costly, as women have to be paid on a monthly basis, for increasingly higher wages. But the reasons for the general air of neglect is because the women employed by Nayars to sweep today are often Izhavas, and they are not allowed to touch anything above the floor level, nor to enter the kitchen. They have a revulsion to the bathrooms as polluting and do not clean them properly. The ladies of the house do not consider housework a suitable occupation, and so only tend to dust and generally clean the house twice a year, just before Onam and Vishu, the two harvest festivals. On both occasions, spring cleaning is mandatory. Christians and Muslims similarly clean thoroughly before their major festivals.

In Sarada Mandiram, great care is taken with the surroundings. The flower garden (used to grow flowers for offering and for cut flowers to decorate the altar) is attractive, and the visitors' room and Hostel office are bright and airy, with crisp curtains and hand embroidered cushions made by free boarders. The temple is a happy combination of deep pastel walls, decorated with religious prints and sculptures, and a shrine flooded with natural light from windows in the dome, which catches the well-polished *pūjā* vessels and brocades on the altar cloth and the polished stone floor. Brightly coloured flower garlands, and gleaming vases of cut flowers and multicoloured leaves add to the brilliance of colour, so different to the dark, oil stained shrines of the usual Kerala temple. All the premises are kept clean and dusted, as both junior monastic inmates and children from the Hostel are obliged to clean daily, as part of Vivekananda's philosophy of the dignity of labour.

Both the Asrama and the church are male domains, and the same care is not taken with 'externals'. The Asrama does not boast the same attractive touches of embellishment as Sarada Mandiram, and even in the temple, the vessels and altar cloths are dull, and the flower offerings lacking artistry. Seldom are garlands or vases used. And, there is no welcoming visitors' room, in which guests are served homemade iced lime cordial or rich, sweet, milk coffee with 'snacks', all served on dainty crockery or glassware. The church, even on Christmas Eve, showed its cobwebs in the candlelight, and five of the Stations of the Cross were broken or missing.

But, the accusation of luxury is levelled especially the President in particular, for the villagers can plainly see that she lives in a different manner from the other inmates. Hostel children study and sleep in badly overcrowded, gloomy 'halls' (dormitories) with an outside toilet block. The halls have dripping clothes hanging over wires high above the children's heads, obscuring the solitary suspended light bulb, while the monastic inmates have neat rooms, with beds and curtains and bookshelves. The children study seated on the floor at low, tiny tables, and at night stack them in a corner. They spread their bedding on the floor, each child almost touching the next. Senior monastic rooms have sturdy wooden bedsteads and internal bathrooms, and even the juniors, though sleeping on the floor, have sufficient space to study and keep their belongings. The President has not only a large bedroom, but a dressing room and private bathroom, an elaborate four poster bed with a ceiling fan above, and foam mattress (a luxury), glass-fronted cupboards, an armchair and large desk and chair. Everything she uses is of fine quality: from her sandals to her heavy silver drinking glass and large metal dinner plate. Early in the morning she is brought a specially prepared beverage, and again mid morning and mid afternoon. Her meals are specially cooked to her taste, and served in an exclusive dining room, reserved for the three or four seniors, who sit at a large dining table instead of on the floor. At her invitation, special visitors join her for meals, while lesser rated guests eat on the floor in line with the children and teachers. While others come for meals at the appointed time, she comes when she pleases, sometimes causing great inconvenience to those who have to serve her, before dining themselves. When she wishes hot water to bathe (or any other service) she calls '*kutty*' (child) and one of the inmates comes running. When she wishes to visit the town or a temple, a taxi will be called by phone and when she wishes to travel interstate or to another town, she has access to funds for the purpose.

During the day she writes letters and chats with visitors. In the afternoon and at night a junior inmate massages her body. They wash and dye her clothes each fortnight, hang them up daily and fold them when dry. Her room is cleaned for her, and her bed prepared at night.[4] So, the villagers working at Sarada Mandiram conclude she has an easy life. To them, she appears to have every luxury, and to do no work. Just the same as the *kāraṇavans* of a generation ago. They only see her if there is trouble. Then she will shout, abuse and even dismiss them. In the latter circumstance they must grovel and plead for mercy, and then she may be gracious enough to reinstate them, after a few days of enduring mental anguish. And, twice a year they must bow at her feet, before she drops a piece of folded clothing into their humbly outstretched hands.

To accuse the President (or any other inmate) of not doing any work is plainly unjust. The rank and file inmates are busy from dawn till ten at night. They work very hard indeed. As for the President, on her shoulders rests the responsibility of a major Institution, with all its departments of work. She does not delegate authority. She has a vast amount of paperwork to attend to, concerning correspondence with both government agencies (who provide grants) and the Headquarters. She replies to all the general enquiries from devotees or potential candidates to the Order, and deals with all problems involving individuals, whether children, inmates, or employees, and the School. She accepts a steady stream of invitations to preach, either at meetings or in homes, and travels widely, including annually by train to Calcutta, in the midst of the blazing summer heat. She also writes numerous articles. Until she became President in 1968 she used to teach, and in the early days of the Institution did her share of heavy physical work. At the time she now had diabetes (aggravated by an unsuitable diet), high blood pressure, and asthma. Whilst I was there, she had the warning symptoms of a possible heart condition. On top of this general ill health, she suffered from severe rheumatism, and walked with a slight limp. Hence, it is not unreasonable for her to have accepted a gift of a comfortable mattress, especially as the traditional kapok ones collect mites and dust, which aggravate asthma. Nor would many reasonable people, seeing how much she suffered from the intense heat, deny her the use of the fan, or even the right to sit on a chair at meals, considering her rheumatism. She has had her years of austerity and now her health was shattered. But still, these concessions are added to non essentials, such as general privileged behaviour. It is this that is resented, plus her attitude towards 'the poor'.

Serving the Poor as God

It is interesting that the villagers complain that the *saṃnyāsinis* not only do not work hard, but that they, as the President herself said, 'have the reputation of only being nice to the rich'. These statements reflect the non-traditional expectations of the public towards the members of the Ramakrishna Order. The villagers agree with me that normally they considered *saṃnyāsins* to be like those who sit outside temples, or are seen walking along the roads, on their way to major pilgrimage centres. They do not expect these *saṃnyāsins* to work hard, nor to work for the poor. They themselves are poor, and live off alms. But the Ramakrishna Mission is different. The *saṃnyāsins* constantly talk of 'work is worship', and 'serving God in the poor'. Annual competitions are held in elocution at the School, during which students mouth Vivekananda's exhortations to uplift the downtrodden of India. 'But', said the villagers, 'they do not practice what they preach. They do not care about the poor at all. They do nothing to show that they have any interest in us.'

'Not only do they not help us', said one villager of quite a respectable position, 'but they antagonise and alienate us'. He and others gave as examples instances when vacancies were available for skilled workers at Sarada Mandiram (such as teachers and kindergarten teaching assistants). On the open employment market a teacher rarely is granted an interview unless 'known' to the Institution. The villagers feel Sarada Mandiram has a responsibility to the village but preference was given to daughters of supporters of Sarada Mandiram rather than to villagers who were qualified and desperate for the money. Apparently, when villagers have been employed, they are dismissed if a newcomer arrives who can take the position and earn a wage for Sarada Mandiram. A recent example was cited. 'It is hypocrites like them who turn God-fearing people into Naxalites'[5] said one embittered party. 'If they treated us properly', said another, 'we would bless them, and worship their Ramakrishna. We have nothing against Ramakrishna. Many boys visit the Asrama temple on their way to school. But not one visits the Sarada Mandiram temple. I don't even think the members of Sarada Mandiram worry about this. Then, what are they here for? Just to live a happy life and make themselves comfortable?'

In reply to my enquiry as to why the Asrama is seen in far more favourable light than Sarada Mandiram, the reply was that the *saṃnyāsins* lead a simple life and help the poor. It is true that the Asrama does not exude the same middle class air as Sarada Mandiram. There is no parlour, and the President is to be found sitting at a desk in one corner of the rundown Asrama office, approachable to anyone who wishes to see him. His manner of behaving towards villagers is markedly different to that of the Sarada Mandiram President. I asked the President of the Asrama how he got on with the villagers. Do they feel at home with him?

'Certainly', he replied. 'I do not allow them to stand. I ask them to sit down. When I go there also I sit along with them and talk to them. They should feel they are one of us. It requires a lot of work . . . Swamiji [Swami Vivekananda] says we must be able to look upon them as part of our own body'. When he spoke of 'going there' he referred to the Harijan Colony started by the Asrama. The Asrama has a small shrine there where once a week *bhajans* are held and stories are told to 'tell them how they can bring themselves up in a different way'. They have trained the boys to take care of the shrine, lighting the lamp both morning and evening and to keep the place clean.

While I was there, a family of 'eight or nine' needed a house badly. They had Rs 2000 saved in their account with the Asrama Saving Incentive Scheme. A devotee came to the Asrama and wanted to spend Rs 4000 on poor feeding (a meritorious act). The President persuaded him to donate it instead to help the family in need. The

Asrama matched the amount, and a house for Rs 10,000 was built. The Asrama also runs a nursery at the Colony to help working mothers, and both employees are from the Colony. Daily 15–18 people receive food in the Colony, at the Asrama's expense. The neat hospital provides free meals twice a day. So, he concluded, 'the people have faith in us, despite propaganda'. By propaganda, he referred obliquely to the Marxists, whose influence is strong in the village. In addition, the government scheme whereby 200 children under five receive bread is administered from the Asrama and therefore identified with it.

In contrast to this, the Sarada Mandiram President only meets villagers who are workers in the Institution, to check on their work or to chastise them. In other words, in situations of confrontation. The *brahmacārini* in the office, generally speaks to the labourers in the tone one would use to a child, but on occasion was both abusive and hurtful. One day a request will be met with 'OK' and the next, with a stinging rebuke. So, workers think twice before humiliating themselves before this 'girl' (though she was over 30 years old). Other villagers stay away from the Institution, as every four days on average whilst I was there, an 'incident' took place at Sarada Mandiram, and news of it spread through the village by the same evening. However petty, the villagers like to recount every detail, thereby reinforcing what they already 'know': that the *samnyāsinis* of Sarada Mandiram are 'not good people'. As one commented, 'outside the ochre robe, but inside, nothing'.

A general attitude of hostility such as this is self-perpetuating. When in the early days of my fieldwork I told the President that I had visited the Harijans,[6] she said, 'If we went there, they would say, "there go the baldheads". We are afraid to walk there'. What she meant was 'would be afraid', since nobody from Sarada Mandiram visits the village at all, except to go to the local Krishna temple, perhaps once a year on its annual festival. The temple is in the 'Nayar' lane, where no Harijans live.

When labourers receive their wages in the evening, they have to stand outside the office, and receive their money through the window bars. When the parents of a free boarder escort her to the Hostel after a vacation, they similarly have to stand or squat outside, if they want to ask anything. Mostly, they just leave the girl at the foot of the stairs, and watch her go up into the Hostel alone. Paying boarder's parents ask to see Mataji, who comes out of her room and sits with them, ordering refreshments and *prasād* to be brought. Mataji will show affection to the daughter if she is in primary school, and any comments about her progress will be couched in mild terms. 'She is a little careless sometimes'. 'She spent so much time practising dance for the competition that her marks are lower.' Parents such as these find Mataji positively charming, and express great faith in the Institution, where the children learn 'all our old values'.

One day, while such a pleasant exchange was taking place in the courtyard near the office, over a cup of coffee, a free boarder arrived with her mother. As the latter turned to leave, she was called roughly by the *brahmacārini* in the office. 'Did you ask her about her marks?' 'Not this time'. 'Why not? We are spending money and how many exams has she passed? Why should she be here?' The mother stood mute and ashamed. At that moment the child's class teacher appeared, and blocking the child's way, waved a hand and said angrily, 'She never passes anything, do you?' The whole scenario was witnessed by the first of the labourers, who had gathered at the window to receive their wages. I was also present, inside the office. Incidents such as these cause immense harm to the relations between the villagers and Sarada Mandiram, but the President is probably unaware that they take place.

However, one incident occurred whilst I was there that the President most certainly knew about. I shall endeavour to describe what transpired as I witnessed it.

In December 1981 Sarada Mandiram planned a Gala Inauguration of the new school auditorium. It was basically a room, with a roof of slab concrete, built on supporting pillars, without walls. Daily it could be used as classrooms, with the use of room dividers, as the School had a shortage of accommodation. A thousand people were officially invited to attend the celebrations, which extended over three days, and included a Womens Conference on 'Our Culture', with a variety of guest speakers. The Governor of the state, a woman, was to be guest of honour.[7] On the second day at the end of the speeches, there was to be 'entertainments', of singing and dancing by the School children, plus a film. That day, there was great excitement as the electrician ran a line from a power pole by the road, and set up coloured lights and a power board for the 'mike set'. In the drab and colourless life of the villagers, this was an event to which to look forward. Usually once a year both the village schools have an 'Anniversary' which is attended by virtually the whole village, and this Inauguration came as an added bonus.

However, as the time drew near, the villagers were told that if they wanted to attend they would be charged Rs 1, 2 or 3 according to the class of seat. All these 'seats' were places on benches outside the actual hall, while inside 400 seats had been placed for the invited guests, who did not have to pay at all. These people were monastic inmates of Sarada Mandiram and the Asrama, plus teachers, devotees from the town, other cities in Kerala, and a few from interstate, plus local notables and donors to the building fund, mostly business proprietors.

At 8.00 p.m., the appointed time, the villagers arrived at the gates. The hall was only half full, even with all the boarders from Sarada Mandiram and the Asrama boys crowded on benches at the rear. All the benches outside were vacant. At the gate sat teachers with books of tickets and a cash box. The villagers must pay, or they would be denied entry. The crowd became angry. The gates were hastily locked. The next thing I knew was that as the children danced away on the stage, the villagers had taken up stones and hurled them at the Institution. One inmate ran to the office and rang the police, whilst the *saṃnyāsinis* took petromax lanterns and patrolled the bushes to make sure nobody had managed to come in without their knowledge, by scaling the fences. The police arrived in their jeep, and the crowd fled in terror. There could well have been a major tragedy that night. As it was, a teacher was injured by stones and had to be taken to the hospital. Meanwhile the dancing went on, with only a few devotees who were staying overnight, and the Hostel children to see. All the work, all the expense of the costumes, all the magic of the event was broken. The children were told to go silently to bed.

During the scuffle, I asked what was happening, and was told that the villagers had been asked to pay, because they are unruly, and would create a disturbance if they could not see, which was not fair to the invited guests. I asked the villagers through a spokesperson in the Harijan lane, the next day, why they were so angry. They told me in a signed statement made by seven villagers of various ages who had witnessed the event and 'supported by many people'. It read as follows:

> Before the auditorium construction commenced, all the students had to give a Rs 5 donation. Then they showed two films, and the students had to attend at a minimum charge of Rs 2. Every student helped the work a lot. They laid the foundations for the floor, carrying stones and sand. On the day before the opening they cleaned the floor of the auditorium.[8] Teachers also had to pay Rs 1 if they wanted to see the film. On Thursday the students came to see the dance programme, but they could not enter because they had no ticket. All of them turned back home. After

> the programme started the people became angry with the *saṃnyāsinis.* They asked, why aren't the pupils at last [sic] given permission, if they are students of the school? Then they were told that if 'you people' see the film,[9] you will understand how to lead a good life! So, they became angry and started to throw stones, in order to stop this cinema from taking place. But, they are very sorry for the teacher who were [sic] injured. They are sorry that they didn't get any of the *saṃnyāsinis* instead.

The inmates of Sarada Mandiram were subdued the next day, and that night Mataji lost her temper and gave a Hostel girl 20 lashes of a flexible cane, for talking during study time. The girl was injured, and kept alone in a Math corridor, and was not allowed to talk to anyone for weeks. The violence of this incident, coupled with the events of the previous day cast fear over the whole Institution. One educated person living there said to me, 'One day, either today or tomorrow, the workers here will rise up. Who will milk the cows? The *brahmacārinis*? One day they will have the courage to do what they must'. News of the Inauguration and Hostel girl spread through the village,[10] and those who worked in Sarada Mandiram were under pressure from others. But, they continued to come to work as usual: very subdued, but afraid to stay away.

The events of these two days have had an incalculable effect on the relations between Sarada Mandiram and the villagers. The villagers from then on used stronger and stronger vocabulary when referring to the *saṃnyāsinis*, and the *saṃnyāsinis* spoke of the ungratefulness of the villagers and their lack of loyalty to the Institution. At the school Anniversary in February, the usual local entrepreneur arrived at the gate with a contraption on wheels from which he sold cheap sweets[11] and peanuts, in cones of discarded notebook paper. The auditorium was full, with students of the Asrama and Sarada Mandiram Hostels and the prizewinners of various exams and competitions held throughout the school year. But the grounds, annually packed with villagers, were empty. They had boycotted the event. Even after dark, when the prizegiving was over and the entertainment by the School children began, the villagers stayed away. This was two and a half months after the fateful Inauguration. Though this time there was no charge, the villagers refused to attend.

The rift between the villagers and Sarada Mandiram is clearly seen at times of crisis. Three weeks after the Inauguration, a temple elephant 'went mad' and in the early hours of the morning escaped from the custody of its *mahut.* After causing havoc and killing a lone cyclist (*Indian Express,* 29 December 1980), it ran towards the village and finally came to a halt in a compound behind Sarada Mandiram. An urgent phone call was made to the Asrama and Sarada Mandiram to warn them of the danger, as the elephant had smashed lorries, buses, houses and walls, and its *mahut* was in hospital. Along the lanes people cried out 'run for your life, the elephant is coming'. Terrified Harijans, grabbing their children in their arms ran, not knowing where, crying out to others to run also. Finally, after fleeing in all directions, a group banged on the gates of the church, which is near their lane. The watchman came out, and informed the priest (not opening the gates until he had done so). The villagers took refuge in the church, and 'all of them prayed to God'. At 7.30 a.m., the elephant was subdued with an injection of sedative fired from a gun. It was tied up, but not taken away. The villagers said they believed that Jesus had protected them, even though they were Hindu. They believed it was his nature to be compassionate to the poor, and that is why he let them in.

The workers arrived late that morning to Sarada Mandiram, looking frightened and exhausted. 'We have been running all night', a worker said to one of the *saṃnyāsinis.* None had eaten breakfast. 'Enough talk about elephants', said the *saṃnyāsini.* 'You are all very late. Get to work now'.

For two days the workers could not sleep, through fear, as the elephant was still not taken away.[12] Even in Sarada Mandiram, the smaller children were taken from their isolated building to sleep with the older girls, because they were so frightened. I was alone and petrified in the guest house, but did not ask to move. The workers said to me, 'See, they couldn't feel our terror. None of us even thought of going to Sarada Mandiram for protection'. At the time of crisis villagers turned to Jesus, not the priest, for mercy, and rejected the *saṃnyāsinis,* not Ramakrishna. This was not the only time that I found evidence of the Hindu villagers expressing faith in Jesus, while having no interest in Christianity as a religion. The church to them *meant* Jesus, while Sarada Mandiram *meant* the *saṃnyāsinis.* Soon after, the father of one of the workers was given a Christian religious medal by a fellow passenger on a local bus. He took this as a special omen, and gave it to his daughter. She wore it on a thread around her neck. One of the *saṃnyāsinis* asked why she, a Hindu, wore it. 'I like Jesus', was the reply. I wondered at her courage. 'They [the *saṃnyāsinis*] preach that all religions are good,' she said to me. 'And, they will not tell *me* what to do.'

'We should care about public opinion', said Mataji one day. 'If they criticise us, we should thank them'. I asked one senior *saṃnyāsini* about the villagers. In the early days they used to visit the Harijan Colony, when Sarada Mandiram was under the control of the Asrama. Now Sarada Mandiram does not seem to concern itself with the uplift of the villagers, especially as the free boarders must come from outside the village, due to government imposed residential rules.

Mataji once told me that the villagers have 'no loyalty to the Institution'. They were in full agreement with this statement. 'They say we don't work when they turn their backs for a few minutes. Maybe it is true. If they paid us properly, we would work hard'. I then asked about certain incidents that had taken place over the years. What about the labourer who seduced an emotionally disturbed orphan? What about the family that was brewing illicit alcohol on the premises at night? What about *every day* when the workers go home, with stolen fruit? That's right, *I have noticed.* So have the *saṃnyāsinis.* But, they don't say a word.

'Yes, that's true', said a villager. 'We have no *sneham* towards Sarada Mandiram'. *Sneham* means both loyalty and goodwill. I think this sentiment is mutual.

The management of Sarada Mandiram has changed its raison d'etre over the years, without in fact recognising it. It started as a means of uplifting local Harijans, by education. The Dedicated Women Workers who threw in their lot with the Institution received status only through the emerging Gandhian Movement, which raised 'service to the poor' to an honourable religious duty. Working for Harijans became a noble cause among the Western educated, while it remained enormously threatening for the local Hindu landlords, who were struggling to keep their property in the face of the partition of *taravāds,* and the distribution of land to the tenant workers. But, as landlords saw that the battle was lost, they too began to support the Gandhians, realising that if the tenants were not given rights, they would seize them by force, as Marxist ideas swept through the Malabar Coast. Thus it was that one of the most powerful landlords gave land for the Harijan Colony, administered by the Asrama.

As the year of Independence grew near, the Sarada Mandiram along with the Asrama had become a focal point of the life of the local aristocracy, and the Dedicated Women Workers had become treated with some respect. They were now fully qualified teachers of an Institution of repute, which now catered not only for Harijans but for caste Hindu girls who, living in rural areas, could stay at Sarada Mandiram to complete their High School education. Parents trusted the Institution, as it was now run largely by caste Hindu workers: respectable women.

The Dedicated Women Workers had fought hard to achieve the status of respectability. After all, they were women living alone, unmarried, and therefore open to speculation as to why they had chosen such a hard life. They lived in near poverty, especially during the War years when food was in short supply, and wore rough cloth produced in the Asrama Industrial Sector. When two of them went to Dwarka, they were met at one of the stations by devotees of the Ramakrishna Order. One of the *saṃnyāsinis* recalled how the hostess took one look at them in their soot-encrusted cheap clothes and dirty hair and treated them as inferiors. She thought they were orphans. By the end of their visit, the family was astounded to find that the pair spoke excellent English, were well-educated, and that one of them was the niece of her next-door neighbour in her home in Kerala. The incident happened about thirty years previously, but the indignity suffered by the *saṃnyāsini* was not forgotten. She was from a *good family*, and not used to be treated otherwise. By the time the Dedicated Women Workers were accepted as *brahmacārinis* of the newly formed Sarada Math, they had already established respectable status by their role of administrators and teachers of a girls boarding School. Their patrons were of good families, and gradually the *brahamacārinis* became accepted into the best homes as desirable guests. After becoming *saṃnyāsinis* their status among devotees was great enhanced: now there was positive advantage in inviting these women to the house. They were no longer ambiguous: they were holy women, representatives of the highest ideals of Hinduism, and now sought after as speakers at pious gatherings.

After Independence the Gandhian people's campaign against Untouchability gave way to legislation, and as Harijans challenged caste Hindus for places in Colleges and in the workforce under the Reservation scheme, helping Harijans became an unpopular cause. In Kerala, landlords not only lost their land to their tenants, but many of the tenants did not pay the compensation required by law. There was now no prestige to be gained by identifying with Harijans, whom caste Hindus suspected were no longer 'hard done by'. Now it was they the former landowners who were suffering, but nobody cared. In Trichur, first Syrian Christians, and later Izhavas, stepped in to fill the power vacuum left by the decline of the Nayar and Nambudiri former landowners.

As the prestige of identifying with the poor declined, at the same time (just post-Independence) the Dedicated Women Workers became part of the Sarada Math, and gained a new form of prestige: as *saṃnyāsinis.* This prestige was based on ancient notions of *saṃnyāsa* as the highest state, and was quite independent of the notion of 'service to the poor', even though Vivekananda had tied these concepts together at the turn of the century. The *saṃnyāsinis* now identified with women of aristocratic homes, whose behaviour they began to emulate, as increased funds (from paying boarders) gave them a higher standard of living. Service to the poor now became a quaint notion, to be relegated to elocution competitions, during which Vivekananda's sentiments on the subject were recited by earnest schoolgirls. Sarada Mandiram, by the time of its separation from the Asrama, had become a boarding School for middle class girls, *with some places available for Harijans.* In 1981 there were 22 Scheduled Caste girls in the Hostel out of a total of 131 students. The Institution employed Scheduled Caste workers as labourers, but it could no longer be said that the Institution existed for the uplift of Harijans. Indeed, the *saṃnyāsinis* did not see this as their primary function. Now that they were *saṃnyāsinis,* their main duty was to attain realisation themselves, and to preach religion to others, in order to stem the tide of atheism and Westernisation. They believe that by educating middle class girls in 'our old traditions', Hindu ideals (whatever that means) will be preserved in the home.

By contrast, the Asrama is active in helping local Harijans, which it still views as one of its primary functions. So, the villagers compare the two Institutions, assume that they operate under the same ideology, and judge one to be sincere, and the other hypocritical. With one eye at the middle class veneer of Sarada Mandiram, the villagers also conclude that Sarada Mandiram is 'out to impress' the wealthy, to attract money. And, this money they use for their own comfort, turning away from the villagers, and their needs.

Whilst the wealthy landowning families have declined to the point of poverty in post-War years, Sarada Mandiram has prospered, through fees, grants and donations. It represents for the women of the 'old families' a relic of the days when *taravāds* functioned in all their glory: well maintained and prosperous. But, part of the glory of the *taravāds* was the retinue of workers and servants, mute and humbled before their masters. I believe this is the heady fantasy that Sarada Mandiram is perpetuating. *It is the last of these great taravāds.* This is how its senior *saṃnyāsinis* behave, mimicking the roles of *kāraṇavan, kāristhan,* seniority etc. However, times are changing, and

I suggest that this fantasy will not endure very long, for Sarada Mandiram is finding out that the patronage of the old aristocracy is no longer worth pursuing. Their future support is beginning to come from another direction, in which the *taravād* model is inappropriate.

Conclusion

Sarada Mandiram is now struggling to retain its self-image. The values of the Nayar aristocracy, with the added ideals of service to the poor (first publicised by Vivekananda and given respectable status by Gandhi) were a workable combination when the Institution was emerging as a separate entity, that is, between 1948–1953. However, the aristocracy exists today only in the minds of its impoverished members, and the ideal of service to the poor is a most unpopular cause with its overtones of condescension.

In the early days Sarada Mandiram was itself poor, and its inmates were unpaid workers and free boarders. But over the years, the majority of its boarders has become paying, government grants have helped to cover the expenses of the free boarders, and monastic inmates have been drawing salaries, paid by the government, as teachers and Wardens. The garden provides crops which are sold by the Sarada Mandiram to its Hostel or even on the open market, and reliable sources of donations in cash and kind are established to ensure the Institution's financial viability.

In the early days of the Institution the aristocracy was already on the decline, and so the women of good *taravāds* enjoyed supporting Sarada Mandiram, as a place where their traditions would be continued. They visited with donations of large vessels, abandoned in their ancestral homes, with grain and cloth. They transported the *brahmacārinis* (who later became *saṃnyāsinis*) to meetings in their chauffeur-driven cars, and arranged for their overnight stays and food when necessary. I often heard seniors say, 'so-and-so was just like a *mother* to us.' These women were in every way patrons of the Institution, as devotion to the ideals of the Ramakrishna Movement was one way of justifying their changing position. Their self-image altered from that of feudal landholders, exercising brutal control over tenants on their land, to that of the new enlightened elite, which was intent on raising their Backward Communities to full equality in the new independent India. Devotees faced their loss of property, ancestral homes, servants and revenue not as a disastrous decline in status (in a society in which family status was all important) but as part of their new spiritual goals, in which personal austerity was recommended, if not prescribed. Devotees viewed themselves not as poor, but austere, and this was reinforced by the Gandhian movement in which positive value was given to simplicity of lifestyle, dress and diet. Their new destiny was to use their superiority (by virtue of heritage) not to *rule over* others, but to *lead them* to education and social refinement. By supporting Sarada Mandiram, which was established for Harijan welfare, they were vicariously working for Harijans themselves, while reaping the benefits of *punya* or religious merit by involving themselves in such lofty ideals.

Sarada Mandiram developed increasingly during the late fifties and sixties into a paying boarding School with 'some free places' for Harijans, and its fees now provided a steady source of income for consolidation and expansion. In the meantime, the patrons had declined rapidly in both financial and social status, as tenants seized land and withheld compensation, and simultaneously new criteria for status evolved, based on education and newly-gained wealth.

Now the tables were turned: the patrons had aged, and in many cases their daughters were not interested in Sarada Mandiram. Often after they secured a 'good' marriage with a well-educated man, they left for interstate or overseas. The new generation sought a life in the city, where there was employment, cinema, modern housing and (for the more adventurous) a social life with a circle of friends. They were the first generation to start living in the nuclear family and derived their income from employment or a profession. For this generation, Sarada Mandiram became a place to visit after a marriage, or the birth of a child, when mother dragged them there to ensure a blessing.

The monastic inmates did not seem to come to grips with the change in attitude that had taken place among Nayars since the break up of the joint families. While the older generation rejoiced to see the existence of an Institution which represented the last vestige of '*taravād* living', the younger generation found it hard to relate to the atmosphere it exuded, at any level. Sarada Mandiram's rigid adherence to hierarchy where youth had always to defer to age was unattractive to the first generation of Nayar nuclear families, who had grown up as the centre of attention in the home.

By the 1960s, daughters of the original patrons of Sarada

Mandiram began looking for suitable schools for their daughters. Young women whose husbands were interstate or abroad sought schools in Kerala where children could speak their mother tongue. Mothers of boarders often recommended Sarada Mandiram and its School, as the main alternative to Catholic 'convents' in the large towns. Until the mid-seventies, Sarada Girls School maintained one division of each standard as English medium, and it was in this division that daughters of the former aristocracy congregated. It was phased out due to the declining number of parents requesting English medium, the trend illustrating the change in the type of paying boarders being admitted to the Institution by this time.

Many of the girls admitted to the Hostel from prosperous families in the mid-seventies begged to be withdrawn within a year. The could not manage communal living in which girls slept and studied in crowded 'halls' with poor ventilation and no fans. They had to wash at open wells, and arise at 5.00 a.m. to bathe. Though the food was good Nayar food, it was vegetarian, though most modern families were now experimenting with eggs, if not fish, as well as other cuisines which were simple to prepare in the absence of servants.

Girls were restricted to wearing very old fashioned skirts and loose overblouses with outmoded undergarments, and slept fully clothed. They also had to attend long prayer sessions and religion classes daily, and to help with domestic, kitchen and garden work. Girls from well-educated families found they had little in common with village girls, and felt the pressures of jealousy that were subtly levelled against them. When the English medium divisions were stopped, parents of close devotees' families who persevered with the Institution found it a good excuse to remove their daughters, and to send them instead to well-known city convents. These were not only English medium, but modern and Westernised in outlook and accommodation, and considered avant-garde. There was always comment at Sarada Mandiram concerning these 'defections', but they were said to be due to the indulgent upbringing the children had undergone, so that their young lives were self centred, making them unable to 'adjust' with other children.

In the mid-seventies, therefore, Sarada Mandiram faced a crisis. Its original patrons were ageing and, their financial situation having declined, no longer retained cars and drivers. Their own daughters (and grand daughters) did not share in the need to rationalize their decline in wealth and prestige. They were busy building up new status based not on family reputation but on education, high-prestige occupations and four figure monthly salaries. As part of this process, they for the most part were hostile to projects for the uplift of Backward Communities.

After the first flush of enthusiasm shown by Nayars (and even some wealthy Nambudiris) in working for the welfare of Backward Communities, a rapid disillusionment set in, culminating in the often-aired opinion that now caste Hindus were backward, and so-called Backward Communities, prosperous. Children who expected to receive a small parcel of land or at least compensation due by tenants when their *taravāds* were divided, found they received nothing. When caste Hindu youth applied for 'seats' in College or for employment, they found that even with a good academic record they often were rejected in favour of candidates from Backward Communities, who were accepted according to the rules of 'Reservations'. Thus, in Kerala, where job opportunities are few and the general level of education high by Indian standards, many well-educated youth face unemployment. Unemployed youth from Backward Communities can fall back on manual work (however humiliating) and even go overseas as contract labourers, but youth of caste Hindu families will not, forcing them either to rely on relatives to support them, or to leave Kerala in search of work in the big cities. Therefore, those who have been raised in post-Independence Kerala feel not compassion and a desire to help those of Backward Communities, but see them as first taking away their property, and now their educational and work opportunities. Any Institution that has a basic tenet the uplift of Backward Communities today, is operating on a seriously dated set of values.

In the meantime, the rapid upward mobility of sections of the Izhava community in particular caused the more affluent of its members to seek at the same time both a modern Westernised lifestyle, and to copy some of the external trappings of the 'good family', such as in dress and 'cultured behaviour'. Izhava businessmen and those who secured contract work overseas (in the Persian Gulf) now sought boarding schools for their daughters, as the Nayars had done since the fifties. Whilst some well-to-do Nayar parents of the post-Independence generation saw Sarada Mandiram as representing an outmoded lifestyle and set of values, these few Izhavas saw the Institution as an excellent means for their daughters to receive a training in 'caste' Hindu refined living, and 'taste'. In this way their daughters would be separated culturally from rank and file Izhavas, and thus hopefully marry a professional or businessman, and gain new social status based on individual achievement rather than community.

Hence, as Sarada Mandiram entered the eighties, it had reached a crucial watershed in its development, a watershed that could determine its very survival, not only as a School and Hostel, but as a religious Institution, and part of the whole Ramakrishna Movement. The place of Sarada Mandiram in present day Kerala, and its possible future direction merits further discussion, to which I shall devote my concluding remarks.

During my stay at Sarada Mandiram, there were widespread rumours that the Marxist-dominated state government intended to take over all private educational Institutions. This only added to the resolve of the Headquarters to remove all monastic staff from Sarada Girls High School as soon as possible.

The recent retirement of the monastic foundation Headmistress of the Girls High School had precipitated the hasty withdrawal of the senior *saṃnyāsinis* from the School. In accordance with the Kerala Education Rules, the seniormost teacher automatically becomes the next Headmistress. This is without any regard to the person's leadership or even teaching ability, commitment to the School or respect for the management or the School's goals. Now, although Sarada Mandiram could continue to appoint a School Manager, the position of Headmistress was lost to the monastic staff. Most lay teachers I spoke to believed that seniority was indeed the fairest method of selection as otherwise bribery would determine the choice. Headmistresses received substantially higher salaries than other teachers, and greatly added prestige. Respect for seniority was universally understood, and in any case, in this way communal bias in selection was neatly avoided.

However, it was the respect due to the Headmistress that hastened the departure of the senior monastic teachers. I was told that 'We are not going to stand when she enters the room'. So, they resigned, leaving a very large gap in the Sarada Mandiram annual revenue. The authorities at Headquarters entirely agreed with the decision to remove all senior *saṃnyāsinis* from the School, and added that the junior monastic inmates should also be withdrawn, for they should not be forced to show respect to a householder.

Even if another *saṃnyāsini* had replaced the retiring Headmistress, the problem would not have been solved for long. All the senior *saṃnyāsinis* were close to retiring age (having been Hostel students at Sarada Mandiram together), and the next generation of Kerala monastic inmates was not qualified for the position. As it was, Karnataka monastic inmates were teaching at the School, without even being able to read or write in Malayalam, as few Malayalam-speaking girls were seeking admission as monastic candidates. The idea had been to keep vacancies open for a set number of monastic inmates, despite transfers to Headquarters and other centres, in order to reach a certain level of salaries, which were used for the running expenses of Sarada Mandiram.

This whole situation was entirely unsatisfactory to the General Secretary of the Order, especially as it was a Rule that no monastic member of the Order was to receive remuneration. However, in other states, monastic inmates did not receive a salary, as payment to teachers in these Institutions was not under government control. In Kerala, to work without pay would simply have meant donating their services to the Marxist-controlled education system. As far as the authorities at Headquarters were concerned, the removal of the monastic inmates from the School was a welcome and overdue move. The School was becoming an increasing cause of concern, with frequent strikes and discipline problems and a lack of qualified monastic staff to retain continuity. The only reservation was the effect this would have on the Sarada Mandiram Hostel.

By 1980, Sarada Mandiram Hostel was finding it difficult to attract and keep students from well known Nayar and aristocratic families, for reasons I have already outlined, and the shortfall in paying boarders was gradually being filled by Izhavas. No doubt, Mataji's presence was an encouraging factor to Izhava parents, who otherwise may have felt quite out of place with the aristocratic Nayar pretensions of the Institution.

However, I cannot see the active recruitment of Izhava girls as the solution for Sarada Mandiram's viability. There may be a brief period during which some Izhava parents wish to emulate Nayars, but I believe this trend is or was shortlived. The overwhelming concern of parents, both Izhava and Nayar, is to find a suitable match for their daughters: on this a family's reputation ultimately depends. No longer is traditional family status the overriding factor in the choice of a spouse. A girl must be well educated, and preferably have paid employment in order to secure a 'good' match. Today's newlyweds will more than likely need to establish a home since few parents have the means to provide one, and this requires both parties to have both a steady income and prospects for the future. Middle class parents will expect their daughters to attend College, as much in the hope that this will help them to secure a match with a young professional man, as for education's own sake.

In the 1960s, when Sarada Mandiram was gradually working towards becoming an independent Institution, parents were still concerned that their daughters have old-fashioned, conservative values, such as they would learn at Sarada Mandiram, as these were still valued. But, numerous parents in 1980–1 expressed their concern to me over the implications of an Asrama-like education. They were worried that the asceticism preached by the Ramakrishna Order would count against their daughter's marriage prospects, since many young men sought a 'modern' wife. A city convent provided a much better education than Sarada Mandiram's village School, and the use of English medium enhanced the student's College prospects. Thus, I cannot see how many parents (Izhava or Nayar) with the capacity to pay, will continue to choose Sarada Mandiram Hostel as it is presently run, especially with the School more and more out of the control of the Institution. But, even more serious than the crisis facing the Hostel, is the lack of general support for Sarada Mandiram in the form of 'devotees'. This amounts to a rejection of the ideals for which the Institution stands, both by the more educated Hindu women of the Trichur region, but even more noticibly, by the caste Hindu and middle class Izhava women of the village. The Institution, which educates all the girls of the village, is in the unique position to gain the goodwill and support of local families of all communities, but instead has succeeded only in alienating itself. If a new direction is not taken, the future for Sarada Mandiram looks very bleak indeed.

Sarada Mandiram needs to enter a new phase in its history, and its revitalisation rests entirely on the judicious choice of President. The choice is narrow, as in an out of the way village, the President needs to speak the local language as well as being able to command respect of outsiders. For, as we have seen, when the President is available it is breach of the rules of seniority for her juniors to receive visitors.

The relations between Sarada Mandiram and the villagers could change with a new President, but this assumes that the *saṃnyāsinis* at Headquarters and the new appointee recognise the need for change. When the office bearers visit, the Institution is a hive of activity. The few devotees are sure to visit and the Institution appears to be thriving. Not even the Annual Report hints at the lack of devotees. The head of Sarada Mandiram shrugged away the lack of devotees as a testimony to the general worldliness of today's generation. She did not take a long hard look at the fact that other local Institutions, (including those run by rival Hindu groups) were indeed thriving, especially those competing for the same 'market', the new middle class. It would take an exceptional leader to admit the Institution's shortcomings and to address them, all within the cumbersome and conservative framework of the Sarada Math administration.

Ultimately, though, the present crisis facing Sarada Mandiram is one which has faced many other socio-religious organisations. It affects those movements which arose as answers for particular problems of their time, and appealed to a particular segment of a population, more than likely one recently alienated from its belief system by rapid social upheaval. But, when the pressures of social upheaval subside, individuals find new direction and adapt to a new lifestyle, and in doing so may no longer need the belief system which sustained them in their period of transition. If the movement can adapt at the same pace as its individual members, it has a chance to retain its followers over a period of time. Otherwise it will languish, as it ceases to be relevant.

It is movements with a broader base of appeal which address themselves to perennial or chronic problems of the 'human condition', that are more likely to endure than those which arise as a response to a particular urgent problem which may be resolved in time.

The Ramakrishna Movement rose and prospered at the time of the dawning of Nationalist consciousness in Colonial India, at a time when a Western education was alienating Hindus from their belief system as then practised. And, over its century of existence, the Movement, through the Ramakrishna Order, has maintained an appeal in its native Bengal, and in particular in Calcutta, much in the same way as the charitable Orders of the Catholic church in the West. Ramakrishna, as a 'saint' is generally known, and his picture appears in many shops, offices and even buses, along with pictures of Vivekananda and Sarada Devi. The charitable, medical and educational work of the Order is especially well known, and Institutions run by the Order dot the city of Calcutta.

But, knowing that 'the Mission' is there, and perhaps on occasion using its services, visiting an Institution or giving a donation, does not make one a devotee. The Ramakrishna Order was founded to spread the teachings of Ramakrishna as *avatār* (the saviour) of the Kali Yuga, the last of the four cyclic ages of Hindu philosophy, which end in the destruction of the world. According to the teachings of the Order, Ramakrishna is *sarva deva devi swarupāya,* that is, 'all gods and goddesses are included in him', meaning that to worship him and follow his teachings is all that is needed to guide one through life in the Kali Yuga. However, very few accept this, and even among staunch devotees, the worship of other deities is common. Total commitment to the Ramakrishna Movement is rare, even among so-called devotees, and even in Calcutta, the Order's stronghold.

The Ramakrishna Order, through its Maths and Missions, sought to spread throughout India and beyond. It was Vivekananda's dream that *saṃnyāsins* and workers would go to even the remotest villages bringing education and medical help. However, this grandiose plan was never to materialise. And, I would like to venture a reason why.

Ramakrishna diagnosed the malady of the Kali Yuga as *kāmini kamcana*, (women and gold) and prescribed celibacy and dispassion as the only remedy. He taught that attachment to family and the cravings for possessions were powers of Maya: illusion. But, what he saw as the ailments of the Kali Yuga, were not necessarily those which motivated most people to seek solace in other deities and philosophies.

At the time of Ramakrishna, there was a rekindling of religious and cultural pride among the educated, as a backlash to the pressures of Westernisation in Calcutta and other major cities of India. This in turn was directed to a Nationalist consciousness, which emerged during Vivekananda's lifetime, and which lasted until Independence was achieved. But, once this era passed, the middle class urban Hindus spent their energies on securing education and 'good' marriages for their children, their own career or business advancement, and the acquisition of possessions. Those who moved to the cities mostly sought to better themselves and to make their lives comfortable with consumer goods undreamed of a generation ago. Most of the modern day *gurus* of Hinduism have realised this trend, and promised their devotees health and success in their worldly pursuits, in return for offerings and devotion. The Hindu temples that have grown to national places of pilgrimages, have become so for the favours and miracles said to be bestowed on the faithful in return for offerings.

Against this, the promise of eventual liberation for the followers of Ramakrishna, in return for chastity, piety and abstemious living seems a meagre reward to the majority of urban Hindus and irrelevant for the poor. While Ramakrishna promised his followers abundant blessings during his lifetime, he would not accept offerings in return for non-spiritual goals. Knowing this, while the centres of the Ramakrishna Order are frequented by those seeking an inspiring discourse or a little peace and solitude, they are avoided by those seeking to be cured of an affliction, to pass examinations, to succeed in a venture or to seek blessings for the 'right match' for their daughters. In short, the product marketed by the Ramakrishna

Movement, namely salvation, is not one in great demand, and Vivekananda's plan for the uplift of the poor finds little sympathy today. This is seen a the task of government. On the other hand, the Marxist parties, popular in Bengal and Kerala in particular, aim not merely at teaching and ennobling the poor, but in destroying the power base of the wealthy: especially landowners and businessmen. In Kerala today, where Marxist rhetoric has permeated every village, religious Orders of all religions and sects are generally viewed as suspect, as they are seen as encouraging the oppressed to accept their lot. The Narayana Guru and Ramakrishna Movements are perhaps the exceptions to this, the former being much admired by Izhavas (although scorned in the main by caste Hindus) while those of all communities who have read Vivekananda's teachings usually have at least some respect for the Order he founded, although ignorant of Ramakrishna.

Few Indians who have read Vivekananda's impassioned pleas for the uplift of India's oppressed masses have failed to be moved, nor those who have read his speeches in which he predicts India will reawaken and be a guiding light to the rest of the world (however unlikely this may seem to the Western observer). Indeed, some of Kerala's leading Marxists harbour nothing but warm feelings towards the Ramakrishna Order in Kerala, some saying that even the great Sankaracarya, founder of the Dasanami Order of *saṃnyāsins*, and a Kerala Brahmin, also believed that in the highest analysis, all men were equal. Thus, Marxists and members of the Ramakrishna Order approach the same problems, but by differing paths. Not one Marxist leader from Trichur town expressed any uneasiness to me over the comfortable lifestyle of the *saṃnyāsinis* of the Ramakrishna Order. Possibly they are not aware that they differ from those of the *saṃnyāsins*. I noticed, though, that leading Marxists themselves lived in considerable style, so perhaps would not feel justified in criticising others, lest their own double standards came under public scrutiny.

But, the villagers, close to Sarada Mandiram, were not so generous. Their children came home mouthing Vivekananda's pious words, to a humble hut, with barely enough to eat or wear. Many hungry village School children sat at lunch time, watching the boarders filing in and out of the Hostel dining room. All knew of the hearty food enjoyed by the senior *saṃnyāsinis* and their guests. The older generation, looking through the massive gates of Sarada Mandiram see not ascetics reaching out to them, as they claim, but rather, people who are not 'real' *saṃnyāsinis* living in luxury, indifferent to their suffering.

Indeed, they see in Sarada Mandiram the last of the *taravād* system, where the poor toil for the landlord, having to accept virtually any conditions. A rebellious worker was all too easy to replace, and dismissal of one was likely to force other workers into submission, albeit sullen and unwilling.

Marxist activists in the village, however, aware of the 'lofty ideals' of Vivekananda, point out to the villagers on every occasion that Sarada Mandiram exists not for the benefit of the village, but for the benefit of its monastic inmates who use the villagers as cheap labour. In this respect the *saṃnyāsinis* are worse than the landlords of the past. The landlords did not even pretend to have the welfare of villagers at heart. Moreover, they belonged to an era in which the intricacies of hierarchy were accepted as part of the existing social order. But, these *saṃnyāsinis*, who are supposed to be without caste or communal affiliation, have set themselves up as a quasi aristocracy. The real land based aristocracy has been destroyed, but Sarada Mandiram remains, as a symbol of the past, at which villagers can readily point a finger. And, to increase the villagers' ire even further, these *saṃnyāsini*-aristocrats for the most part come from very humble backgrounds, from the ranks of the oppressed and exploited themselves.

* * *

To return to my opening observations:

The *saṃnyāsin* as an 'individual-outside-the-world' exists I suspect only in the realm of folklore. He is 'of such stuff as myths are made' [sic]. The bold, independent *saṃnyāsin*, who truly has no thought for caste, kin, status, or concerns for ritual purity, must be exceedingly rare.[2] Yet, honour him, as is the Hindu practice, showering him with gifts, a fine home, clothes and a retinue of helpers (*sevikas*), disciples and lay devotees, and he will vanish. Thus once more ensnared in the social world (*saṃsāra*), he ceases to exist. He has become his own antithesis: the celebrity-*saṃnyāsin*, so often to be later 'exposed' and shamed by disillusioned disciples.

Certainly the *saṃnyāsins* of the established sects and monastic Orders live squarely within the parameters of Hindu society. Once living communally, their food, clothes, speech, devotees, and even the deities they worship all label them as related to a particular secular community. Thus, the Trichur Sarada Mandiram exists as a quasi-Nayar Institution: moreover modelled on the former aristocratic *taravād*. The Order established in the name of Narayana Guru, (represented throughout Kerala and in neighbouring states) is unmistakably Izhavas, as was its Guru. Although the Ramakrishna Order claims that devotees from a community of their own, we have seen that one local community ('dominant caste') tends to dominate each branch of the Order.

Moreover, once accepted as a monastic inmate in any Institution, a candidate for *saṃnyāsa* becomes part of a hierarchical structure, at the apex of which is the monastery's head, whether known as President, Guru or traditional Mahant. Part of this structure indeed involves a hierarchy of purity, with once again the same apex.

In discussing these topics, I have opened the way for a new understanding, emphasising not dichotomies and closure, but a 'valve' system, in which the 'higher' purity is actively encouraged to flow through to the lower levels, but prevents where possible the lower levels from contaminating the higher. This indeed, is the underlying principle of hierarchy in Hindu society.

Notes

Introduction

1 I use the term 'asceticism' (and 'ascetic') in preference to Dumont's 'renunciation' and 'renouncer', to cover all categories of people who have forsaken kinship ties and social obligations, to devote themselves to religious exercises.
2 The others are *brahmacāri*, *gṛhastha* and *vanaprastha*, or celibate student, householder and forest hermit.
3 *Saṃnyāsa* refers only to those who have, by means of appropriate ritual, entered a religious Order. Not all ascetics have taken this step, especially women, for whom the option of *saṃnyāsa* is not always available.
4 Even non-academic 'seekers' (Vandana 1978 and Murray 1980), in works on various *gurus* and *āśramas* are unaware of the existence of a female Hindu religious Order, even though the former, a Catholic sister, visited Sri Sarada Mandiram, the very Institution examined in this book.
5 A feminine form of *saṃnyāsin.*
6 Sri is a respectful title, but the Institution is commonly referred to as 'Sarada Mandiram'. 'Sri' is usually omitted in similar contexts also.
7 Ancestral home of a Nayar, member of a major Kerala community.

Chapter One

1 The reputed author of an ancient book of Hindu law.
2 The practice of a wife mounting her husband's funeral pyre.
3 Born Gadadhar Chattopadhyaya.
4 The 'authorized' sources published by the Ramakrishna Order.
5 Wheels.
6 Cereals, fish, meat, wine and sexual union (*Abridged GSR*:587).
7 Even during menstrual periods. Ramakrishna is said to have told her 'purity and impurity reside in the mind' (Gambhirananda 1977:87).
8 Sanskrit formula used for repetition during meditation.

Chapter Two

1 Founded by Sankaracarya, possibly in the eighth century.
2 Emphasis mine.

3 Berger and Luckman (1966) have noted that 'insertion' is common in religious biography: 'Since it is relatively easier to invent things that never happened than to forget those that actually did, the individual may fabricate and insert events wherever they are needed to harmonize the remembered with the reinterpreted past' (p. 180).
4 Since he had not renounced his Brahmo pledge.
5 Much of it regarding *satī* and 'idol worship'.
6 Leon Landsberg became Swami Kripananda and Marie Louise, Swami Abhayananda (*LSV*:56).
7 These are dealt with extensively in the *Complete Works of Swami Vivekananda*, Vols I–IV.
8 The last of the four cyclic eras, typified by decay of moral values and ultimate world destruction.
9 A play on words in Bengali, meaning 'man' and 'God' in the wider sense.
10 Ceremonial offering of 'five elements' during worship.
11 My emphasis.
12 Alternate spelling.
13 According to which, all are divine, but do not realize this.
14 'As many ways, as many paths'.
15 Published as *Sri Ramakrishna the Great Master* in English.
16 The work is best described as a 'hagiography'.
17 Thus setting up the necessary *guru*-disciple *parampara* or succession.
18 Specifically of Siva and Sakti (*SGM*:497) though in hymns by monks of the Order, also of Rama and Krishna (*Altar Flowers* pp. 175 and 161).
19 Which encouraged locally made goods – especially 'homespun' cloth.

Chapter Three

1 Comprising Malabar, Cochin and Travancore.
2 Malayalam speaking regions, known today as Kerala.
3 I use the word *community* throughout in the sense it is used in India, that is, to denote the main caste/religious/regional group to which an individual belongs by virtue of birth. It is a term used in official parlance, and the various communities are well defined within a given region, by means of lists.
4 Whom we shall meet later in Chapter Four.
5 Outcaste.
6 Tamil is the main language of Madras, but the group members, being Western educated, knew English, the *lingua franca* in major cities.
7 It is customary to sit on the floor whilst dining with leaf plates set out in rows.
8 The Lord.
9 Discrimination between the Real and the Unreal.
10 Told to me by one of the senior Swamis from the village.
11 Today candidature is nine years for men, but not at the time under discussion.
12 Not to be confused with the 4 Maths he founded in 4 parts of India (*see* ch 8, note 5).
13 Based on linguistic, archaeological and other evidence.
14 All these data were collected from conversations with members of former royal and aristocratic Nayar households.

15 Gained from informants.
16 Ezhuttachan are highly literate as both teaching and building require reading skills.
17 Not all Nayar women. Those of high-ranking *taravāds* have various other titles.
18 The name of the schools in Vedic times where *bramacāris* resided with their *gurus*
19 Used by men and women towards females of similar family status, of the same generation, but senior in age.
20 She came to Trichur to stay with her father, when Australian sailors came to Cochin port during World War II.

Chapter Four

1 Holy Mother, as Sarada Devi was called.
2 *saṃnyāsins.*
3 A feminine form of *Sādhu.*
4 Sages.
5 She appeared genuinely 'attached' to them. Holy Mother is reported to have said without this 'attachment' she would have left the world with Ramakrishna (Gambhirananda, 1977, pp. 191–2).
6 Marie Louise, referred to previously.
7 She was only, in reality, associated in the 'public mind'.
8 Association or fellowship.
9 Especially by the older, conservative *saṃnyāsins.*
10 Lay disciples, and members of the Order.
11 'lac', as is sometimes customary after the death of a *guru*, before the body is cremated.
12 As they are in the Bangalore Ramakrishna Asrama.
13 Numbering six.
14 The printing press has helped spread Sanskrit learning to all.
15 It is considered meritorious to arise before dawn and bathe fully.
16 Especially those run by the certain Orders of the Catholic Church.

Chapter Five

1 These are official figures from the Order's 1981 General Report.
2 A term which includes Pre Probationers, Probationers, *brahmacārinis* and *saṃnyāsinis.*
3 Though fathers of children in the Mission's institutions are welcome to visit them. Parents are also invited to school functions.
4 Sri Sarada Math Calcutta.
5 The Mission branch in Kerala, for example, had 45 monthly donors for 1978–9, the majority donating between Rs 50 and Rs 150. The smallest donation was Rs 10 and the largest Rs 600.
6 *The Hindu*, 26th December 1980, discussing Sabarimala Temple.
7 US 80G of Income Tax Act of 1961.
8 It is customary for seniors to travel with at least another *saṃnyāsini* or *brahmacārini*, who tends to her needs.
9 It is possible, but less popular, to receive the *mantra* of Holy Mother.

10 Such as *papadums*, lentil wafers, fried and eaten with rice meals.
11 These are usually the gifts or offerings of lay devotees, especially at the time of receiving *mantra* initiation.
12 I discuss this further in Chapter Ten.
13 She visited Headquarters to pay her respects on the death of the *saṃnyāsa guru*, the first President of the Order. She came and left without uttering a word.
14 Especially of a conservative Brahmin background.
15 For Nayars, this would be the *taravād* name.
16 In summer the schools are closed for long vacation. Many schools have no water in summer, as the wells are dry.
17 Voting is not compulsory.
18 This is an oversimplification, but I mention the case of Gandhi to bring the RSS into respective.
19 I arrived in Kerala to begin fieldwork on the day of a General Strike, and ended up having to carry my heavy case and typewriter for an hour, in driving rain, to my destination.
20 It was common practice for girls to avoid using their caste titles (if any) and in many cases even parents had dropped both titles and the use of house names. Often the community of a caste Hindu could be worked out from the house name as, for example, the house of a Nambudiri was composed of the family name plus *mana* or *illam* while a Nayar's house was often a *veedu*, or other regional Nayar term.
21 The premises were repaired by Sarada Mandiram, which paid Rs 68,000 for them 'and Rs 5,000 black', the latter statement referring to unaccounted for money paid in cash for which no receipt was given. The transaction was told to me in a matter-of-fact manner by the *brahmacārini* in charge of accounts in the Sarada Mandiram office. The inclusion of a sum of black money in large transactions is almost standard practice in many parts of India, including Trichur, which has a thriving 'parallel economy'.
22 Each day when the milkman arrived, a *brahmacārini* placed a special meter in the milk which indicated the added water content. Only when this reached an outrageous proportion, something was said, and for a while the percentage of milk rose. The availability of such a meter gives some indication of how common such adulteration must be.

Chapter Six

1 The final school leaving certificate.
2 It was only after I had interviewed six candidates that discussion among the inmates began to arise. Was I going to publish everything they said? I assured them that I was interested in establishing patterns, and that is why I was asking everyone the same questions. After that, I resumed my task more cautiously, introducing the subject of joining while engaged in chores together, perhaps one question at a time, until over a period of three or four months, the cards that I had compiled for each inmate were satisfactorily completed.
3 A second daughter joined five years ago.
4 The ochre colour of the *saṃnyāsinis* robes, known as *gerua* in northern India.
5 I was delighted to show my Research Assistant that as a 'White Jew' (as I

appear on the Indian Census for 1981) I was, like her, from a Backward Community also!

6 A usage coined by M.N. Srinivas (see 1960:7).

7 By contrast, not one Kerala candidate's family has a phone at home.

8 Campbell-Jones, quotes a Catholic nun, who states, 'a good nun is someone who could have been married and would have made a good wife.' 1979:77.

Chapter Seven

1 The old cowshed was abandoned after the death of a good milch cow. The cowshed has been visible from the nearby road, and passers-by, casting envious looks, were thought to have caused the cow's death.

2 This is from *Bhagavad Gita* IV:24.

3 Jai Sri Guru Maharaj ji ki Jai, Jai Mahamayi ki Jai, Jai Swamiji Maharaj ji ki jai. Jai Vadakumnathan Siv, Kali Mayi ki Jai! Victory to Guru Maharaj (Ramakrishna, the teacher monk), Victory to Holy Mother, Victory to Swami Vivekandanda, Victory to Siva, Lord of the North (the presiding deity of Trichur), Victory to Kali (his consort).

4 Worship with symbols of the five elements: a lighted lamp, a conch filled with water, a handkerchief, a flower and a yak's tail fan.

5 Harmonium, drums, bells, cymbals, gong and perhaps, tampura.

6 Two hymns to Ramakrishna, one to Holy Mother, a short salutation to Swami Vivekananda, an invocation to Divine Mother, a locally-composed hymn to the incarnations of Visnu (culminating in Ramakrishna) and a Vedic chant for auspiciousness and peace.

7 Inmates of Sarada Mandiram never refer to it as an 'Asram', which is the name by which the Ramakrishna Asrama opposite is known.

8 *Bhajans* are devotional songs and hymns.

9 A short sacred formula given at initiation.

10 Pouring water on the head and hair. However, the hair is only actually washed with soap once a week. Daily, oil is applied to the hair, before rinsing it during the 'headbath'. By the end of the week it smells rancid.

11 The first worship of the day, similar to the evening *ārati*.

12 The shrine itself is separated from and elevated above the prayer hall. Although shrine entry is not permitted, entry into the prayer hall is to those who are ritually polluted.

13 Its alternate, and more common meaning, is 'faith'.

14 Campbell-Jones, in her study of catholic nuns comments that, 'In the minds of the sisters I spoke to, it was the petty rules and restrictions which made the most impression . . .' 1979:89.

15 Not her real name. I have changed names throughout.

16 Despite an explicit ban on this by Headquarters, following the wishes of the founder of the Order, Vivekananda.

17 The word used in Kerala for an 'envelope'.

18 On the birthdays of direct disciples of Ramakrishna, a few pages of their life or writings are read at 'Reading' instead of the *Gospel* or *Great Master*.

19 I taped this entire incident and thus quote verbatim.

20 The evening *pāyasam* is made from roasted semolina simmered in milk, and sweetened with sugar. *Luchis* are deep fried bread, like small, round, air-filled cushions.

21 A plate of cut fruit is covered by an inverted plate. A saucer of water is kept on Mataji's shelf, and an empty cup placed in it. The plate of fruit is balanced on the cup. The idea is that the moat of water around the cup prevents ants from reaching the fruit.
22 One *saṃnyāsin* remarked, however, 'It used to be "plain thinking and high living", now it is "high living and plane going".'
23 Though a pseudonym, Grand stands for the chain of businesses owned by Madhavan.
24 Tapping palm trees for juice, which is fermented into toddy, is the traditional occupation of Izhavas, and one looked down on by higher ranking communities.
25 Gold bars.
26 *Madamu* is the local word for a 'European' woman of respectable background.
27 Bleaching is done by soaking the cloth in cow dung, rinsing, and spreading in the sun for 2–3 days, keeping constantly wet with a solution of soap and soda.
28 The first President of the Order wore neither stitched garments nor footwear.
29 Campbell Jones' study documents similar rules in a Catholic teaching Order (1979:71).

Chapter Eight

1 This is confusing, so other 'Math' centres are often referred to as 'Madras Math' etc.
2 But, seniors do not borrow from their juniors, as this is against the accepted 'flow' of articles.
3 In Kerala, new cloth is most auspicious if worn unbleached and unwashed.
4 Sacrificial fire.
5 *Bhadrinath, Sringeri, Puri and Dwaraka* (in North, South, East and West respectively). *See* Mahadevan 1968:52–4.
6 *Atmano moksartham, jagad hitayaca.* For one's own salvation, and the good of the world.
7 Emphasis mine.
8 Despite the Order's refusal to take a political stand in the Nationalist struggle.
9 In branches of the Order outside Kerala no marks are permitted on the forehead, as these are considered an indicator of householder status. However, in Kerala where there is a sizeable Christian and Muslim population, the use of *bhasmam*, sandalpaste or red *kumkum*, marks out the wearer as a Hindu. In the village in which Sarada Mandiram is situated over half the population is Christian and, under pressure from local Marxists, many Hindu girls and women of Backward Communities refuse to adorn their foreheads. Thus, all inmates of Sarada Mandiram (monastic and otherwise) are compelled by seniors to adorn their foreheads in order to set an example, in the hope that others will follow. However, many young women today wear not the sacred *prasād* powders and pastes of temples, but cosmetic preparations in a myriad of colours to match their sarees or perhaps nail polish, and add allure to their *kohl* laden eyes.

10 Hail to the Guru-monk (Ramakrishna). Hail to the Divine Mother, Hail to Swamiji (Vivekananda). Durga Durga (a goddess who protects travellers in the Order's tradition).
11 Otherwise lumps of clay will leave rusty stains on clothes.
12 One *saṃnyāsini* has grown her hair again. Nobody has forced her to keep it shaved.
13 This sentiment is repeated in each verse of these *mantras*, used during *saṃnyāsa* rites.
14 Popularised by Dumont 1966, 1970 who sanctioned this in English translations of his work.
15 One *saṃnyāsini* solved the problem by borrowing tampons. Blood remaining *within* bodily margins does not pollute.
16 Though this by no means represents the norm.

Chapter Nine

1 I am not myself suggesting that 'timeless tradition' in fact exists or existed.
2 Monastic inmates of Sarada Mandiram and Ramakrishna Asrama vote in all elections. In other centres they do not vote.
3 This in itself is a very complex issue which I have merely outlined here.
4 Meaning 'fair in complexion', not necessarily 'foreigners'.
5 Again, this is a very complex issue.
6 Not necessarily 'cooked'. Sometimes merely 'cut'.
7 I personally encountered similar problems to the newcomers, while residing in the home of an aristocratic Kerala family. I soon learned that the members of the family did not expect to be asked for assistance, whether to suggest a tailor to make blouses for me, or to agree to interviews when I asked. If I did not ask, they would talk of their own accord. The final afront came when the lady of the house admired a set of very expensive clothes in a local shop. I returned and purchased it for her. She looked at me and said, 'Why do you give me this present, *cloth*, like a *child*!' She did wear it, however, to a family wedding that same week. The point that I had missed was that cloth, of all prestations, is the gift of seniors to their juniors of higher to lesser ranks, *par excellence*. The *kāranavan* gave it to members of his *taravād*, and to all tenants, servants and other workers on the major festivals. A gift of cloth from a man to a woman signified (and still does in the Nayar marriage) the commencement of cohabitation, *sambandham*. The male partner was formerly of superior family or communal status to the female, and older. The exception was the custom of wealthy and influential *taravāds* giving a feast of Brahmins, on such occasions as a sixtieth birthday of a *kāraṇavan*. This would include the gift of cloth to each Brahmin: a meritorious act. I was told of one occasion a few Nambudiri men received their cloth from the host, a Prince, before one stood up and announced, 'this head bows to none but God' and sat down. All those who had accepted before him (all from higher ranking *manas* than the protester) were severely embarrassed: which was the object of the mutinous gesture. *Saṃnyāsins* also have traditionally been recipients of cloth on similar occasions, for it is the duty of householders to support both the priestly caste and monks; the latter having (ideally) no source of income except alms. Although the gift of cloth to Brahmins is an all India custom, the

Nambudiri – member of a community that was known as 'Gods on earth' – realised that the custom would put a Nambudiri Brahmin on a lower rank than the Prince. Despite tradition, this was totally against prevailing rules of hierarchy, and so not to be tolerated: upholding one's prestige was more important than a piece of cloth, no matter how fine.

Chapter Ten

1 Water sanctified by the seven sacred rivers and ritually offered for Ramakrishna's bath, by pouring spoon by spoon over and *lingam* placed in a vessel as a bell is rung.
2 No centres outside Kerala allow the daily wearing of sandalwood paste or *bhasmam*, as this is a sign of householder status.
3 One toilet soap and 1½ bars of laundry soap. Each bar is 23 cm long.
4 Some orthodox Brahmin widows refrain from eating boiled rice for life. This is not the case among communities in which widows do not have to remain celibate.
5 She named the parties concerned. I must stress that I have no means of verifying this account. I merely am repeating it as told to me.
6 Her term, but clearly the relationship was physical.
7 In one instance, before the nightly reading had begun, a *brahmacārini* was sitting with her fist clenched, thumb side uppermost. Another *brahmacārini* came and sat by her, thrusting her own thumb in and out of the hole in the fist. 'Nice, isn't it', she commented. They blushed and giggled. A junior inmate observing this said, 'I don't understand'. They enlightened her in a whisper. The junior was very embarrassed. The mother of a *saṃnyāsini* was also present. She lowered her head and sniggered. None realised that I had witnessed the incident. There were other isolated similar instances of such behaviour, but unless I missed a great deal of what was happening, these were minor, compared for example with the behaviour of the Hostel girls in another branch of the Order. Here, couples of girls could regularly be found in mutual embrace, with besotted expressions, and even loss of appetite, due to the violence of their 'love'. Numerous cheap romantic English novels, concealed behind plain covers were confiscated in the Hostel, and fell open easily at the most lurid descriptions of sex. Indeed, many such passages had been neatly underlined. The confiscated books were, incidentally, read by some of the monastic inmates.
Against the undercurrent of sexual tension in this centre (due no doubt to the presence of fifty of so teenage College girls) Sarada Mandiram appeared an oasis of innocence. A hundred and fifty girls, ranging from four to fourteen would listen solemnly as Mataji regularly exhorted them to be pure, and to pray if ever an impure thought crossed their minds. I doubt whether such a subject would be raised in the other centre, lest it disturb a hornet's nest!
8 Campbell-Jones (1979:100) states that in a Catholic convent, 'outsiders were polluting. . . . No sister ever took food or drink with a stranger, not even the convent priest.'
9 I had purchased my own stainless steel plate and tumbler.
10 This excludes gifts to Brahmins and *saṃnyāsins* as alms.
11 Or ten in the case of women, as Hindu feminists point out.

Chapter Eleven

1 This information was obtained from the small lane in which 23 small houses built by the Asrama for Harijan and Backward Community members were situated. Ten of the households had at least one member working at Sarada Mandiram as a daily wage labourer, two as 'sweepers' and the rest, (including two young men who tended the cows as part of the labour pool) involved in daily but seasonal agricultural or construction work. With the aid of an informant from the lane, I obtained a detailed profile of each household, its financial situation, and its attitude towards both Sarada Mandiram and the Asrama. This was a project spanning six months, and included discussions between the local men at the end of the day in the village's tea shops, and between the women, as they went about their daily routine. Any incident occurring daily the day would be promptly reported to me the next morning, in a most efficient manner.
2 Two slices of bread per day on school days.
3 Ramakrishna's.
4 When she wants any medicine she just asks, and it is purchased.
5 An extreme form of Chinese-inspired Marxism.
6 Later my continued visits and friendship caused a good deal of tension between me and Sarada Mandiram.
7 She called on the day to say she could not come.
8 This is hard work as it requires a 'bucket brigade' from the well to the auditorium.
9 An old black and white Bengali film on Irish *brahmacārini* Sister Nivedita, was to be shown.
10 The village Catholic priest told me that 'all the teachers were injured'.
11 'Lollies', not Indian sweetmeats.
12 I was later told it was given a laxative and died of diarrhoea, but this may have been one of the wild rumours I encountered from time to time.

Conclusion

1 Apart from the continuing concern for fairness of complexion.
2 Ramakrishna at an early stage of his youth was reputed to be one such 'holyman'.

Bibliography

General

Aiyappan, A. 1965. *Social Revolution in a Kerala Village.* Asia Publishing House, New York.

Ayyar, Jagadisa. 1925. *South Indian Customs.* Diocesan Press.

Basu, Sankari Prasad (ed.). 1969. *Vivekananda in Indian Newspapers 1893–1902.* Bookland Private Ltd., Calcutta.

Beals, Alan, R. and John T. Hitchcock. 1960. *Field Guide to India.* National Academy of Sciences. National Research Council Publication 704. Washington, DC.

Berger, Peter and Thomas Luckmann. 1966. *The Social Construction of Reality.* Peregrine Books. The Penguin Press, Harmondsworth.

Bharati, Agehananda. 1961. *The Ochre Robe.* George Allen and Unwin, London.

Bose, Nemai Sadhan. 1969. *The Indian Awakening and Bengal.* Firma K.L. Mukhopadhyay, Calcutta. Second revised and enlarged edition, 1969.

Burman, Debajyoti. 1968. Sister Nivedita and Indian Revolution, in *Nivedita Commemoration Volume,* Amiya Kumar Mazumdar (ed.). Vivekananda Janmotsava Samiti, Calcutta.

Campbell, Gabriel J. 1976. *Saints and Householders.* Ratna Pustak Bhandar, Kathmandu.

Campbell-Jones, Suzanne. 1979. *In Habit: An Anthropological Study of Working Nuns.* Faber & Faber, London.

Cantlie, Audrey. 1977. Aspects of Hindu Asceticism, in *Symbols and Sentiments,* Ioan Lewis (ed.). Academic Press, London.

Carstairs, G. Morris. 1957. *The Twice Born: A Study of a Community of High-Caste Hindus.* The Hogarth Press, London.

Chatterjee, Rakhahari. 1968. Sister Nivedita in the Background of Contemporary Indian Politics, in *Nivedita Commemoration Volume,* Amiya Kumar Mazumdar (ed.). Vivekananda Jammotsava Samiti, Calcutta.

Chattopadhyayya, Kamaladevi et al. 1939. *The Awakening of Indian Women.* Everymans Press, Madras.

Daner, Francine Jeanne. 1976. *The American Children of Krsna.* A study of the Hare Krsna Movement. Holt, Rinehart & Winston, New York.

Das, Veena. 1976. The Uses of Liminality: Society and Cosmos in Hinduism. *Contributions to Indian Sociology* 10(2).

—— 1977. *Structure and Cognition: Aspects of Hindu Caste and Ritual.* Oxford University Press, Delhi.

Dougal, Sonia. 1974. *The Nun Runners.* Sterling Publishers, New Delhi.

Douglas, Mary. 1966. *Purity and Danger.* Routledge and Kegan Paul, London.

Dumont, L. 1970. World Renunciation in Indian Religion, in *Religion, Politics and History in India.* Mouton Publishers, Paris.

—— 1972. *Homo Hierarchicus.* Paladin, London.

Fawcett, F. 1901. *Madras Museum Bulletin* III:3. Madras.

Foxe, Barbara. 1975. *Long Journey Home: A Biography of Margaret Noble (Sister Nivedita).* Rider & Co., London.

Fuller, C.J. 1976. *The Nayars Today.* Cambridge University Press, Cambridge.

Geertz, Clifford. 1977. Ideology as a Cultural System, in *Symbols and Society,* Carole E. Hill (ed.). SAS Proceedings No.9, Athens.

Gennep, Arnold van. 1975. *The Rites of Passage* (tr. Monica B. Vizedom and Gabrielle L. Caffee). The University of Chicago Press, Chicago.

Ghurye, G.S. 1964. *Indian Sadhus* Popular Prakashan, Bombay.

Golde, Peggy. 1970. *Women in the Field.* Aldine Publishing Co., Chicago.

Gough, Kathleen E. 1952. Changing Kinship Usages in the Setting of Political and Economic Change among the Nayars of Malabar. *Journal of the Royal Anthropological Institute* 82:71–87.

—— 1959a. The Nayar definition of Marriage. *Journal of the Royal Anthropological Institute* 89:23–34.

—— 1961. Nayar: Central Kerala, in *Matrilineal Kinship,* David M. Schneider and Kathleen Gough (eds). University of California Press, Los Angeles.

—— 1975. Changing Households in Kerala, in *Explorations in the Family and Other Essays,* Dhirendra Narain (ed.). Thacker & Co. Ltd., Bombay.

Iyer, L.A. Krishna. 1968. *Social History of Kerala.* I. The Pre-Dravidians. Book Centre Publications, Madras.

—— 1970. *Social History of Kerala.* II. The Dravidians. Book Centre Publications, Madras.

Iyer, L.K. Anantha Krishna. *The Cochin Tribes and Castes.* Vol.I. 1909. Vol.II 1912. Higginbotham and Co. Madras. Reprint: Johnson Reprint Corporation New York, 1969.

Kakar, Sudhir. 1978. *The Inner World: A Psycho-analytical Study of Childhood and Society in India.* Oxford University Press, Delhi.

Leach, Edmund. 1976. *Culture and Communication: The Logic by which Symbols are Connected.* Cambridge University Press, Cambridge.

Mahadevan, T.M.P. 1968. *Sankaracharya.* National Book Trust. New Delhi.

Majumdar, R.C. 1951. *The History and Culture of the Indian People.* Vol. I. The Vedic Age. Allen and Unwin, London.

Marglin, F.A. 1977. Power, Purity and Pollution: Aspects of the Caste System Reconsidered, in *Contributions to Indian Sociology.* 11, 2, 245–270.

Mazumdar, Vina (ed.). 1979. *Symbols of Power: Studies on the Political Status of Women in India.* Allied Publishers Private Limited, Bombay.

Mencher, Joan P. 1965. The Nayars of South Malabar, in *Comparative Family Systems,* M.F. Nimkoff (ed.). Houghton Mifflin Company, Boston.

—— 1973. Namboodiri Brahmans of Kerala, in *Man's Many Ways,* Richard A. Gould (ed.). Harper & Row, New York.

Mencher, Joan P. and Helen Goldberg. 1974. Kinship and Marriage

Regulations among the Namboodiri, in *The Family in India*, George Kurian (ed.). Mouton, The Hague.

Menen, Aubrey. 1974. *The New Mystics.* Thames and Hudson, London.

Menon, A. Sreedhara. 1967. *A Survey of Kerala History.* Sahitya Pravarthaka Co-operative Society Ltd, Kottayam.

—— 1978. *Cultural Heritage of Kerala: an Introduction.* East-West Publications Private Ltd., Cochin.

Miller, David A. and Dorothy C. Wertz. 1976. *Hindu Monastic Life: the Monks and Monasteries of Bhubaneswar.* McGill-Queens University Press, Montreal.

Miller, Jeanine. 1974. *The Vedas.* Rider and Company, London.

Moorhouse, Geoffrey. 1969. *Against All Reason* Weidenfeld and N.

Mukherjee, S.N. 1977. *Calcutta: Myths and History.* Subarnarekha, Calcutta.

Murray, Muz. 1980. *Seeking the Master: a Guide to the Ashrams of India.* Neville Spearman, Jersey.

Nair, R. Ramakrishnan. 1976. *Social Structure and Political Development in Kerala.* The Kerala Academy of Political Science, Trivandrum.

Nandy, Ashis. 1980. *At the Edge of Psychology: Essays in Politics and Culture.* Oxford University Press, Delhi.

Neevel, William Jr. 1976. The Transformation of Sri Ramakrishna, in *Hinduism: New Essays in the History of Religions,* Bardwell L. Smith (ed.). E.J. Brill, Leiden.

Ojha, Catherine. 1981. Female Asceticism in Hinduism: Its Tradition and Present Condition, in *Man in India.* Vol 61, No.3: 254–285.

O'Flaherty, Wendy Doniger. 1973. *Siva: The Erotic Ascetic.* Oxford University Press, London.

Orenstein, Henry. 1965. The Structure of Hindu Caste Values: A Preliminary Study of Hierarchy and Ritual Defilement. *Ethology* 4.

—— 1968. Towards a Grammar of Defilement in Hindu Sacred Law, in *Structure and Change in Indian Society,* Milton Singer and Bernard S. Cohen (eds). Viking Fund Publications in Anthropology, Chicago.

—— 1970. Logical Congruence in Hindu Sacred Law: Another Interpretation. *Contributions to Indian Sociology* 4:22–35.

Pandey, P.R. 1979. *The Concept of Avatars.* B.R. Publishing Corp., Delhi.

Pandey, Dr Raj Bali. 1969. *Hindu Samskaras.* Motilal Banarsidas, Delhi.

Pannikar, T.K. Gopal. 1901. *Malabar and Its Folk.* G.A. Natesan & Co., Madras.

Puthenkalam Fr. J. 1977. Marriage and Family in Kerala. *Journal of Comparative Family Studies Monograph.* Series General Editor: George Kurian. University of Calgary, Calgary.

Rajendran, G. 1974. *The Ezhava Community and Kerala Politics.* The Kerala Academy of Political Science, Trivandrum.

Rao, M.S.A. 1957. *Social Change in Malabar.* Popular Book Depot, Bombay.

Ray, Renuka (ed.). 1978. *Role and Status of Women in Indian Society.* Firma KLM Private Limited, Calcutta.

Raymond, Lizelle. 1953. *The Dedicated.* John Day Co., New York.

Roy Choudhury, Girijashankar. 1956. *Sri Aurobindo o' Bangalay Swadeshi Yug.* Navabharat Publishers, Calcutta.

Sanoo, M.K. 1978. *Narayana Guru.* Bharatiya Vidya Bhavan, Bombay.

Schneiderman, Leo. 1969. Ramakrishna: Personality and Social Factors in the Growth of a Religious Movement. *Journal of the Scientific Study of Religion* VIII(1): Spring. University of Connecticut.

Sengupta, Padmini. 1974. *The Story of Women of India.* Indian Book Company, New Delhi.
Sinclair, Wendy. 1979. *Nambudiri and Nayar Death Rites: a Comparative Analysis.* Unpublished thesis. University of Sydney.
—— 1982. *How to Deal with Women*: According to Bengali mystic Sri Ramakrishna. Asian Studies Association of Australia. 4th National Conference. Monash University.
Spratt, P. 1966. *Hindu Culture and Personality.* Manaktalas, Bombay.
Srinivas, M.N. 1952. *Religion and Society among the Coorgs of South India.* MPP, Bombay.
—— (ed.). 1960. *India's Villages.* 2nd edition. MPP, Bombay.
—— 1962. *Caste in Modern India and Other Essays.* Asia Publishing House, London.
—— 1966. *Social Change in Modern India.* University of California Press, Berkeley.
—— 1976. *The Remembered Village.* Oxford University Press, Delhi.
—— 1978. *The Changing Position of Indian Women.* Oxford University Press, Delhi.
—— n.d. *The Dual Cultures of Independent India.* Raman Research Institute, Bangalore.
Stevenson, Sinclair. 1971. *The Rites of the Twice Born.* Oriental Books Reprint Corporation, New Delhi. Distributor: Munshiram Manoharlal.
Tambiah, S.J. 1975. From Varna to Caste through Mixed Unions, in *The Character of Kinship*, Jack Goody (ed.). Cambridge University Press, Cambridge.
Thurston, Edgar. 1906. *Ethnographic Notes in Southern India.* Government Press, Madras.
—— 1909. *Castes and Tribes of Southern India. Vol.V – M to P. Government Press, Madras.*
Tripathi, B.D. 1978. *Sadhus of India.* Popular Prakashan, Bombay.
Turner, Victor W. 1975. Ritual as Communication and Potency, in *Symbols and Society*, Carole E. Hill (ed.). SAS Proceedings No. 9, Athens.
Uberoi, Jit Singh. 1966. *On Being Unshorn.* Seminar on Guru Gobind Singh, Sikhism and Indian Society. Indian Institute of Advanced Study, Simla.
Unnithan, T.K.N. 1974. Contemporary Nayar Family in Kerala, in *The Family in India: A Regional View*, George Kurian (ed.). Mouton, The Hague.
Vandana, Sister. 1978. *Gurus Ashrams and Christians.* Darton, Longman and Todd, London.
Walker, Benjamin. 1968. *The Hindu World: An Encyclopaedic Survey of Hinduism.* 2 volumes. George, Allen and Unwin, London.
Wax, Rosalie H. 1971. *Doing Fieldwork.* The University of Chicago Press, Chicago.
Yale, John. 1961. *A Yankee and the Swamis.* George Allen and Unwin, London.
Yalman, Nur. 1967. *Under the Bo Tree: Studies in Caste, Kinship and Marriage in the Interior of Ceylon.* University of California Press, Berkeley.

Mission Literature

Altar Flowers. A Bouquet of Choicest Sanskrit Hymns. Advaita Ashrama, Calcutta, 1974, sixth edition.
Atmaprana Pravrajika. 1961. *Sister Nivedita.* Sister Nivedita Girls' School, Calcutta.

Gambhirananda Swami. 1957. *History of the Ramakrishna Math and Mission.* Advaita Ashrama, Calcutta.
—— 1977 (third edition). *Holy Mother Sri Sarada Devi.* Sri Ramakrishna Math, Madras.
The Gospel of Sri Ramakrishna. (Abridged GSR) 1958 Abridged edition, (tr. Swami Nikhilananda). Ramakrishna-Vivekananda Center, New York.
Gospel of Sri Ramakrishna. (GSR) 1974 sixth edition, (tr. Swami Nikhilananda). Sri Ramakrishna Math, Madras.
Life of Sri Ramakrishna (LSR) (Compiled from Various Authentic Sources) 1924 (2nd edition 1928). Advaita Ashrama, Calcutta.
Life of Swami Vivekananda. (LSV) 1981 5th edition, (By His Eastern and Western Disciples) Vol.I and II. Advaita Ashrama, Calcutta.
Menon, A. Karunakaran. 1978. Sri Ramakrishna Ashrama, Trichur, Then and Now, in *Golden Jubilee Souvenir.* Sri Ramakrishna Ashrama, Puranattukara, Trichur.
Pravrajika Bharatiprana. Sri Sarada Math, Calcutta, 1973 (no author).
Reminiscences of Swami Vivekananda 1961 (2nd edition 1964). (By His Eastern and Western Admirers). Advaita Ashrama, Calcutta.
Satprakashananda Swami, 1978. *Swami Vivekananda's Contributions to the Present Age.* The Vedanta Society of St Louis, St Louis.
Selections from Swami Vivekananda. 1963. Swami Gambhirananda (ed.). Advaita Ashrama, Calcutta.
Siddhinathananda Swami. 1978. Influence of Sri Ramakrishna and Swami Vivekananda in Kerala, in *Golden Jubilee Souvenir.* Sri Ramakrishna Ashrama, Puranattukara Trichur.
Sri Ramakrishna The Great Master. (SRGM) 1978 5th revised edition (By Swami Saradananda) (tr. Swami Jagadananda) Vols I and II. Sri Ramakrishna Math, Madras.
Suddhasattwananda Swami. 1969. *Worship of Sri Ramakrishna.* Sri Ramakrishna Math, Myalpore, Madras.
Tapasyananda Swami. 1977. *Sri Sarada Devi the Holy Mother.* Vols I and II. Sri Ramakrishna Math, Madras.
Vivekananda Swami. *The Complete Works of Swami Vivekananda.* Mayavati Memorial Edition. Advaita Ashrama, Calcutta.
—— 1960 edn. *Letters of Swami Vivekananda.* Advaita Ashrama, Calcutta.
—— 1978. *Our Women.* Advaita Ashrama, Calcutta.

Reports

Family Planning and the Status of Women in India. Report of a Seminar of Central Institute of Research and Training in Public Cooperation, New Delhi, August 1969. CIRTPC, Delhi.
The General Report of Sri Sarada Math and Ramakrishna Sarada Mission. Calcutta, 1968–70, 1980, 1981.
Golden Jubilee Souvenir. Sri Ramakrishna Ashrama. Trichur, 1978.
The Hindu. 26th December 1980.
Report for 1975–1976. Sri Sarada Mandiram. Puranattukara, 1976.
Report for April 1978 to March 1980. Sri Sarada Mandiram. Trichur.
Report for 1977–1979. Ramakrishna Sarada Mission, Trivandrum.
Samvit. Ramakrishna Sarada Mission. New Delhi, March 1980.

Sri Ramakrishna Ashrama Bangalore and Its Activities. Sri Ramakrishna Ashrama, Bangalore.

Sri Ramakrishna Gurukul and Vidya Mandir, The Vilangans, Trichur. Report for 1933–35, 1935–36, 1937–38, 1939–40, 1943, 1945.

Sanskrit Sources

[The] Bhagavadgita (tr. Adidevananda Swami). Mangalore Trading Association Private Ltd. Mangalore, 1968.

Eight Upanisads (tr. Gambhirananda Swami). Vol.I. 1965. Vol.II. Advaita Ashrama, Calcutta, 1966.

[The] Laws of Manu (tr. Georg Buhler). Dover Publications, Inc., New York, 1969.

Mahanarayanopanisad (tr. Vimalananda Swami). Sri Ramakrishna Math, Madras, 1979.

[The] Message of the Upanisads (Swami Ranganathananda). Bharatiya Vidya Bhavan, Bombay, 1968.

[The] Principal Upanisads (ed. S. Radhakrishnan). George Allen and Unwin, London, 1953.

Sankara Digvijaya of Madhava Vidyaranya (tr. Swami Tapasyananda). Sri Ramakrishna Math, Madras, 1978.

[The] Upanishads (tr. Prabhavananda Swami). New American Library (Mentor Book). New York, 1957.

Vivekacudamani of Sri Sankaracarya (tr. Swami Madhavananda). Advaita Ashrama Calcutta, 1974.

Zaehner, R.C. *Hindu Scriptures.* J.M. Dent and Sons Ltd., London, 1966.

Dictionaries

MacDonnell, A.A. *A Practical Sanskrit Dictionary.* Oxford University Press, London, 1971.

Pillai, Madhavan. *Assisi English-Malayalam Dictionary.* Assisi Printing and Publishing House, Changanacherry, 1978.

Pillai, Mekkolla Parameswaran. *Assisi Malayalam-English Dictionary.* Assisi Printing and Publishing House, Changanacherry, 1978.

Stutley, M. & J. *A Dictionary of Hinduism.* Routledge and Kegan Paul, London, 1977.

Index